COMBATING TERRORISTS IN THE USA

PROTECTING THE CONUS FROM TERRORISTS

ROBERT T. UDA, MS, MBA

CONTRIBUTING AUTHORS:

BRICE A. GYURISKO, SR., MPA
DAVID P. HALE, PHD
1ST LT. MICHAEL W. HALTER JR., US ARMY, MBA
CARL R. HOSPEDALES, BS AVIATION
KEVIN SCOTT, MBA, MA
DARRIN L. TODD, MS
WILLIAM R. TUBBS, JR., MPA

IUNIVERSE, INC.
NEW YORK   BLOOMINGTON

Combating Terrorists in the USA
Protecting the CONUS from Terrorists

iUniverse books may be ordered through booksellers or by contacting:

iUniverse
1663 Liberty Drive
Bloomington, IN 47403
www.iuniverse.com
1-800-Authors (1-800-288-4677)

ISBN: 978-1-4401-1771-8 (sc)
ISBN: 978-1-4401-1772-5 (ebook)

Printed in the United States of America

iUniverse rev. date: 1/27/2009

DEDICATION

To Dr. Wafa Sultan, formerly a Middle Eastern woman,
now a great American.

CONTENTS

PREFACE

Combating Terrorists in the USA provides all Americans with basic information on how to deal with terrorists who are currently living in clandestine cells within the USA. We provide information on the enemy and the associated threat. *Combating Terrorists in the USA* provides strategy and the importance of intelligence. We delve into combating terrorism, risk management, security planning, and countermeasures. *Combating Terrorists in the USA* considers protecting our critical infrastructure, cyber-security (including cyber-crime, cyber-terrorism, and cyber-warfare), terrorist profiling, maritime piracy, abortion clinic bombings, Ku Klux Klan, Al-Qaeda, and naval militias. This book includes 443 reference citations of ideas from many of the greatest minds worldwide in homeland security and combating terrorists.

Seven subject matter experts who are highly qualified practitioners contributed one or more chapters to *Combating Terrorists in the USA*. Their contributions add tremendously to the quality and technical content of this book. I owe a debt of gratitude to them for the valuable information they provide for everyone's benefit.

All chapters and opinions written therein by contributing authors are solely those of each contributing author. Their writings are theirs only, and I may or may not agree with what each wrote. However, all of my chapter writings and opinions in this book are solely mine. Any error would be my error only. If you find errors, please bring them to my attention.

I love the kind of dialogue that can occur between two matured, objective, unemotional, honest people. I like people who question my writings, statements, and beliefs, because it allows me to:

- Determine if people understand what I write or say.
- Clarify my statements that they don't understand to facilitate understanding.
- Think deeply of what I write or say and to develop sensible rationale for my statements.
- Be able to respond in a professional, objective, logical manner that facilitates understanding.
- Gain a better understanding of other peoples' viewpoints.
- Learn and grow from the experience.

All of these are good results of having an honest dialogue between us.

Therefore, if you disagree with anything that I have written in this book, I encourage you to write me and voice your disagreement. I always like to hear and learn about other people's views on whatever I write. Never do I believe that I know all truth on anything. I am always willing to change my views if someone presents contrary responses that make sense to me. That being said, I look forward to hearing from you. Thank you.

Robert T. Uda
San Marcos, California
January 2009

CHAPTER 1
INTRODUCTORY VIEWPOINTS
AND REFLECTIONS

Robert T. Uda, MS, MBA

I cannot understand why many Muslims were so upset with Pope Benedict XVI when he made the statement characterizing Muhammad. The violent actions of extremist Muslims burning down Christian churches, killing of a nun, protests, and threats because they were offended by the Pope's statements just appear to verify and validate what the Pope had said. Look how people characterize God, Jesus Christ, and Christianity, yet Christians don't burn, kill, protest, and threaten. Something is not right with the way things are going in this country and the world.

One Nation under Surveillance

A person I know made the following statement: "One nation under surveillance." I asked him what was that all about. He said that the satirical statement is a play on words contained within the Pledge of Allegiance. He further said that, "It makes reference to how a culture of suspicion, paranoia, and omnipresent police is robbing our nation of the basic freedoms upon which it was formed. There are those in our nation who believe it is necessary to destroy our freedoms in order to protect them. The more we cave in to this line of reasoning, the less we can be distinguished from our feared enemies."

One Nation under God

Personally, I prefer "One nation under God" as stated in the Pledge of Allegiance to the Flag. On the other hand, a culture of total rights and total freedom develops an environment that has developed such as in San Francisco, where they look down upon those being judgmental and, instead, everything and anything goes. Everyone is able to think, say, and do whatever he or she pleases, thereby developing a totally permissive society. In other words, if it feels good, do it! So, what do we have in Frisco? We have a high rate of homelessness, cops being killed on the streets, prostitution, diseases, crime, abortions, babies thrown into trash bins or flushed down toilets after being purposefully aborted and killed, and rape. You name it. It all goes on in San Francisco. Furthermore, this *modus operandi* is creeping through every city and town in the United States.

Total Freedom. Totally free sex allows people to do anything and everything they feel like doing, thereby, resulting in unwanted pregnancy, which increases abortions (i.e., killing of innocent human lives). Total freedom in sexual liaisons, whether it is with human, same sex, animals, or young children, creates all kinds of societal problems such as homosexuality/ homophobia, same-sex marriages, pedophilia, adults marrying children, sex slaves, making sexual orientation at the same level as racial orientation, and child sexual abuse. We now have teachers having sex with underage students/ children; cheerleaders doing crazy, sexual, and wild things; Britney Spears serving as a poor role model for our kids by flashing her you-know-what to the paparazzo; and it goes on-and-on-and-on.

Sad State of Affairs. Totally free speech by politicians has eliminated civility in the Halls of Congress. Politics is now a pure blood sport. Total freedom of athletes to act the way they do on the basketball and other courts and the gridiron has set a very poor example for our children in youth athletics who mimic those antics on their own courts and fields. Hence, we have athletes killed in drive-by shootings, throwing games to win side bets, dogs killed in gambling dogfights, taking steroids to build strength to break performance records unethically and lying to Congress, performing all kinds of extramarital illicit relationships, and accidentally shooting oneself in the leg while illegally carrying a firearm. I can go on *ad infinitum* on this sad state of affairs.

Total Permissiveness without Responsibility. Newspapers and television possess no propriety any more showing in photos and videos our soldiers explicitly shot and killed by enemy snipers, people having sex on beaches, and gory deaths of victims. We do not need to be subject to such freedoms. I prefer not to have the right or freedom to watch such X-rated film with children in our midst in the living room. Our schools distribute condoms to students, politicians seeking to keep parents from knowing that their pregnant children may be getting an abortion, children suing parents on outlandish child-abuse charges, and euthanasia. This is what happens when we allow and create such a permissive society of total rights and total freedom without any associated limits or personal responsibility.

Return to Lawlessness. Soon, we will allow shouting "Fire" in a crowded theater. We will allow obscenities and the "F" word on the news reports and in TV shows. We will allow those who rape the right to do what they do simply because they were born that way, and they cannot help but raping people. We will allow multiple spouses and marrying our own children. We will allow freedom of stalking. We will allow people not to stop at traffic signals or stop signs because stopping limits their freedom of movement and passage. We will create a society with absolutely no boundaries, no laws, no rules, no manners, no nothing. We will achieve full circle and return to the caveman days where "survival of the fittest" reigned. We will have absolutely no limits to our freedoms and rights. We will return to the wild, Wild West. Those are some of the conditions that prevail in Somalia and other such lawless countries.

Secular Progressivism. People desire total freedom but without any associated responsibility. The Bill of Rights gives us freedom of religion, yet societal forces are gradually eliminating religion from our government, schools, and lives and replacing it with secular progressivism. The Bill of Rights gives us the freedom to bear arms, yet societal forces are moving to take this right away from individual citizens. The Bill of Rights gives us freedom of speech, yet Columbia University student radicals and students at other such universities curtail and shout down free speech on their campuses made by both Democrat and Republican guest speakers. Those students want their total rights to speak up, assemble, and dissent, yet they will not allow anyone else the same rights if guest speakers' thinking and words are opposite to theirs. Congress and the new Administration are trying to revive and pass the Fairness Doctrine. Soon talk radio may be eliminated or curtailed. This kind of reaction is where our country is heading against all of the freedoms we hold so dear.

Culture of Total Rights and Freedom. The statement "a culture of suspicion, paranoia, and omnipresent police is robbing our nation of the basic freedoms upon which it was formed" flies in the face of what is really happening in society. On the contrary, a culture of total rights and freedom without associated responsibility and propriety robs us of the basic freedoms that formed our nation. Total permissiveness void of any limitations whatsoever has created most of our societal ills we are experiencing today.

A Society Gone Wild. The police do not rob our nation of basic freedoms. It is a "society gone wild" that robs us of basic freedoms. We do not have enough police to keep this wild society in check. That is why we are losing our freedoms. The campus police stood by while the radical students shouted down, assaulted, and mistreated the guest speakers at Columbia University. What kind of freedom is that? The students had their total freedom of speech, but they robbed the guest speakers of their freedom of speech. That is not a free society as I see it. If the campus police did their job, these incidents would not happen. This was not the "omnipresent police robbing" anyone of their rights. This was a bunch of *laissez faire* campus police. Nothing would

3

have changed if they were not there at all. Hence, how can the police rob anyone of their freedoms if they do nothing?

Radical Students. The radical students are robbing us of our freedom of speech. The errant students with unfettered rights and freedom had robbed the guest speakers of their rights and freedom. On a national television show held after that fiasco at Columbia University, one of the guest speakers stated that he had "feared for his life" during that incident. What kind of freedom is that, anyway?

An Opposite Perspective. I totally agree with the statement, "There are those in our nation who believe it is necessary to destroy our freedoms in order to protect them." Yes, it is the secular progressives and the total rights and total freedom folks who are "destroying our freedoms in order to protect" their own freedoms. I also totally agree with the final statement, "The more we cave-in to this line of reasoning, the less we can be distinguished from our feared enemies." These are the reasons why I agree with most of those thoughts. However, I fear I might be viewing it from a rather different perspective from the total rights folks.

Where are we heading? Yes, our feared enemies are the secular progressives, "the enemy within," and the terrorists or Islamo-fascists who have openly professed to kill all infidels and dominate the world with a one-world government and one-world religion. When they accomplish their ultimate goal, they will have their total freedom and rights. Those of us who survive, but are retained in bondage, will have absolutely no freedoms or rights. That is the way things are heading in America today.

Dealing with Islamo-fascists

Asynchronous Warfare. Asynchronous warfare is combating terrorism. Guerrilla warfare, paramilitary warfare, and insurgent warfare are all forms of asymmetrical warfare … and so is combating terrorism. Hence, asymmetrical warfare and asynchronous warfare are the same. World War III is going to be, if it is not already, an asymmetrical or asynchronous war. It is a war of ideology, a war of philosophy, a war of culture, and a war for the survival of the Western way of life.

Contrasting View of Things. When I talk about a war of ideology, a war of philosophy, a war of culture, and a war of the survival of the Western way of life, I am referring to the vastly contrasting ideologies, philosophies, cultures, and way of life between the Islamo-fascists (terrorists) and the civilized world (i.e., Western society). If we did not have such a vastly different view of these things, we would not have the resulting conflict.

Conventional Warfare. Synchronous or symmetrical warfare is conventional warfare. Asynchronous or asymmetrical warfare is unconventional warfare. Conventional warfare is what we fought in World War I, World War II, and the Korean War. Unconventional warfare is what we fought in the Vietnam War and are currently fighting in the War in Afghanistan, War in Iraq, and the Global War on Terrorism (GWOT). Therefore, not all warfare is asymmetrical warfare.

Definition of Words. I fully understand that misunderstandings and confusion can result when people cannot agree on the definition of words they use in their discussions. For example, take conventional, synchronous, or symmetrical warfare. The reasons why I designated WW I, WW II, and the Korean War as conventional, synchronous, or symmetrical warfare include the following:

1. The combatants on each side wore military uniforms with military insignia on them.
2. Each side was signatory to the Geneva Convention.
3. Each side followed a clear chain-of-command from top to bottom.
4. Both sides used advanced weapons and tactics.
5. There was a battlefront and lines that separated the enemy from friendly forces.

Terrorists Characterized. Whereas, for unconventional, asynchronous, or unsymmetrical warfare, a significant difference exists between what one side (the terrorists, for example) uses and what the other side (the West) uses in the way of weapons, tactics, uniforms, adhering to the Geneva Convention, lines of authority, and battle lines. The terrorists do not use a consistent uniform. You cannot differentiate the terrorists' uniforms from those of ordinary Arab-Muslim-Islamist (AMI) civilians. They do not follow the Geneva Convention. They are intentionally indiscriminate on who they kill. They do not care about collateral damage. They do not even care about fratricide of their own people. In fact, they believe in and practice genocide of the Jews and the entire Western civilization. Finally, urban warfare does not lend itself to battlefronts or battle lines.

Principles of Asymmetrical Warfare. From this premise, I have devised certain principles of asymmetrical warfare that demonstrate how to beat the Islamo-fascists at their own game. If these principles are taken seriously by our political and military leaders, we will win all future asymmetrical or asynchronous wars. These principles of asymmetrical warfare were not derived from deep study, military doctrine, or complex military theories. They were derived from simple common sense and from the ideas expounded by my greatest military hero, General George S. Patton, Jr., who said, "A leader is a man who can adapt principles to circumstances." The principles are what you will find in this book. The circumstances are asymmetrical warfare.[1]

"Islamo-fascists" Defined. Before we go any further, however, I must define what I mean by "Islamo-fascists." I call them "Isfasts" for short. Isfasts are comprised of a smaller percentage of all Arabs, Muslims, and Islamists in the world. The Isfasts attacked the United States on September 11, 2001, destroyed the World Trade Center Twin Towers, and killed nearly 3,000 innocent non-combatant civilians in the process including those at the Pentagon and those in a field in Pennsylvania.[2]

A Hijacked Religion. The Isfasts want to wipe Israel off the face of the map. They desire to kill all infidels, i.e., Americans, Westerners, and the non-believers of the Islamic religion. They hijacked the Islamic religion and twisted the passages of the Quran (In the literature, this is also spelled Qur'an, Quraan, Koran, Koraan, Qoraan, or Qoran) to support their own extremist ends. They celebrated and danced in the streets when the Twin Towers came down. They include the nations and people that finance and support the terrorists. Their goal is to dominate the world.[3]

Who are the Isfasts? The Isfasts comprise about 10 percent of the AMI population of the world. Since there are approximately 1 billion of these people, the Isfasts is comprised of about 100 million people. That is a formidable group with which to contend. The Isfasts include the members of al-Qaeda, Taliban, Hezbollah, HAMAS, and the anti-American peoples of Iran, Syria, Saudi Arabia, Egypt, and other Middle Eastern, East Asian, and Pacific Rim countries that believe in and expound the goal of "Death to America" … America to them being "The Great Satan."[4]

---

1   Uda, R. T. (2007). *Principles of Asymmetrical Warfare: How to Beat Islamo-fascists at Their Own Game*. Lincoln, Nebraska: iUniverse, Inc.

2   Ibid.

3   Ibid.

4   Ibid.

Who the Isfasts are Not. The Isfasts do not include the approximately 90 percent of all Arabs, Muslims, and Islamists in the world who are peace-loving and tolerant of other religions and peoples of the world. President George W. Bush said, "Islam is peace, and the United States is not against the religion of Islam, but those who pervert the religion to support terrorism and mass murder."[5]

Isfasts' Goal. Because of the intolerance displayed by the Isfasts toward the West as well as the ultimate goal of the Isfasts (i.e., world domination), we have a problem that cannot be resolved through debate, discussion, diplomacy, or compromise. The Isfasts do not believe in compromise. It is all their way or the highway for us. It is impossible for diplomacy to work with such an unyielding position held by the Isfasts.

Conventional Warfare. Yes, if anyone defines no war as "conventional," then we cannot intelligently discuss about what is conventional and what is unconventional. I have defined what I mean by conventional warfare, and if one cannot accept and/or disregards my definition and insist that no war is "conventional," then there can be no further logical discussion about conventional and unconventional warfare.

Death to America. The Isfasts believe that Americanism provides a decadent way to live. They do not believe that America is great. They only believe that America is the Great Satan, and they preach "death to America." However, I do not believe that it is a generally accepted opinion throughout the world … lest why are so many foreigners trying to come to America both legally and illegally?

Terrorist Attack against the US

> What is the current threat of a terrorist attack against the US or our western allies? How will it manifest itself, and when will it occur?

Current Major Threat. The current major threat against our American warfighters and coalition forces in the two war zones (i.e., Afghanistan and Iraq) is the deadly improvised explosive devices (IEDs). The current major threat in other countries (i.e., our Western allies) of the world is the suicide bomber, car bombs, and other vehicle-borne IEDs (VBIEDs). The current major threat in the continental United States (CONUS) is the weapons of mass destruction (WMDs) including chemical, biological, radiological (dirty

---

5   Garamonde, J. (2001, October 4). Islam growing in America, US military. *DefenseLINK News*. Retrieved on September 5, 2006, from http://www.defenselink.mil/news/Oct2001/n10042001_200110043.html.

bombs), and nuclear (CBRN) weapons. The terrorist attacks on the US were projected to have occurred in the summer of 2007. However, here we are, and they have not yet transpired. However, rest assured, they shall occur. It is not a matter of "if" they will happen but "when" they will happen.

More Attacks in Europe. I think more attacks will occur in European countries before they start in the CONUS. Terrorists have attacked Spain, England, France, and Germany. I estimate that more major attacks will occur in Europe. A major, coordinated attack recently occurred in India in December 2008. A major attack in the CONUS will probably occur in 2009.

Al-Qaeda Emboldened. I read in *The Al-Qaeda Connection,* written by Paul Williams, that the Clinton Administration did nothing after al-Qaeda terrorists attacked the USS Cole. At that time, the Clinton Administration should have made an all-out effort to go after and capture or kill Osama bin Laden (OBL) and those perpetrators of that attack. All our inaction did was to embolden al-Qaeda to plan more attacks such as the huge one that occurred on 9/11/01.[6]

We Help Those Who Work to Destroy Us. Again, upon reading *The Al-Qaeda Connection,* I was appalled to read that OBL had issued his *fatwas* #1 and #2 years before we had supported OBL and his al-Qaeda followers and the Albanians to destroy the Serbs.[7] We were helping those who had the goal to destroy the US! Later, after the Serbian war was over because the US and NATO blew up all Serb resistance, the Muslims who took over their country themselves proceeded to perform ethnic cleansing, which is the same thing the Serbs was accused of doing! Somehow, I don't see the Clinton Administration doing the right thing in that case. We, again, helped and emboldened the Islamic fundamentalists to carry out their *fatwa* on us on 9/11!

Human Intelligence (HUMINT). Regarding needing "superior HUMINT" to get OBL, it was also during the Clinton Administration that HUMINT in the Central Intelligence Agency (CIA) was emasculated because of insufficient funding. That was sad because we have been playing a catch-up game on acquiring effective HUMINT on terrorists ever since Clinton left office.

Reactive Congress. I believe that only after the first barrage of dirty nukes in a few of our big cities, then our politicians will wake up and develop an approach to mitigating this threat. Hence, very few people if any will be concerned about dense population centers until after the fact. As usual, our Congress is reactive, not proactive.

---

6   Williams, P. L. (2005). *The Al-Qaeda connection: International terrorism, organized crime, and the coming apocalypse.* Amherst, New York: Prometheus Books.
7   Ibid.

The Enemy Within. No one really knows when, where, and how the terrorists will attack. The reasons that contribute to our ignorance is that there are internal forces (e.g., politicians, a particular political party, anti-Americans, anti-military, and the Hollywood elite/mafia) in the US that fight to eliminate the Patriot Act, eliminate wiretapping of incoming cell phone calls from overseas suspected terrorists, and disallow racial/religious profiling of suspected terrorists. Why do these forces (some call them "enemies within") want to tie our own hands behind our backs and expect to fight and win a GWOT is way beyond me. The terrorists only need to succeed once; we must succeed thwarting their attempts every time ... or many Americans will be killed. To minimize the terrorist threat, we should do two things:

1. *Eradicate Terrorists One at a Time.* We should eradicate terrorists one at a time ... without fanfare. Publicity kills us every time. We should kill the terrorists and not publicize their elimination. The press/media will discover and publicize enough of what happens in the GWOT anyway. The FBI, CIA, federal government, and US armed forces do not need to add to the media frenzies by feeding them any information ... except disinformation. We should take no prisoners, thereby not needing the Guantanamo (or Gitmo for short) prison and eliminating it as Barack Obama will be doing.

2. *Demonize the Demons.* We (the US) should plan and implement a methodical media campaign to discredit al-Qaeda, all terrorist groups, and individual terrorists. Our adversaries have been doing a superb job in demonizing the US. It is about time we started demonizing those demons of terror. We should conduct a massive world-wide, but subtle, campaign to demonize OBL, al-Qaeda, Iran, Syria, and other such people, organizations, and terror-financing countries. Whenever they err or do something really atrocious, we should put our propaganda machine in full swing and demonize them and the incident. We should also implement a massive disinformation campaign. Whatever they do, we can and will do better.

We Must Seek a Happy Median. We have so much freedom and rights in this country that we work ourselves to a point where not only our hands but our legs also are tied behind our backs. Then, we are unable to defend ourselves, and we all will either be killed or held in bondage. So, we will make full circle from full and complete rights and freedom to death, bondage, and no rights. There has got to be a happy median in there somewhere.

Solving the Energy Problem Solves the Terrorism Problem

Force and Violence. To solve the terrorism problem, we need to understand and know how to deal with terrorists. Bob Taubert said, "Unfortunately, people of this ilk only respect force and violence. So be it."[8] Hence, to solve or kill the terrorism problem, we must use "force and violence" because those are the only things terrorists understand and respect. Another way to defeat terrorism is to follow the terrorists and eliminate them one at a time without fanfare. Then, one day, there will be none.

Alternative Fuels. I'm so sick of Middle Eastern oil and Venezuelan oil that I strongly believe we should seek alternative fuels to petrol. Even coal and natural gas, both of which we have an overabundance of in the US, would be better than continuing to deal with the Arabs, Venezuelans, and Russians to buy their oil. Since the USA has a huge amount of coal and natural gas, we should exploit those energy sources we currently have and ignore the Middle East. That would be a tactical solution to the problem.

Strategic Solution. What the US should really do is to conduct a 10-year project, similar to the Manhattan Project, and create an alternative fuel source such as converting water into hydrogen (fuel) and oxygen (oxidizer), both of which burn clean without any pollution. Water is plentiful in the world. We NEED to get off being dependent on oil ... particularly, Middle Eastern oil. That's the strategic solution to eradicate terrorism.

Water is an Alternative. Once we solve the problem of economically converting good old H_2O (i.e., water), of which there is an unlimited supply in the world, into hydrogen and oxygen, we won't need to depend on hydrocarbons any longer. Hydrogen and oxygen combusts clean and generates heat and water (recycling again), which would be environmentally friendly. I say, let's not deal with petroleum any longer than we absolutely must. If we become independent of petroleum, we can counter all of those adversaries who are continually sticking it to us. Let them find another reason to blackmail us.

Alternative Fuel

Manhattan Project. I am for the US conducting a Manhattan-Project-like effort to develop a way to use water (H_2O) as a fuel within 10 years. The hydrogen (2H) is separated from the oxygen (O), and the hydrogen (2H) is

---

8   Taubert, R. (2006, Summer). Piracy's perils: Marine marshals. *The Journal of Counterterrorism and Homeland Security International, 12(2)*.

used as the propellant and the oxygen (O) as the oxidizer or the hydrogen (H) can be used as propellant and the hydroxyl ion (OH) used as the oxidizer. When we do that, we won't need Middle Eastern oil any longer. Fuel will be plentiful as water is all around us and also is recyclable.

Crux of the Problem. This solution will prove whether oil and our presence in the Middle East are the crux of the problem. We may find out that jealousy may actually be the crux of the problem because I feel that al-Qaeda will still want to destroy the USA even after we are out of the Middle East and not bothering them any longer.

Motivation. The motivation to get a Manhattan-Project-type project going to accomplish the task within 10 years would need to be a major WMD attack on the US by the Islamo-fascists. As I have stated before, our US politicians/leaders are reactive not proactive in nature. They do nothing significant unless motivated by major catastrophes. That approach is sad, but that's the way they operate.

If we move at the current snail's pace that we are moving, hydrogen power is 50 years away from today. However, a Manhattan-like project would contract those 50 years into a mere decade. The development of the atomic bomb was also 50 years off at the snail's pace that they were moving. However, with the brewing of WW II on the horizon in the mid-30s, that was the motivator for a 10-year Manhattan Project.

Also, remember when President Kennedy said in 1960 that we would go to the Moon within the decade? When Congress and the Aerospace Industry got behind it, the US made it to the Moon even before the 10 years were up. WW II motivated the development of long-range rockets (e.g., the Germans developed the V-1 buzz bomb and the V-2 rocket) and the jet-engine aircraft (again, the Germans led the world in this area). By the time the Korean Conflict started in the early 1950s, the Russians had the MIG-15, and we had the F-86 Sabre Jet.

Attacking Our Schools

School Districts. Henry Morgenstern, president of Security Solutions International (SSI), stated: "Another early sign of the terrorists will to attack soft targets was the discovery in October 2004 in Iraq when US troops found two computer disks containing photographs, evacuation plans, and crisis management related information regarding eight school districts in the USA: Fort Myers, Florida; Salem, Oregon; Jones County, Georgia; Rumson and Franklin Township in New Jersey; Birch Run, Michigan; San Diego, California; and one [other] district in California that remained unidentified, so great was the estimated threat level."[9] My guess is that unknown school district in California is the Los Angeles Unified School District.

Morgenstern goes on to write, "With terrorists looking to bring the US to its psychological knees, it is clear that they understand the value of hitting the US where every American, not just big city Americans live. LA has identified more than 605 critical terror targets."[10]

San Diego and "The Enemy Within." It is interesting to note how important the city where I live, i.e., San Diego, is to the terrorists. After all, we are close to the Mexican border (where al Qaeda infiltrators are coming in droves), we have a huge Naval Base in San Diego, and some of the 19 al-Qaeda 9/11 terrorists that attacked the WTC had lived in San Diego planning their dastardly deed. When the attack happens, our country would also need to deal with all of the traitors in Congress, i.e., the enemy within.

Targeting 2,000,000 Children. As expected, our normal *modus operandi* (MO) is "business as usual." Only when something like a 9/11-type attack actually happens, then and only then, will the American populace feel that something should have been done and say, "Why wasn't it done a long time ago?" OBL has targeted 2 million children in this upcoming attack. Then, it'll be time to shed that mental fat. Sad, but that's exactly the way it will happen. We are not a proactive society; we are a reactive society. When you have the mentality of our leaders feeling that the GWOT is just police action, not a war; if it is a war, we have already lost; and that the war is just a bumper sticker slogan; do you wonder why the populace has that "Who cares?" head-in-the-sand, cavalier attitude?

Coming Attack. I read Paul Williams' book titled *The Al Qaeda Connection*, which is on international crime and terrorism. The Russians and al-Qaeda have numerous suitcase nukes already hidden (buried underground) throughout the US.[11] A few of these will be use to wipe out our schools and will kill millions of children. It is not a question of "if" but "when." People do not want to hear of talk about this topic, but few of us need to be prepared for this eventuality to help save the country when it does happen.

---

9   Morgenstern, H. (2007, Winter). Hardening targets: How do you respond to alert levels. *Counter Terrorism: The Journal of Counterterrorism and Homeland Security International, 13(4)*, 10-12.

10   Ibid.

11   Williams, P. L. (2005). *The Al-Qaeda connection: International terrorism, organized crime, and the coming apocalypse.* Amherst, New York: Prometheus Books.

Research. I have yet to find any info on the schools' blueprints that they have found. I am continuing my research into all of these important details about al Qaeda's pending attack on the CONUS motherland.

Learning from the Russians. Tomas Hunter wrote that the Beslan School Hostage Crisis, initiated by Chechen gunmen on September 1, 2004, remains one of the deadliest attacks against civilians in the age of modern terrorism. It once again brought the specter of militant Islamism to the global consciousness. It is a painful reminder of the vicious and cruel lengths to which some extremist organizations are willing to undertake in order to convey their twisted message to the public. It also highlights the myriad obstacles and difficulties faced by state security forces when confronting extremists who intend on carrying out complex, lethal terrorist actions.[12] We can learn many relevant lessons by studying the Beslan School #1 hostage crisis.

World War

It is a known fact (per Paul Williams) that we have many suitcase nukes already hidden in the ground throughout the USA.[13] When the word is given, WW III or WW IV (depending on how you look at it) will start after the terrorists blow up seven of our major metropolitan cities.

Russia and China. Russia and China have thousands of nuclear-tipped warheads on intercontinental ballistic missiles (ICBMs) and submarine-launched intermediate range ballistic missiles (IRBMs). Trust me, more than one or two will get through. China is building the largest navy in the world while the US naval fleet is diminishing in size and numbers. In 10 years, China will surpass us in the total number of ships.

SLBMs. It is not the ICBMs that we need to worry about, but it is the sub-launched IRBMs. They will be located closer to our shores, and detection/response times are a whole lot shorter than the 25-30 minutes we will have for the ICBMs. Submarine-launched ballistic missiles (SLBMs) will reach their CONUS targets in 5-10 minutes. I don't think our response forces could respond quickly enough to get all of our nuclear bombers in the air in 5 minutes … maybe 10 is possible.

First Strike. If the US starts with a first strike, we win. If we start after the first strike by an enemy, we may lose. Even though we say we have done away with mutual assured destruction (MAD) and massive retaliation, that

---

12   Hunter, T. B. (2008, Winter issue). A look back at the Beslan school hostage crisis. *Counter Terrorism: Journal of Counterterrorism & Homeland Security International, 14(4)*, 30-34.

13   Williams, P. L. (2005). *The Al-Qaeda connection: International terrorism, organized crime, and the coming apocalypse*. Amherst, New York: Prometheus Books.

doesn't mean that we still cannot do it. First strike is not out of the question. Remember, we did it in Iraq. We can do it again in Iran. At any rate, if the Israelis start the war with a First Strike approach, the US will automatically join in and help implement The Plan. If we strike with nukes first, we win. If we strike only in retaliation, we may lose.

Pacifists. It appears that the pacifists want us to take the first barrage and then retaliate with whatever we have left to throw at them. By then, it may be too late for any kind of defensive action. But that is what they want by waiting to be hit first. Only time will tell whether that is the right strategy as I don't believe that the US will strike first. After all, we don't appear to want to win ... just to survive ... and maybe barely.

Apparently, "gloom and doom" are upon us. Whatever happens, I believe that we shall survive. Since Barack Obama is now our president, guess who will be responsible for the upcoming war? Pacifists will be unable to blame it on the Republicans any longer. It will be in the laps of the cut-and-run pacifists. Scary times are ahead of us. Thus, we must be forever vigilant.

Negative vs. Positive Attitude. Remember the old 1971 Charlton Heston movie titled "The Omega Man"? You have seen too many doomsday movies such as "The Day After." All of these kinds of movies that are created by the Hollywood mafia/elite have brainwashed the population to display a negative attitude that a nuclear war will be the end of the world.

Bernard Brodie (1919-78) wrote *The Absolute Weapon* (1946), which was the first book on nuclear strategy. He thought that a nuclear war couldn't be won[14] ... the "glass half empty" mindset. On the other hand, Herman Kahn (1922-83) wrote *On Thermonuclear War* (1961), but unlike Brodie, he believed that nuclear war could be won[15] ... the "glass half full" mindset. Kahn founded the Hudson Institute in 1961.

Nuclear Warfare. Tactical nukes can be effectively used to end a war. Democrat President Harry Truman effectively used two nukes (Little Boy and Fat Man) to obliterate Hiroshima and Nagasaki to bring the war in the Pacific (WW II) to an abrupt end. There was no nuclear holocaust. The bomb on Hiroshima was about 13 kiloton yield, and the one on Nagasaki was a smaller yield. After five years from the bombings, approximately 200,000 people had died as a result of the two bombs. Note that the residual radiation didn't last very long. Japan started to flourish after five years from the end of the War. By ending the war with nuclear weapons, Truman saved the loss of millions of lives (on both sides) in a prolonged war.

---

14   Brodie, B. (Ed.). (1946). *The absolute weapon: Atomic power and world order*. New York: Harcourt, Brace and Co., 214 pp.

15   Kahn, H. (1961). *On thermonuclear war*. New York: Princeton University Press.

Atomic bombs would have lasting radiation effects, but not hundreds of years as some people say. However, at one time we had developed the neutron bomb, which when exploded, would not have as much lingering radioactive effects as would thermonuclear weapons (atomic fission bombs and hydrogen fusion bombs). President George H. W. Bush terminated the development of those weapons. However, other nations have continued the development of such enhanced radiation weapons (ERWs), which they would definitely use on us so that it wouldn't make the US a wasteland.

Impacts. No matter what major manmade or natural disaster occurs, there are always impacts on the supply of food and gas, and they always affect financial markets. These are given as results of major manmade or natural disasters. What I am also concerned about are other impacts on our country and population. These concerns include such items as first response, survival of our national defense infrastructure, dealing with "the enemy within," neutralizing the effects of WMDs, retaliatory response, and really closing the borders after the first attack.

Survival of Mankind. We need to think about more than just economic matters, money, and day-to-day individual survival. We need to think about the overall survival of our nation and way of life. That's what I am concerned more about than where my next meal is coming from, filling my car with gasoline, or whether the stock market tanks. We need to go beyond those things and work for the survival of mankind, and how we are going to deal with the enemy tearing down the front gate to get at us.

Preparation

Some of the things that we can do to prepare include the following:

1. Get knowledgeable about the enemy (To defeat they enemy, you must "know thy enemy") and what they can/will do so we won't be surprised and will, instead, be prepared as are Boy Scouts, for when you are prepared, you need not fear.

2. Not keep our heads buried deep in the sand (like an ostrich) thinking that it will not happen, or it will go away by ignoring it.

3. Not maintain the doom's day attitude but, instead, know that we will survive and will prevail ... if we prepare for it.

4. Maintain a year's supply of stored food to provide for your family, relatives, friends, and neighbors should a dire need for food arise after a disaster. Also, keep a supply of bottled water and rotate them regularly.

5. Keep a supply of dry cell batteries needed for the many gadgets you may have that require batteries.

6. Keep a 72-hour kit in the trunk of your cars of important items you will need during emergencies.

7. Never let the gasoline level in your cars' tanks go below 1/4th full.

8. Know the escape routes in your home.

9. Stay vigilant continuously so you are never blindsided. Always be aware of your surroundings.

10. Educate others of the threat so that they will also be better prepared.

11. Work to help strengthen our country in dealing with the terrorist threat (I have a litany of things that I am doing here).

12. Keep physically, mentally, and morally healthy.

13. Pray to God for his continual protection.

14. Many others can be added from here onward.

All other items, except one (i.e., canned food), will be the next level of action should the GWOT really get "hot," and we are thrust into WW III (or WW IV as some people say since they consider the Cold War as WW III, which we have already won). We don't need to panic. All we need to do is to be aware, become trained, be vigilant, and be calm when an attack or disaster occurs. Some people will need to direct all of the others who are unprepared. I hope to be part of that smaller group who are ready for action when it becomes necessary.

I didn't think we needed to be in the survivalist mode, so I suggest this simple, initial list. Note that these things could be used for any natural or manmade disaster. Of course, I assume that we are not dealing with a nuclear holocaust, which I don't suggest that the preparation of things to do would prepare you for such an event. Being vigilant, having dry cell batteries, and no less than a quarter tank of gas won't do much good if we had a nuclear holocaust. However, if we got into a tactical nuclear conflict, I suggest that we take these simple survivalist actions.

The Will to Win. If we all took the denial approach to what could happen, we all would be unprepared for a nuclear event such as a terrorist dirty bomb (radiological weapon). Thinking that it is impossible to defend against a tactical nuclear conflict is taking the defeatist approach. If everybody thought that way, we certainly would lose. Winning wars is based on *the will to win*. If we lose the will to win, we definitely would lose and would never win. I would never take the approach to believe these events won't happen or believe they will happen and still do nothing. That is the defeatist approach. Thinking something will not happen is taking the "head-in-the-sand approach" used by ostriches. I totally disagree with anyone's assertion that we are in for years of posturing and saber-rattling. Ahmadinejad has been doing all of the saber-rattling for months/years, but I don't think he will be doing that for years on end.

War is Hell

General William Tecumseh Sherman said, "War is Hell." Remember, Iran's President Mahmoud Ahmadinajad said that he will blow Israel off the map and attack the US with nukes. Osama bin Laden wants al-Qaeda to kill 4 million Americans including 2 million children soon. When they do that, we will massively retaliate and wipe out Iran and locations where OBL is hiding out in the borders of Pakistan and Afghanistan. The US military already has plans for such an occurrence. Israel has a "doom's day" plan that it will initiate should the first Iranian-sponsored nuke explode in Israel as perpetrated by al-Qaeda terrorists.

Ahmadinajad's Antics. Iran's President Mahmoud Ahmadinajad came to the UN in New York City (NYC) to lambaste the US. He also had plans to visit Ground Zero in NYC to pay his respects to the 19 terrorists (led by Mohamed or Muhammad Atta) who destroyed the World Trade Center (WTC) twin towers. Further, like fools, we were about to allow him to do that. However, NYC Mayor Michael Bloomberg objected followed by an outcry of the citizenry, and Ahmadinajad decided not to do it. Do you think President George W. Bush could go to Tehran, Iran, and make anti-Iran speeches … and live? He'd be deader than a door knob!

Ahmadinajad also went to the left-wing Columbia University to praise the "hate-America-first" crowd of students who won't even let our own leaders speak there without being drowned out with noise and being attacked on stage. They really believe in freedom of speech. If you believe that, I have some marshlands in Florida to sell you. The world's war condition is heating up drastically … much faster than Al Gore's global warming is happening. Be vigilant.

Conclusion

We had better prepare ourselves for the coming attacks. The chapters of this book can help to educate American citizens and prepare them to combat terrorists in the United States of America. If we are prepared, we have no need to fear. We must not bury our collective heads in the sand. We must eradicate the enemy within. We must be forever vigilant.

CHAPTER 2
US NATIONAL SECURITY
AND HOMELAND SECURITY
STRATEGIES

Robert T. Uda, MS, MBA

Introduction

In this chapter, I analyzed the various strategy documents and compared their objectives and other major points to answer the question: Do the US national security and homeland security strategies complement each other? To begin with, I defined the word "strategy." Then, I explored the salient points of *The National Security Strategy of the United States of America* document. I did likewise with the *National Strategy for Homeland Security* document and identified important features. However, sandwiched between the national security strategy and homeland security strategy, I analyzed the *National Strategy for Combating Terrorism* document. It was interesting to note how these three documents worked synergistically together as an integrated strategy.

What is Strategy?

Strategy Defined. *Strategy* is the science of planning and directing large-scale military operations, specifically (as distinguished from tactics) of maneuvering forces into the most advantageous position prior to actual engagement with the enemy. *Strategy* is a plan or action based on this. *Strategy* is skill in managing or planning, especially by using stratagems. *Strategy* is a stratagem or artful means to some end.[16] As stated in the problem statement above, *strategy* provides a plan for action to combat a threat, and that threat today is the attacking terrorists and their weapons of mass destruction

---

16   Neufeldt, V. (Editor in Chief), & Guralnik, D. B. (Editor in Chief Emeritus), (Eds.). (1989). *Webster's New World Dictionary of American English (Third College Edition)*. New York: Simon & Schuster, Inc.

(WMDs)[17] and cyber-warfare.[18] WMDs include chemical, biological, radiological, nuclear, and enhanced effects (CBRNE) weapons. An example of an "enhanced effects weapon"[19] is when terrorists use commercial airliners[20] as missiles and crash them into large buildings as they did on 9/11.

Asymmetrical Warfare Strategy. In today's Global War on Terrorism (GWOT), strategy using "large-scale military operations" is only large scale in the sense that the war is worldwide or global. However, in fighting terrorists, we do not marshal large-scale forces to meet at a battlefront as we did in conventional warfare in World War I, World War II, and the Korean Conflict. Unconventional or asymmetrical warfare uses a different kind of strategy. The enemy does not dress in a military uniform with insignia on it. The enemy does not respect national boundaries. The enemy does not abide by the tenets of the Geneva Convention. The enemy is not afraid of dying for his twisted cause. The enemy is brutal and vicious and will kill anyone they consider as infidels or who are non-believers of their special brand of fundamentalist Islamic beliefs. They are Islamo-fascists. We must possess a strategy that can effectively counter that kind of unconventional, asymmetrical warfare. We tried to fight an unconventional war in Vietnam with conventional weapons, strategies, and tactics … and we failed miserably at it. To win, we must fight the Islamo-fascist terrorists using unconventional weapons, strategies, and tactics.

National Security Strategy

National Security Policy. It is the *policy* of the United States to seek and support democratic movements and institutions in every nation and culture, with the ultimate goal of ending tyranny in our world. In the world today, the fundamental character of regimes matters as much as the distribution of power among them. The *goal* of our statecraft is to help create a world of democratic, well-governed states that can meet the needs of their citizens and

---

17   The White House (2002, December). *National Strategy to Combat Weapons of Mass Destruction.* Washington, DC.

18   The White House (2003, February). *The National Strategy to Secure Cyberspace.* Washington, DC.

19   Larsen, R., & McIntyre, D. (n.d.). A primer on homeland security: Strategic functions, threats, and mission areas. ANSER Institute for Homeland Security. Retrieved June 14, 2008, from http://www.homelanddefense.org/bulletin/strategic_functions.htm.

20   DHS (2007, March 26). *National Strategy for Aviation Security.* Washington, DC: US Department of Homeland Security (DHS).

conduct themselves responsibly in the international arena. This is the best way to provide enduring security for the American people.[21]

There Will Always Be Wars. "Ending tyranny in our world" may be a lofty vision statement but an unachievable task. Since there is opposition in all things, there will always be protagonists and antagonists. Like Newton's Third Law of Motion, "For every action, there is an equal and opposite reaction,"[22] no force will ever go on forever without meeting an opposing force in due time. As long as this dichotomy exists, there will be disagreements and eventual conflicts. It is like ending poverty in the world. That will never happen because one defines the other. For a certain people to be considered as rich there must be another set of people considered as poor. One defines the other. From history, we see that there will always be wars. Yes, there may be short periods of world peace. However, a short period of peace usually ends with the start of ongoing wars somewhere throughout the world.

War on Islamo-fascist Terrorists. The war on poverty will never be solved because poverty is a concept, and you cannot triumph over a concept. Likewise, the war on drugs will never be solved because you cannot fight and triumph over drugs. Drugs are inanimate chemicals. Additionally, the war on *terrorism* or the war on *terror* will never be won because you cannot triumph over the concept of terrorism or terror. However, we are fighting a war against human beings (if you can call them that) ... a war against Islamo-fascist terrorists. A war on terrorists can be won because all we need to do is to kill all terrorists, destroy their will to continue the fight, or persuade them that there are better alternatives ... alternatives that are peaceful in nature in a co-existing world. If they cannot and will not accept the peaceful co-existence alternative, then we must either destroy their will to fight or eliminate them altogether.

The Goal of Our Statecraft. Achieving this goal is the work of generations. The United States is in the early years of a long struggle, similar to what our country faced in the early years of the Cold War (which lasted for about 45 years). The 20th Century witnessed the triumph of freedom over the threats of totalitarianism including fascism, Nazism, and communism. Yet a new totalitarian ideology now threatens, an ideology grounded not in secular philosophy but in the perversion of a proud religion (Islam). Its content may be different from the ideologies of the last century. However, its means are

---

21   The White House (2006, March). *The National Security Strategy of the United States of America*. Washington, DC.

22   Anonymous (n.d.). Newton's Third Law: Applied to aerodynamics. National Aeronautics and Space Administration Glenn Research Center website. Retrieved June 14, 2008, from http://www.grc.nasa.gov/WWW/K-12/airplane/newton3.html.

similar, i.e., intolerance, murder, terror, enslavement, and repression. National strategy provides the vision for all elements of power to combine to protect national interests.[23]

Our National Security Strategy. In a letter to the American people, President George W. Bush wrote:[24] Our national security strategy is founded upon two pillars:

- **The first pillar** is promoting freedom, justice, and human dignity – working to end tyranny, to promote effective democracies, and to extend prosperity through free and fair trade and wise development policies. Free governments are accountable to their people, govern their territory effectively, and pursue economic and political policies that benefit their citizens. Free governments do not oppress their people or attack other free nations. Peace and international stability are most reliably built on a foundation of freedom.
- **The second pillar** of our strategy is confronting the challenges of our time by leading a growing community of democracies. Many of the problems we face – from the threat of pandemic disease, to proliferation of weapons of mass destruction, to terrorism, to human trafficking, to natural disasters – reach across borders. Effective multinational efforts are essential to solve these problems. Yet, history has shown that only when we do our part will others do theirs. America must continue to lead.

Hence, we have our work cut out for us. We must lead, follow, or get out of the way. But we have no choice. Either we lead to win or we lose. Given those two alternatives, we must lead.

Idealistic Goals and Realistic Means. The challenges America faces are great, yet we have enormous power and influence to address those challenges. The times require an ambitious national security strategy, yet one recognizing the limits that even a nation as powerful as the United States can achieve by itself. Our national security strategy is idealistic about goals, and realistic about means. There was a time when two oceans seemed to provide protection from problems in other lands, leaving America to lead by example alone. That time has long since passed. America cannot know peace, security, and prosperity by retreating from the world. America must lead by deed as well as

---

23   The White House (2006, March). *The National Security Strategy of the United States of America.* Washington, DC.

24   Ibid.

by example. This is how we plan to lead, and this is the legacy we will leave to those who follow.[25]

Combating Terrorism Strategy

National Strategy for Combating Terrorism. America is at war with a transnational terrorist movement fueled by a radical ideology of hatred, oppression, and murder. Our September 2006 *National Strategy for Combating Terrorism*, first published in February 2003,[26] recognizes that we are at war and that protecting and defending the Homeland, the American people, and their livelihoods remains our first and most solemn obligation.[27] In conjunction with *The National Security Strategy of the United States of America*, our *National Strategy for Combating Terrorism* focuses specifically on the terrorist threat.

A Different Kind of War. Our strategy also recognizes that the War on Terror is a different kind of war. From the beginning, it has been both a battle of arms and a battle of ideas. Not only do we fight our terrorist enemies on the battlefield, but we promote freedom and human dignity as alternatives to the terrorists' perverse vision of oppression and totalitarian rule. The paradigm for combating terrorism now involves the application of all elements of our national power and influence. Not only do we employ military power, we use diplomatic, financial, intelligence, and law enforcement activities to protect the Homeland and extend our defenses, disrupt terrorist operations, and deprive our enemies of what they need to operate and survive. We have broken old orthodoxies that once confined our counterterrorism efforts primarily to the criminal justice domain.[28]

Winning the Battle of Ideas. From the beginning, the War on Terror has been both a battle of arms and a battle of ideas – a fight against the terrorists and their murderous ideology. In the short run, the fight involves the application of all instruments of national power and influence to kill or capture the terrorists, deny them safe haven and control of any nation, prevent them from gaining access to WMD, render potential terrorist targets less attractive by strengthening security, and cut off their sources of funding and other resources they need to operate and survive. In the long run, winning the War on Terror means winning the battle of ideas. Ideas can transform the

---

25   Ibid.

26   The White House (2003, February). *National Strategy for Combating Terrorism.* Washington, DC.

27   The White House (2006, September). *National Strategy for Combating Terrorism.* Washington, DC.

28   Ibid.

embittered and disillusioned either into murderers willing to kill innocents or into free peoples living harmoniously in a diverse society.[29]

Two-pronged Vision. The battle of ideas helps to define the strategic intent of our *National Strategy for Combating Terrorism.* The United States will continue to lead an expansive international effort in pursuit of a two-pronged vision:[30]

- The defeat of violent extremism as a threat to our way of life as a free and open society
- The creation of a global environment inhospitable to violent extremists and all who support them

Safer but Not Yet Safe. Since the September 11 attacks, America is safer, but we are not yet safe. We have done much to degrade al-Qaeda and its affiliates and to undercut the perceived legitimacy of terrorism. Our Muslim partners are speaking out against those who seek to use their religion to justify violence and a totalitarian vision of the world. We have significantly expanded our counterterrorism coalition, transforming old adversaries into new and vital partners in the War on Terror. We have liberated more than 50 million Afghans and Iraqis from despotism, terrorism, and oppression, permitting the first free elections in recorded history for either nation. In addition, we have transformed our governmental institutions and framework to wage a generational struggle. Challenges will continue to exist, but along with our partners, we will attack terrorism and its twisted ideology and bring hope and freedom to the people of the world. This is how we will win the War on Terror.[31]

Homeland Security Strategy

Overview. America is at war with terrorist enemies who are intent on attacking our Homeland and destroying our way of life. The lives and livelihoods of the American people also remain at risk from natural catastrophes, including naturally occurring infectious diseases and hazards such as hurricanes and earthquakes, and man-made accidents. Our *National Strategy for Homeland Security* recognizes that while we must continue to focus on the persistent and evolving terrorist threat, we also must address the

---

29 Ibid.
30 Ibid.
31 Ibid.

full range of potential catastrophic events, including man-made and natural disasters, due to their implications on homeland security.[32]

Purpose of Our Strategy. The purpose of our Homeland Security Strategy is to guide, organize, and unify our Nation's homeland security efforts. It provides a common framework by which our entire Nation should focus its efforts on the following four goals:[33]

- Prevent and disrupt terrorist attacks
- Protect the American people, our critical infrastructure, and key resources[34],[35]
- Respond to and recover from incidents that do occur
- Continue to strengthen the foundation to ensure our long-term success

Our Borders are Unsecured. In accordance with the problem statement, Homeland security strategy should complement national security strategy and address specific requirements associated with defending the nation's borders. Page 5 of the *National Strategy for Homeland Security* makes the following statement: "We have made our borders more secure and developed an effective system of layered defense by strengthening the screening of people and goods overseas and by tracking and disrupting the international travel of terrorists."[36],[37] I take total umbrage to this statement. It is blatantly false! We absolutely have not made our porous borders secure[38] from terrorist infiltrations, not to mention the millions of illegal aliens who have entered the United States.

Terrorists Infiltrate Our Borders. Texas Governor Rick Perry said, "Nationwide, 650 people from 'special interest countries' were caught last

---

32   HSC (2007, October). *National Strategy for Homeland Security*. Washington, DC: Homeland Security Council (HSC).

33   Ibid.

34   The White House (2003, February). *The National Strategy for the Physical Protection of Critical Infrastructures and Key Assets*. Washington, DC.

35   DHS (2006). *National Infrastructure Protection Plan*. Washington, DC: US Department of Homeland Security (DHS).

36   HSC (2007, October). *National Strategy for Homeland Security*. Washington, DC: Homeland Security Council (HSC).

37   NCTC (2006, May 2). *National Strategy to Combat Terrorist Travel*. McLean, VA: National Counterterrorism Center (NCTC).

38   Anonymous (2007). *The Secure Borders, Economic Opportunity, and Immigration Reform Act of 2007: Section 127, National Strategy for Border Security*. The Heritage Foundation. Retrieved June 15, 2008, from http://www.heritage.org/research/immigration/im62007.cfm?page=22.

year [2005] entering the country illegally. This shows the potential of terrorist organizations to infiltrate our border is a real threat that must be taken seriously."[39],[40] Since 1994, the Border Patrol has made more than 11.3 million apprehensions nationwide. In FY 2001, Border Patrol agents apprehended almost 1.2 million persons for illegally entering our country.[41],[42]

Port and Maritime Security. Along with border security,[43] we must be concerned about port and maritime security.[44] Department of Homeland Security Secretary Michael Chertoff said that the threat of a *USS Cole*-type attack on US ports – where a small boat packed with explosives detonates in a harbor – is one of his top concerns.[45],[46] We historically know that terrorists like al-Qaeda use small vessels to conduct attack operations. They attempted to do so with respect to the *USS The Sullivans*. They successfully did so with respect to the *USS Cole*. They did so with respect to the French tanker *Limburg*. Hence, this is certainly a threat with some historic legacy.[47],[48]

A Truly National Effort Needed. Homeland security requires a truly national effort, with shared goals and responsibilities for protecting and defending the Homeland. Our *National Strategy for Homeland Security* leverages the unique strengths and capabilities of all levels of government, the

39   Anonymous (2006, October 20). High-intensity joint operations help Texas improve security at border. *Crime Control Digest, 40(41)*, pp. 1-2.

40   Uda, R. T. (2008). *Terrorism and Counterterrorism: Victory Over Islamo-fascist Jihadists*. Bloomington, IN: iUniverse, Inc.

41   Bullock, J. A., Haddow, G. D., Coppola, D., Ergin, E., Westerman, L., & Yeletaysi, S. (2006). *Introduction to Homeland Security, Second Edition*. Oxford, United Kingdom: Elsevier Butterworth-Heinemann.

42   Uda, R. T. (2008). *Terrorism and Counterterrorism: Victory Over Islamo-fascist Jihadists*. Bloomington, IN: iUniverse, Inc.

43   Anonymous (2007). *The Secure Borders, Economic Opportunity, and Immigration Reform Act of 2007: Section 127, National Strategy for Border Security*. The Heritage Foundation. Retrieved June 15, 2008, from http://www.heritage.org/research/immigration/im62007.cfm?page=22.

44   The White House (2005, September). *The National Strategy for Maritime Security*. Washington, DC.

45   Anonymous (2007, September 10). Chertoff: We're preparing for nuclear attack. Newsfront. Retrieved June 15, 2008 from http://www.newsmax.com/newsfront/chertoff_nuclear/2007/09/10/31560.html?s=al&promo_code=39CB-1.

46   Uda, R. T. (2008). *Terrorism and Counterterrorism: Victory Over Islamo-fascist Jihadists*. Bloomington, IN: iUniverse, Inc.

47   Chertoff, M. (2007, July 20). Chertoff addresses port security & supply chain protection. *News Room*, Equity International, Inc. Retrieved June 15, 2008, from http://www.worldinvest.us/details.asp?id=597.

48   Uda, R. T. (2008). *Terrorism and Counterterrorism: Victory Over Islamo-fascist Jihadists*. Bloomington, IN: iUniverse, Inc.

private and non-profit sectors, communities, and individual citizens. Mindful that many of the threats we face do not recognize geographic boundaries, we also continue to work closely with our international partners throughout the world. Our first and most solemn obligation is to protect the American people. The *National Strategy for Homeland Security* guides our Nation as we honor this commitment and achieve a more secure Homeland that sustains our way of life as a free, prosperous, and welcoming America.[49]

Our Work is far from Over. Since the turn of the millennium, our Nation has endured history's deadliest attack of international terrorism and the most destructive natural disaster to strike American soil. In the face of these challenges, America has responded courageously, with focus and clarity of purpose. Today, we are safer, stronger, and better prepared to address the full range of catastrophic events that threaten us, including man-made accidents and natural disasters. Our work, however, is far from over. We remain resolute in our commitment to prevent and disrupt terrorist attacks in the Homeland, protect the American people and the Nation's critical infrastructure and key resources,[50],[51] and effectively respond to and recover from those incidents that do occur. Working together, our Nation will secure the Homeland in order to sustain our way of life – now and for generations to come.[52]

Are the Two Strategies Complementary?

Combating Terrorism Strategy Builds Directly from National Security Strategy. The updated September 2006 *National Strategy for Combating Terrorism* sets the course for winning the War on Terror. It builds directly from the March 2006 *National Security Strategy* as well as the February 2003 *National Strategy for Combating Terrorism*, and incorporates our increased understanding of the enemy. From the beginning, we understood that the War on Terror involved more than simply finding and bringing to justice those who had planned and executed the terrorist attacks on September 11, 2001. Our strategy involved destroying the larger al-Qaeda network and also

49   HSC (2007, October). *National Strategy for Homeland Security*. Washington, DC: Homeland Security Council (HSC).

50   The White House (2003, February). *The National Strategy for the Physical Protection of Critical Infrastructures and Key Assets*. Washington, DC.

51   DHS (2006). *National Infrastructure Protection Plan*. Washington, DC: US Department of Homeland Security (DHS).

52   HSC (2007, October). *National Strategy for Homeland Security*. Washington, DC: Homeland Security Council (HSC).

confronting the radical ideology that inspires others to join or support the terrorist movement.[53]

Homeland Security Strategy Complements Combating Terrorism Strategy. The updated October 2007 *National Strategy for Homeland Security* builds directly from the first July 2002 *National Strategy for Homeland Security*.[54] Additionally, it reflects increased understanding of the terrorist threats confronting the United States today. Furthermore, it incorporates lessons learned from exercises and real-world catastrophes – including Hurricane Katrina. Finally, it proposes new initiatives and approaches that enable the Nation to achieve our homeland security objectives. This *National Strategy for Homeland Security* also complements both the March 2006 *National Security Strategy* and the September 2006 *National Strategy for Combating Terrorism*.[55] As can be seen, the *National Security Strategy* not only complements the *National Strategy for Combating Terrorism*, but it also complements the *National Strategy for Homeland Security*. In other words, all three strategies work in unison, in coordination, and in correlation with each other.

Conclusion

Strategy provides a plan for action to combat a threat. The US must possess a strategy that effectively counters unconventional or asymmetrical warfare. The Global War on Terrorism (GWOT) is both a battle of arms and a battle of ideas. The battle of ideas helps to define the strategic intent of our *National Strategy for Combating Terrorism. The National Security Strategy of the United States of America, National Strategy for Combating Terrorism,* and *National Strategy for Homeland Security* work in unison, in coordination, and in correlation among each other. Because of that synergism and since the September 11 attacks, America is now safer but not yet safe.

---

53   The White House (2006, September). *National Strategy for Combating Terrorism.* Washington, DC.

54   Anonymous (2002, July). *National Strategy for Homeland Security.* Washington, DC: Office of Homeland Security.

55   HSC (2007, October). *National Strategy for Homeland Security.* Washington, DC: Homeland Security Council (HSC).

CHAPTER 3
US NATIONAL & HOMELAND SECURITY INTELLIGENCE POLICIES

Robert T. Uda, MS, MBA

Introduction

In this chapter, I analyze the US homeland security intelligence strategy and compare it to published homeland security strategy documents. Furthermore, this paper covers a discussion of US national and homeland security intelligence policies. Intelligence operations and plans support the accomplishment of the objectives as documented in the *National Strategy for Homeland Security*.

Published Homeland Security Strategy Documents

July 2002 National Strategy for Homeland Security. The Office of Homeland Security (OHS) published the first *National Strategy for Homeland Security* document dated July 2002. The purpose of the *Strategy* is to mobilize and organize our Nation to secure the US homeland from terrorist attacks. This is a complex mission that requires coordinated and focused effort from our entire society including the federal government, state and local governments, private sector, and American people.[56]

October 2007 National Strategy for Homeland Security. The Homeland Security Council (HSC) published the second *National Strategy for Homeland Security* document dated October 2007. The purpose of our *Strategy* is to guide, organize, and unify our nation's homeland security efforts. It provides a common framework by which our entire nation should focus its efforts on the following four goals:[57]

- Prevent and disrupt terrorist attacks

---

56   OHS (2002, July). *National Strategy for Homeland Security*. Washington, DC: Office of Homeland Security (OHS).

57   HSC (2007, October). *National Strategy for Homeland Security*. Washington, DC: Homeland Security Council (HSC).

- Protect the American people, our critical infrastructure, and key resources
- Respond to and recover from incidents that do occur
- Continue to strengthen the foundation to ensure our long-term success.

This updated *Strategy*, which builds directly from the first *National Strategy for Homeland Security* (NSHS) issued in July 2002, reflects our increased understanding of the terrorist threats confronting the US today. This *Strategy* also complements both the *National Security Strategy* issued in March 2006[58] and the *National Strategy for Combating Terrorism* issued in September 2006.[59]

DHS Intelligence Enterprise Strategic Plan. The *DHS Intelligence Enterprise Strategic Plan* indicates our commitment to integrate the broad intelligence capabilities of the Department. Our stakeholders expect us to warn them of threats to the Homeland, support operational missions and policy initiatives, and develop the collection, analysis, and dissemination capabilities that make the DHS Intelligence Enterprise a first-class operation.[60] The *DHS Intelligence Enterprise Strategic Plan* works in unison with *The National Intelligence Strategy of the USA*.[61]

Homeland Security Strategic Planning: Mission Area Analysis. This report explains the Homeland Security Institute (HSI) approach to conduct the homeland security (HS) mission area analysis (MAA) and documents the results of that analysis. The HS MAA provides a hierarchical breakdown of the activities required to achieve the goal of securing the homeland. These activities include the objectives, functions, and tasks specified for the missions identified in the NSHS. These five categories of activities (Goal, Mission, Objective, Function, and Task) describe the HS operational mission space with sufficient clarity, which enable the MAA to be an effective analysis and

---

58   The White House (2006, March). *The National Security Strategy of the United States of America*. Washington, DC.

59   The White House (2006, September). *National Strategy for Combating Terrorism*. Washington, DC.

60   DHS (2006, January). *DHS Intelligence Enterprise Strategic Plan*. Washington, DC: U.S. Department of Homeland Security (DHS).

61   ODNI (2005, October). *The National Intelligence Strategy of the United States of America: Transformation through Integration and Innovation*. Washington, DC: Office of the Director of National Intelligence.

measurement tool. Collectively, the five MAA categories indicate what must be done to secure the homeland.[62]

DHS Information Sharing Strategy. In October 2007, President George W. Bush announced the *National Strategy for Information Sharing.*[63] The *National Strategy* and the updated 2007 *National Strategy for Homeland Security* envision a coordinated and integrated information sharing environment (ISE) to fight terrorism effectively and to respond to both manmade and natural disasters. Both strategies give the DHS a central role in ensuring that critical information is shared rapidly to the fullest extent allowed by law.[64] Additionally, the *DHS Information Sharing Strategy* is consistent with other information sharing strategies such as the recently released *United States Intelligence Community Information Sharing Strategy.*[65],[66]

Analysis of US Homeland Security Intelligence Strategy

Concerns about DHS Intelligence. Back in August 2003, there were concerns about DHS intelligence. Despite enactment of the Homeland Security Act, it is clear that significant concerns persisted within the executive branch about the new department's ability to analyze intelligence and law enforcement information. Media accounts suggest that these concerns center on DHS's status as a new and untested agency and the potential risks involved in forwarding "raw" intelligence to the DHS intelligence component.[67],[68] Another concern is that a new entity, rather than long-established intelligence

---

62   HSI (2007, March 28). *Homeland Security Strategic Planning: Mission Area Analysis (Final)*. Arlington, VA: Homeland Security Institute (HSI).

63   The White House (2007, October). *National Strategy for Information Sharing: Successes and Challenges in Improving Terrorism-Related Information Sharing.* Washington, DC.

64   DHS (2008, April 18). *Department of Homeland Security Information Sharing Strategy: Securing the Homeland Through Information Sharing and Collaboration.* Washington, DC: US Department of Homeland Security (DHS).

65   ONDI (2008, February 22). *United States Intelligence Community Information Sharing Strategy.* Washington, DC: Office of the Director of National Intelligence (ONDI).

66   DHS (2008, April 18). *Department of Homeland Security Information Sharing Strategy: Securing the Homeland Through Information Sharing and Collaboration.* Washington, DC: US Department of Homeland Security (DHS).

67   Eggen, D., & Mintz, J. (2002, December 6). Homeland security won't have diet of raw intelligence; rules being drafted to preclude interagency conflict. *Washington Post*, p. A43.

68   Best, R. A., Jr. (2003, August 6). Homeland security: Intelligence support. Congressional Research Service (CRS) Report for Congress, Order Code RS21283.

and law enforcement agencies, would be relied on to produce all-source intelligence relating to the most serious threats facing the country.[69]

Intelligence Reform. Charles E. Allen, Assistant Secretary for Intelligence and Analysis and Chief Intelligence Officer of the DHS, when he arrived at DHS in late 2005, stated that he would deliver results against these five priorities:[70]

- Improving the quality of intelligence analysis across the DHS
- Integrating DHS Intelligence across its several components
- Strengthening DHS's support to state, local, and tribal authorities as well as to the private sector
- Ensuring that DHS Intelligence takes its full place in the Intelligence Community (IC)
- Solidifying the DHS relationship with Congress by improving our transparency and responsiveness

All of these priorities ensure that the direction of DHS Intelligence is firmly aligned with the intent of intelligence reform within the DHS and in the IC.

Countering the Threat of Nuclear Terrorism. Charles E. Allen, Undersecretary for Intelligence and Analysis, testifying before the Senate Committee on Homeland Security and Governmental Affairs, said that the DHS, working closely with our IC colleagues, is making progress in countering the threat of nuclear terrorism. DHS Intelligence continues to provide actionable and tailored assessments to ensure that Departmental operations – especially border detection – are prepared to counter the threat of a nuclear device entering the United States. We also will remain vigilant in working with state, local, tribal, and private sector partners to ensure they maintain situational awareness and possess the necessary information to recognize and thwart nuclear-related activity in the homeland.[71]

Domestic Intelligence Agency for the US? The challenge in developing a viable domestic intelligence capability for the United States centers on:

---

69   Ibid.

70   Allen, C. E. (2007, January 25). Intelligence reform and homeland security intelligence. Written testimony to the US Senate Select Committee on Intelligence.

71   Allen, C. E. (2008, April 2). Testimony of Under Secretary for Intelligence and Analysis Charles E. Allen before the Senate Committee on Homeland Security and Governmental Affairs, "assessing the nuclear attack threat." Retrieved July 25, 2008, from http://www.dhs.gov/xnews/testimony/testimony_1207151676007.shtm.

- **Organizational Mechanisms.** How to organize these capabilities optimally within the larger US intelligence framework,
- **Information Sharing.** How to ensure streamlined information sharing between foreign intelligence and the multitude of law enforcement agencies, and
- **Oversight.** How best to implement oversight mechanisms to protect civil liberties and ensure accountability of intelligence operations.

Organizational mechanisms, information sharing, and *oversight* are the three critical components to instituting an effective domestic intelligence capability.[72]

One of the proposed constructs to meet these organizational and information sharing challenges is to create a domestic intelligence agency. The US is unique among Western or highly industrialized countries in that it does not possess one. James Burch examines the feasibility, suitability, and acceptability of instituting a domestic intelligence agency in the US from the viewpoint of organization, information sharing, and oversight.[73]

The National Intelligence Strategy of the USA. Passed by Congress in 2004, the Intelligence Reform and Terrorism Prevention Act codified our new concept of "national intelligence." This new concept originates from the tragedy of September 11, 2001, and President Bush's *National Security Strategy of the United States of America.* The President signed the new law with the expectation that "our vast intelligence enterprise will become more unified, coordinated, and effective." Our charge is clear:[74]

- Integrate the domestic and foreign dimensions of US intelligence so that there are no gaps in our understanding of threats to our national security,
- Bring more depth and accuracy to intelligence analysis, and
- Ensure that US intelligence resources generate future capabilities as well as present results.

The National Intelligence Strategy and Homeland Security Intelligence. By definition, any national strategy focuses on and provides direction to

---

72   Burch, J. (2007, June). A domestic intelligence agency for the United States? A comparative analysis of domestic intelligence agencies and their implications for homeland security. *Homeland Security Affairs, 3(2).*

73   Ibid.

74   ODNI (2005, October). *The National Intelligence Strategy of the United States of America: Transformation through Integration and Innovation.* Washington, DC: Office of the Director of National Intelligence.

the entities and agencies that the federal government controls. A broader reach or direction to entities beyond this purview might run the risk that the communities agree with the national strategy and possess the resources to implement such direction. The *National Intelligence Strategy* recognizes a homeland security intelligence role for state, local, and tribal entities as well as the private sector. Therefore, it does so only in a general manner but does not stipulate the activities these communities will implement to protect US national security.[75]

State, local, and tribal entities can be connected to our homeland security and intelligence efforts. The *National Intelligence Strategy* categorizes homeland security intelligence as driven by the federal entities most associated with the domestic intelligence mission. This mission includes the activities undertaken by the intelligence elements of the Departments of Justice and Homeland Security. "Connected" implies communication among federal, state, and local intelligence officials. However, the quantity and quality of this communication is a subject of debate among federal, state, and local officials.[76] Moving forward, *The National Intelligence Strategy of the USA* correlates well with *The National Counterintelligence Strategy of the United States of America.*

The National Counterintelligence Strategy of the United States of America. *The National Counterintelligence Strategy of the United States of America* elaborates the fundamental responsibility for US intelligence to warn of and help prevent terrorist attacks against the homeland, engage other asymmetric threats, and provide reliable intelligence on traditional and enduring strategic issues. It also describes a way forward by which the counterintelligence organizations of the US government will engage elements in the public and private sectors to address the threat posed by the intelligence activities of foreign powers and groups and protect our nation's secrets and the means by which we obtain those secrets.[77] The *Defense Intelligence Strategy* supports and coordinates with all of the above plans and strategies.

Defense Intelligence Strategy. The Defense Intelligence Enterprise must be poised at all times to provide our national, military, and civilian leaders with information sufficient to fully enable their anticipation, knowledge, understanding, management, and when possible, mitigation of the risks

---

75   Masse, T. (2006, August 18). Homeland security intelligence: Perceptions, statutory definitions, and approaches. Congressional Research Service (CRS) Report for Congress, 26 pp.

76   Ibid.

77   NCIX (2007). *The National Counterintelligence Strategy of the United States of America.* Washington, DC: National Counterintelligence Executive (NCIX).

associated with their choices. This *Defense Intelligence Strategy* provides us with the framework to meet these challenges.[78]

Comparison of US HS Intelligence Strategy to HS Strategy Documents

DHS Intelligence Enterprise Strategic Plan Vision and Mission. The vision is an integrated DHS Intelligence Enterprise that provides a decisive information advantage to the guardians of our homeland security. The mission of the DHS Intelligence Enterprise is to provide valuable, actionable intelligence and intelligence-related information for and among the National leadership, all components of DHS, our federal partners, and state, local, territorial, tribal, and private sector customers. We ensure that information is gathered from all relevant DHS field operations and is fused with information from other members of the Intelligence Community to produce accurate, timely, and actionable intelligence products and services. We independently collate, analyze, coordinate, disseminate, and manage threat information affecting the homeland.[79] The DHS Intelligence Enterprise vision and mission compare well with the homeland security vision and strategy discussed in the following paragraph.

Our Vision and Strategy for Homeland Security. Along with our partners in the international community, the US works to achieve a secure homeland that sustains our way of life as a free, prosperous, and welcoming America. We accomplish this through:[80]

- A concerted national effort that galvanizes the strengths and capabilities of federal, state, local, and tribal governments
- The private and non-profit sectors
- Regions, communities, and individual citizens

To realize this vision, the US uses all instruments of national power and influence. These instruments include diplomatic, information, military, economic, financial, intelligence, and law enforcement. Our strategic goals include to:

---

78   OUSD(I) (2008, March 31). *Defense Intelligence Strategy*. Washington, DC: Office of the Under Secretary of Defense for Intelligence (OUSD(I)).

79   DHS (2006, January). *DHS Intelligence Enterprise Strategic Plan*. Washington, DC: U.S. Department of Homeland Security (DHS).

80   HSC (2007, October). *National Strategy for Homeland Security*. Washington, DC: Homeland Security Council (HSC).

- Prevent and disrupt terrorist attacks
- Protect the American people, critical infrastructure, and key resources
- Respond to and recover from incidents that do occur

We also continue to create, strengthen, and transform the principles, systems, structures, and institutions to secure our nation over the long term. This is our strategy for homeland security.[81]

Does the US HS Intelligence Strategy Support the HS Strategy?

Information Sharing Environment. Working in a collaborative environment, the federal government recommends priorities for state, local, and tribal homeland security activities. These activities focus resources on the most pressing problems, adopt a formal intelligence process with requirements generation and information collection, and analyze/disseminate the information. Underlying our efforts to achieve domain awareness and to identify and locate terrorists and terrorist activity in the homeland is a fully developed and integrated Information Sharing Environment (ISE). This ISE supports the vertical and horizontal distribution of terrorism-related information among federal, state, local, tribal, and foreign governments as well as the private sector.[82]

DHS Information Sharing Strategy. The Intelligence Reform and Terrorism Prevention Act of 2004 (IRTPA), as amended, gives DHS a central part in the ISE. Shortly after establishing the ISE, President George W. Bush established the Office of the Program Manager for the ISE (PM-ISE). The PM-ISE currently reports to the Office of the Director of National Intelligence (ODNI). The DHS works closely with the PM-ISE to coordinate and develop a common national framework for information sharing. The DHS also possesses major responsibilities with respect to the *National Response Framework* (which replaced the *National Response Plan*), which outlines how information is to be shared in response to all incidents including terrorist attacks and natural disasters.[83] This paragraph indicates that the DHS national intelligence strategy indeed supports the HS strategy.

81　Ibid.

82　Ibid.

83　DHS (2008, April 18). *Department of Homeland Security Information Sharing Strategy: Securing the Homeland Through Information Sharing and Collaboration.* Washington, DC: US Department of Homeland Security (DHS).

Intelligence Operations and Plans Support Achieving Strategy Document Objectives

National Counterterrorism Center. In August 2004, President Bush established the National Counterterrorism Center (NCTC) to serve as the primary organization in the United States Government for integrating and analyzing all intelligence pertaining to terrorism and counterterrorism and to conduct strategic operational planning by integrating all instruments of national power. In December 2004, Congress codified the NCTC in the IRTPA and placed the NCTC in the ODNI. Located at the Liberty Crossing Building in Northern Virginia, the NCTC is a multi-agency organization dedicated to eliminating the terrorist threat to US interests at home and abroad.[84] The NCTC supports the achievement of NSHS objectives.

National Response Framework. The *National Response Framework* is required by, and integrates under, the larger *National Strategy for Homeland Security (Strategy)*, which serves to guide, organize, and unify our nation's homeland security efforts. The *Strategy* reflects our increased understanding of the threats confronting the United States, incorporates lessons learned from exercises and real-world catastrophes, and articulates how we should ensure our long-term success by strengthening the homeland security foundation that we have built.[85]

Objectives Outlined in a Strategy Document

Objectives Matrix. The matrix below shows the best depiction of objectives outlined in a strategy document. The homeland security (HS) mission area analysis (MAA) identifies the activities required to conduct the missions identified in the *National Strategy for Homeland Security* (NSHS). Accordingly, the HS MAA focuses specifically on the NSHS missions without regard for organizational or jurisdictional boundaries, either inside or outside the federal government.[86]

---

84   NCTC (2008, March 26). About the National Counterterrorism Center. National Counterterrorism Center (NCTC) website. Retrieved August 2, 2008, from http://www.nctc.gov/about_us/about_nctc.html.

85   DHS (2008, January). *National Response Framework.* Washington, DC: US Department of Homeland Security (DHS).

86   HSI (2007, March 28). *Homeland Security Strategic Planning: Mission Area Analysis (Final).* Arlington, VA: Homeland Security Institute (HSI).

	Mission Area			
	Prevent	**Protect**	**Respond**	**Recover**
Objective A	Detect Threats	Assess Critical Infrastructure and Key Assets	Assess Incident	Assist Public
Objective B	Control Access	Implement Protective Programs for Assets & Systems	Minimize Impact	Restore Environment
Objective C	Eliminate Threats	Mitigate Risk to Public	Care for Public	Restore Infrastructure

Conclusion

In this chapter, I analyzed the US homeland security intelligence strategy and compared it to published homeland security strategy documents. I also discussed US national and homeland security intelligence policies. All of the national and homeland security intelligence documents and policies coordinate and correlate well with the national security and homeland security documents, which is an amazing accomplishment.

CHAPTER 4
COMBATING TERRORISM –
A CHALLENGE FOR MANY
NATIONS

Robert T. Uda, MS, MBA

Introduction

Yes, combating terrorism is certainly a challenge for many nations …
particularly the United States of America. By the very nature of the
threat against the US, the US's strategy, intelligence operations, and
counterterrorism operations must be different from those of other nations.
Basically, this is because the US must protect its vast homeland, the continental
US (CONUS), as well as its assets, citizens, and friends throughout the
world. The US has been successful in averting another direct attack against
its homeland for the past seven years since 9/11. Spain, England, France,
and Germany, on the other hand, have all experienced direct attacks on their
homeland since 9/11. The US has been preoccupied with fighting terrorists
in Afghanistan and Iraq. Indeed, we are the policemen of the world, because
if we do not serve in that role, no other nation will.

The US strategy, intelligence operations, and counterterrorism operations
indicate a wide contrast with those of Israel, for example. Israel fights terrorism
right in its own backyard. They depend on human intelligence (HUMINT)
much more so than the US does. The US is more prone to use open-source
intelligence (OSINT) and technical satellite intelligence, surveillance, and
reconnaissance (ISR). The technical means that the US uses include signals
intelligence (SIGINT), measurement and signatures intelligence (MASINT),
and imagery intelligence (IMINT).[87]

This chapter covers how the US's strategy, intelligence operations, and
counterterrorism operations compare to other nations' efforts to defeat
terrorism. It also contains an evaluation of strategies, intelligence operations,
and measures taken by the US and other nations to conduct counterterrorism

---

87   Masse, T. (2006, August 18). Homeland security intelligence: Perceptions,
statutory definitions, and approaches. Congressional Research Service (CRS) Report
for Congress, Order Code RL33616.

operations and to unite government agencies in order to ensure national security.

US Strategy Compared to Other Nations' Efforts

US Strategy for Combating Terrorism. The *National Strategy for Combating Terrorism* contains the US strategy for winning the War on Terror. Our strategy consists of both a long-range approach and a short-term approach. Our long-term approach is *advancing effective democracy*. The long-term solution for winning the War on Terror is the advancement of freedom and human dignity through effective democracy. Elections are the most visible sign of a free society and can play a critical role in advancing effective democracy. However, elections alone are not enough. Effective democracies honor and uphold basic human rights, including freedom of religion, conscience, speech, assembly, association, and press. They are responsive to their citizens, submitting to the will of the people. Effective democracies exercise effective sovereignty and maintain order within their own borders, address causes of conflict peacefully, protect independent and impartial systems of justice, punish crime, embrace the rule of law, and resist corruption. Effective democracies also limit the reach of government, protecting the institutions of civil society. In effective democracies, freedom is indivisible. They are the long-term antidote to the ideology of terrorism today. This is the battle of ideas.[88]

Our short-term approach consists of the following *four priorities of action*:[89]

1. **Prevent attacks by terrorist networks**
   a. Attack terrorists and their capacity to operate
   b. Deny terrorists entry to the US and disrupt their travel internationally
   c. Defend potential targets of attack
2. **Deny WMD to rogue states and terrorist allies who seek to use them**
   a. Determine terrorists' intentions, capabilities, and plans to develop or acquire WMD
   b. Deny terrorists access to the materials, expertise, and other enabling capabilities required to develop WMD
   c. Deter terrorist from employing WMD

---

88   The White House (2006, September). *National Strategy for Combating Terrorism*. Washington, DC.

89   Ibid.

    d.   Detect and disrupt terrorists' attempted movement of WMD-related materials, weapons, and personnel

    e.   Prevent and respond to a WMD-related terrorist attack

    f.   Define the nature and source of a terrorist-employed WMD device

3. Deny terrorists the support and sanctuary of rogue states

    a.   End state sponsorship of terrorism

    b.   Disrupt the flow of resources from rogue states to terrorists

4. Deny terrorists control of any nation they would use as a base and launching pad for terror

    a.   Eliminate physical safe-havens

    b.   Eliminate legal safe-havens

    c.   Eliminate cyber safe-havens

    d.   Eliminate financial safe-havens

UK's Counterterrorism Strategy. Laws alone will not stop terrorism. However, since we must be prepared to deal with terrorism, the United Kingdom (UK) devised a strategy in 2003 (known within government as CONTEST) for countering terrorism. With it, the UK aims to reduce the risk from international terrorism so that people can go about their daily lives freely and with confidence. The strategy affects multiple branches of the UK government. They base their strategy on four pillars: (1) Prevent, (2) Pursue, (3) Protect, and (4) Prepare. Each is discussed as follows:[90]

1. **Prevent** is meant to show people that Brits are not that bad. They plan to win the hearts and minds of Muslims by supporting reform, deterring terrorism facilitators, and engaging in the battle of ideas.

2. **Pursue** is meant to take away the option to harm the UK and its interests by gathering intelligence, disrupting terrorist activity, and international cooperation.

3. **Protect** is meant to reduce the vulnerability within the UK and of its assets by strengthening border security, protecting key utilities, protecting transportation assets, and protecting crowded places.

4. **Prepare** is meant to ensure that the UK can mitigate the effects of an attack and can find the perpetrators by identifying the potential risks and mitigating them and continually evaluating and testing preparedness.

---

90 Anonymous (2008a, January 21). About the UK's counter-terrorism strategy. *Global Security Challenge* (GSC). Retrieved August 7, 2008, from http://www.globalsecuritychallenge.com/2008/01/about -the-uks-counterterrorism.html.

German Cabinet Approves Controversial Anti-terror Law. The German government has approved a new law that would revamp the role of the country's federal criminal police in the international fight against terror. Some think the changes are going too far. For the first time, the proposed legislation, which still needs to be approved by parliament, would give federal police officers the right to take preventive measures in cases of suspected terrorism. The bill calls for video surveillance of private apartments and online computer searches. German Interior Minister Wolfgang Schaeuble defended the proposed law after the meeting. "It's an important building block for Germany's security architecture," he said, adding that the bill was in line with Germany's constitution.[91]

Israel's Strategy for Combating Palestinian Terror. Israel's strategy for combating Palestinian terror consists of five elements: (1) altering perceptions among Arabs (particularly Palestinians), (2) negotiating with responsible Palestinians to achieve a mutually beneficial agreement, (3) reasserting the ultimate responsibility of the state to protect its citizens, (4) destroying terror by force, and (5) engendering international support. Each of these elements is discussed as follows:[92]

1. **The Arab Mindset** – The result of the war on terrorism must change the outlook of Arab nations … especially among Palestinians. Israelis are ready to negotiate, but neither threats nor violence will evoke concessions. Three conditions are vital to achieving this goal:
   a. Steadfastness
   b. Israel must not be pressured to give up anything
   c. Determination
2. **A Responsible Partner** – Israel must have a legitimate negotiating partner with four qualities:
   a. The Palestinians must fight terrorism regardless of its source
   b. Palestinians must work to change public discourse on Israel
   c. A new leadership must move toward accountability
   d. Palestinians should renounce the desire for a massive return of refugees
3. **Self Defense** – The state is ultimately responsible for defending its citizens by whatever means necessary.

---

91 Anonymous (2008b, April 6). German cabinet approves controversial anti-terror law. DW-World. Retrieved August 9, 2008, from http://www.dw-world.de/dw/article/0,,3384037,00.html.

92 Amidror, J. (2002, Autumn). Israel's strategy for combating Palestinian terror. *JFQ*, pp. 117-123.

4. **Destroying Terrorism** – Terrorists must be met by force. Because terrorism cannot be completely prevented, terrorists and their supporters must be defeated.
5. **International Support** – A small country like Israel needs as much international support as possible without risking its vital interests.

Pakistan's Comprehensive Strategy. Until he recently resigned, President Musharraf had a comprehensive strategy aimed at eradicating extremism in the federally-administered tribal areas, which combines these three critical components:[93]

1. Strengthened governance
2. Increased economic development
3. Improved security

That is it … short and simple but comprehensive. However, apparently, the extremists won.

US Intelligence Operations Compared to Other Nations' Efforts

Terrorist Threat Integration Center. On January 28, 2003, in his State of the Union address, President George W. Bush called for the establishment of a new Terrorist Threat Integration Center (TTIC) that would merge and analyze all threat information in a single location under the direction of the director of central intelligence (DCI). On May 1, 2003, TTIC began operations at CIA Headquarters under the leadership of John O. Brennan, who had previously served as the CIA's deputy executive director.[94]

National Counterterrorism Center. On August 27, 2004, President Bush signed Executive Order (EO) 13354, *National Counterterrorism Center.* This EO established the National Counterterrorism Center (NCTC). The EO further stipulated roles for the NCTC and its leadership and reporting relationships among the NCTC leadership, NCTC member agencies, and

---

93 Office of the Press Secretary (2007, August 6). Fact sheet: Combating terrorism worldwide. Washington, DC: The White House. Retrieved August 5, 2008, from http://www.whitehouse.gov/news/releases/2007/08/print/20070806-1.html.

94 Best, R. A., Jr. (2003, August 6). Homeland security: Intelligence support. Congressional Research Service (CRS) Report for Congress, Order Code RS21283.

the White House. The TTIC and its fusion functions have been absorbed into the NCTC Directorate of Intelligence.[95]

Director of National Intelligence. On December 17, 2004, the President approved the Intelligence Reform and Terrorism Prevention Act of 2004 (IRTPA, PL 108-458). The Act incorporated many of the proposals of the 9/11 Commission including the establishment of a Director of National Intelligence (DNI) separate from the director of the CIA or DCI. The DNI serves as head of the Intelligence Community (IC) and as the principal adviser to the President, the National Security Council (NSC), and the Homeland Security Council for intelligence matters related to the national security.[96]

State and Local Fusion Center Program. The State and Local Fusion Center Program is an outgrowth of the Homeland Security Act (HSA) of 2002 and the IRTPA. With the support of both the DNI and the Department of Justice (DOJ), the Department of Homeland Security (DHS) has created the State and Local Fusion Center Program, which places DHS homeland security intelligence professionals in state and local fusion centers that are part of the national network of fusion centers. As of January 2007, we had 12 fusion centers around the country. The plan is to deploy 35 additional fusion centers by the end of FY 2008.[97]

Foreign Network at Front of CIA's Terror Fight. The CIA has established joint operation centers in more than 24 countries where US and foreign intelligence officers work side-by-side to track and capture suspected terrorists and to destroy or penetrate their networks. The secret Counterterrorist Intelligence Centers (CTICs) are financed mostly by the CIA and employ some of the best espionage technology the CIA has to offer. This technology includes secure communications gear, computers linked to the CIA's central databases, and access to highly classified intercepts once shared only with the nation's closest Western allies. The Americans and their counterparts at the CTICs make daily decisions on when and how to apprehend suspects, whether to whisk them off to other countries for interrogation and detention, and how to disrupt al-Qaeda's logistical and financial support.[98]

---

95   Masse, T. M. (2005, March 24). The National Counterterrorism Center: Implementation challenges and issues for Congress. Congressional Research Service (CRS) Report for Congress, Order Code RL32816.

96   Best, R. A., Jr. (2005, February 11). The director of national intelligence and intelligence analysis. Congressional Research Service (CRS) Report for Congress, Order Code RS21948.

97   Allen, C. E. (2007, January 25). Intelligence reform and homeland security intelligence. Written testimony to the US Senate Select Committee on Intelligence.

98   Priest, D. (2005, November 18). Foreign network at front of CIA's terror fight. *Washingtonpost.com*. Retrieved August 9, 2008, from http://www.washington-

Germany Combating Terrorism. Combating Islamist extremism and terrorism will for the foreseeable future be the core task of the German security authorities. Germany is part of a global danger zone facing the risk of terrorism. Preventive intelligence-gathering and defense measures are, therefore, the most important weapons in the fight against extremism and terrorism. Imposing bans on new and existing associations and their activities has proven particularly effective. The fight against terrorism must continue to be expanded using all means available under the rule of law. Measures to prevent terrorist activity before it occurs are especially important in this regard. That includes new technology such as biometrics for identifying travelers during border checks.[99]

US Counterterrorism Operations Compared to Other Nations' Efforts

Doctrine of Preemption. Throughout the course of history, few, if any, wars against groups using terrorist-type tactics have been won by defensive operations. Accordingly, the US anti-terrorism strategy relies heavily on the doctrine of preemption. As a subset of this framework of preemption, US anti-terrorism strategy targets the financing of terrorism. In the 9/11 Commission report's recommendations, two overarching issues relate to financing of terror:[100]

1. What strategy – or strategy mix – best addresses the issue of terrorist financing, and
2. To what degree are the goals and objectives sought by such a strategy realistically achievable, cost-effective, and in-tandem with other counterterrorism and foreign and domestic policy objectives.

Terrorism Financing. Arguably, in the global war on terror, the man with the money is as dangerous as the man with the gun. Despite the difficulties of interdicting terrorist financing, policies which ignore or downplay the

---

post.com/wp-dyn/content/article/2005/11/17/AR2005111702070_pf.html.

99   Anonymous (n.d.). Combating terrorism. German Federal Ministry of the Interior. Retrieved August 9, 2008 from http://www.bmi.bund.de/cln_012/nn_122730/sid_CA874214EF42CE8C593C6619BB01BB63/nsc_true/Internet/Content/Themen/Innere__Sicherheit__allgemein/PolitischeZiele/Combating__Terrorism__en,templateId=renderPrint.html.

100   Perl, R. (2005, January 7). Anti-terror strategy, the 9/11 Commission report & terrorism financing: Implications for U.S. policymakers. *Strategic Insights, IV(1)*, 12 pp.

importance of money to terrorist operations appear unwise, since successful interdiction of funds can derail terrorist operations. Moreover, detecting and tracking illicit transactions can yield valuable intelligence which may be unavailable from other sources. Since Islam and other world religions require charitable contributions from adherents, implying unstoppable cash flows, it is imperative that donations be channeled away from terrorist causes towards legitimate charities.[101]

How Five Foreign Countries are Organized to Combat Terrorism. The five countries (Canada, France, Germany, Israel, and the United Kingdom) examined have similarities in how they are organized to combat terrorism:[102]

- The countries generally have the majority of organizations used to combat terrorism under one lead government ministry. However, because many other ministries are also involved, the countries have created interagency coordination bodies to coordinate both within and across ministries. For example, while many countries generally have their intelligence and law enforcement organizations under their ministries of interior or equivalent, they also need to coordinate with their ministries of foreign affairs, defense, and health or emergency services.
- The countries have clearly designated who is in charge during a terrorist incident – typically their national or local police.
- The countries have national policies that emphasize prevention of terrorism. To achieve their policies, the countries use a variety of strategies including intelligence collection, police presence, and various security measures such as physical barriers at the entrances to public buildings.
- These countries primarily use their general criminal laws (e.g., those for murder or arson) to prosecute terrorists. The countries also have special terrorism-related laws that allow for special investigations or prosecution mechanisms and increased penalties.
- The countries' executive branches provide the primary oversight of organizations involved in combating terrorism. This oversight involves reviewing the programs and resources for effectiveness, efficiency, and legality.

---

101 Ibid.

102 GAO (2000, April). Combating terrorism: How five foreign countries are organized to combat terrorism. United States General Accounting Office (GAO) Report to Congressional Requesters, GAO/NSIAD-00-85, 30 pp.

Conclusion

For effective democracies, freedom is indivisible. Those democracies provide the long-term antidote to the ideology of today's terrorism. This, then, becomes a battle of ideas and winning the hearts and minds of people. We know that laws alone will not stop terrorism. Preventive intelligence-gathering and defense measures comprise the most important weapons in the fight against extremism and terrorism. Few, if any, wars against groups using terrorist-type tactics have been won purely by defensive operations. Hence, the US anti-terrorism strategy relies heavily on the doctrine of preemption. The US has employed that doctrine in Iraq. Further, in the global war on terror, the man with the money is as dangerous as the man with the gun. Thus, the successful interdiction of funds can derail terrorist operations.

CHAPTER 5
ISRAELI SECURITY AND RISK
MANAGEMENT MEASURES

Robert T. Uda, MS, MBA

Introduction

This chapter presents an analysis and conclusions regarding what security and risk management measures (1) that I would use in response to an imminent terrorist threat and (2) that are currently being implemented in a foreign country. The foreign country that I selected was Israel because Israel has both faced and dealt with a wide variety of terrorist threats. In fact, next to the United States (US), Israel is the second priority target (a very close second) of terrorists.

First, the terrorist threats to the US were considered and analyzed. The major threat to the US today is the threat of weapons of mass destruction (WMD) or chemical, biological, radiological, and nuclear (CBRN) attacks. Next, the threats against Israel were analyzed and presented. Needless to say, should Iran develop the nuclear bomb, the terrorists would obtain the bomb and unleash it on Israel. Hence, like the US today, the WMD threat is also Israel's greatest threat. Next, the security and risk management measures currently being implemented in Israel were considered and analyzed. Finally, I selected the Israeli security and risk management measures to use in the US.

The Terrorist Threat

This section presents the terrorist threats to both the US and Israel.

Today's Threat Environment in the US. Our nation faces complex and dynamic threats from terrorists. Despite concerted worldwide efforts in the aftermath of September 11 that have disrupted terrorist plots and constrained al-Qaeda's ability to strike our homeland, the US faces a persistent and evolving terrorist threat primarily from violent Islamo-fascist terrorist groups and cells. Currently, the most serious and dangerous manifestation of this threat remains al-Qaeda, which is driven by an undiminished strategic intent to attack our homeland. We must never lose sight of al-Qaeda's persistent desire for WMD as that group continues to try to acquire and use CBRN material.[103]

The terrorist threat to our homeland is not restricted to violent Islamo-fascist extremist groups. We also confront an ongoing threat posed by domestic terrorists based and operating strictly within the US. Often referred to as "single-issue" groups, they include white supremacist groups, animal rights extremists, and eco-terrorist groups, among others.[104]

For our terrorist enemies, violence is not only justified, it is necessary and even glorified – judged the only means to achieve a world vision darkened by hate, fear, and oppression. They use suicide bombings, beheadings, and other atrocities against innocent people as a means to promote their creed. Our enemy's demonstrated indifference to human life and desire to inflict catastrophic damage on the US and its friends and allies around the world have fueled their desire for WMDs. We cannot permit the world's most dangerous terrorists and their regime sponsors to threaten us with the world's most destructive weapons.[105]

WMD Threat against the US. Weapons of mass destruction (WMDs) – CBRN – in the possession of hostile states and terrorists represent one of the greatest security challenges facing the US. We must pursue a comprehensive strategy to counter this threat in all of its dimensions. We will not permit the world's most dangerous regimes (Iran, Syria, and North Korea) and terrorists to threaten us with the world's most destructive weapons. We must accord the highest priority to the protection of the US, our forces, and our friends and allies from the existing and growing WMD threat.[106]

Low-intensity Warfare against Israel. The kinds of terrorists threats that Israel experienced over the years include airplane hijackings, bus bombings, kidnappings (as in the case of the Israeli athletes at the Munich Olympics in 1972), attacks on schools (such as Ma'alot on the Lebanese border in 1974, in which 22 children were killed), and other kinds of terror.[107] After the next

---

103 HSC (2007, October). *National Strategy for Homeland Security*. Washington, DC: Homeland Security Council (HSC).

104 Ibid.

105 The White House (2006, September). *National Strategy for Combating Terrorism*. Washington, DC.

106 The White House (2002, December). *National Strategy to Combat Weapons of Mass Destruction*. Washington, DC.

107 Steinberg, G. M. (2008, June). Israel at sixty: Asymmetry, vulnerability, and the search for security. Jerusalem Center for Public Affairs (JCPA). Retrieved August 18, 2008, from http://www.jcpa.org/JCPA/Templates/ShowPage.asp?DRIT =2&DBID=1&LNGID=1&TMID=111&FID=283&PID=0&IID=2206&TTL=I srael_at_Sixty:_Asymmetry,_Vulnerability,_and_the_Search_for_Security.

election, we may experience similar terrorist threats within the continental United States (CONUS).

In addition to deterrence, which used such tactics as expulsion of terrorists, their families, and supporters, the Israel Defense Forces (IDF) also applied passive defensive measures at roads, airports, markets, schools, sports arenas, embassies, and other potential targets. In Europe and other areas where the Palestinians had easy access to Israeli targets, security increased (particularly around El Al aircraft, which ended hijackings), while Mossad "hit squads" sought out and killed Palestinians in Europe who had participated in attacks such as at the Munich Olympics.[108]

Targeted killing of major terror leaders from the different organizations forced the terrorist groups to invest resources in hiding and defending themselves, reducing the terror attacks further. And a formidable separation barrier was constructed around much of the West Bank and all of Gaza, making infiltration more difficult and further decreasing the attacks. This barrier highlights the importance of defensible borders in any peace negotiations, as stipulated in United Nations (UN) Security Council Resolution 242.[109] The US, on the other hand, has failed miserably to close its northern and southern borders from terrorist infiltrations.

WMD Threat against Israel. Having faced a growing WMD threat for the past several decades, Israel was forced to make counter-proliferation a top national defense priority. *Counter-proliferation* refers to policies enacted to oppose the potential use of WMD. To understand what policies Israel has devised and employed in order to counter WMD proliferation, it is imperative to analyze the threats Israeli security planners have considered when formulating these strategies. The gravity of the situation for Israel lies in a combination of factors that play to Israel's disadvantage. The first factor is the country's small geographic size (just over 20,000 square kilometers) and its small number of highly valued targets (e.g., three major seaports, one major civilian airport, and four central power stations). This is then compounded by the country's extremely high population density, with two-thirds of its residents living within a 75-km radius in three major metropolitan areas.[110]

---

108 Ibid.

109 Ibid.

110 Brown, C. (2004, September). Israel and the WMD threat: Lessons for Europe. *Middle East Review of International Affairs (MERIA) Journal, 8(3)*, 28 pp. Retrieved on August 19, 2008, from http://meria.idc.ac.il/journal/2004/issue3/jv8n3a4.html.

Security and Risk Management Measures Being Used in Israel

This section identifies some of the more prevalent security and risk management measures being used in Israel. Most of them are quite effective and have kept Israel secure for many years.

Israel at War Only with Perpetrators, not the Palestinian People. No country has been subjected to more relentless terrorism than Israel; nor has any country been subjected to greater scrutiny or vilification. Though the terrorist war was launched by the official Palestinian leadership – and polls have consistently shown a Palestinian majority in support of suicide attacks – Israel considers itself at war with only the perpetrators of terrorism, not with the Palestinian people. Israel has not resorted to indiscriminate bombings, mass expulsions, blockades of food and fuel that modern states have frequently adopted in wartime. Despite intense fighting, no city in the West Bank or Gaza remotely resembles Dresden in 1945, Hanoi in 1972, or Grozny, Chechnya, in 1994 and 1999. The Palestinian terrorists' goal is to kill the maximum number of Israeli civilians. In contrast, Israeli soldiers have risked their lives to minimize civilian Palestinian casualties by searching out terrorists in house-to-house fighting rather than calling in artillery.[111]

Anti-terror Tactics. Israeli security forces developed and applied anti-terror tactics including (1) interrogation, (2) checkpoints, and (3) punishments directed against terrorists and their families designed to deter such attacks. This was a different type of warfare, necessitating different training and weapons. Large tank formations and mobile ground forces were no longer required, and the mass army based on universal conscription (including women) was also reduced.[112],[113] Hence, Israel transitioned to a very vulnerable position.

---

111 Halevi, Y. K., & Oren, M. B. (2004, September 20). Israel's unexpected victory over terrorism: How Sharon beat the intifada – and what the United States can learn. *Jewish World Review.* Retrieved August 21, 2008, from http://www.jewish-worldreview.com/0904/halevi_israeli_victory.php3.

112 Cohen, E. A., Eisenstadt, M. J., & Bacevich, A. J. (1998). *Knives, tanks, and missiles: Israel's security revolution.* Washington Institute for Near East Policy. Retrieved August 18, 2008, from http://www.jcpa.org/JCPA/Templates/ShowPage.asp?DRIT=2&DBID=1&LNGID=1&TMID=111&FID=283&PID=0&IID=2206&TTL=Israel_at_Sixty:_Asymmetry,_Vulnerability,_and_the_Search_for_Security.

113 Steinberg, G. M. (2008, June). Israel at sixty: Asymmetry, vulnerability, and the search for security. Jerusalem Center for Public Affairs (JCPA). Retrieved August 18, 2008, from http://www.jcpa.org/JCPA/Templates/ShowPage.asp?DRIT=2&DBID=1&LNGID=1&TMID=111&FID=283&PID=0&IID=2206&TTL=Israel_at_Sixty:_Asymmetry,_Vulnerability,_and_the_Search_for_Security.

Operations against Infrastructure Used to Support Terrorist Activity.
In Israel's battles against Hezbollah, the guiding principle adopted by the
Israel Defense Forces (IDF) was to target only infrastructure that was making
a significant contribution to the operational capabilities of the Hezbollah
terrorists. This meant that, for the most part, Israeli attacks were limited to
the transportation infrastructure. Most of the other infrastructure (medical,
cultural, railroad, tunnels, ports, banking, manufacturing, farming, tourism,
sewage, financial, electricity, drainage, water, and the like) was left almost
completely untouched.[114]

Runways at Beirut International Airport. In the IDF's viewpoint,
rendering runways unusable constituted one of the most important and
appropriate methods of preventing reinforcements and supplies of weaponry
and military materiel reaching the terrorist organizations. It was also a response
to reports that the Hezbollah terrorists intended to fly the kidnapped Israelis
out of Lebanon.[115] Airports are widely recognized to be legitimate military
targets. The Canadian Law of Armed Conflict Manual,[116],[117] for example, notes
that "ports and airfields are generally accepted as being military objectives"
while the International Committee of the Red Cross (ICRC) list of generally
recognized military objectives includes "airfields, rocket launching ramps,
and naval base installations."[118],[119]

114 MFA (2007, April 1). Preserving humanitarian principles while combating
terrorism: Israel's struggle with Hezbollah in the Lebanon war. Diplomatic Notes No.
1. Israel Ministry of Foreign Affairs (MFA). Retrieved on August 19, 2008, from http://
www.mfa.gov.il/MFA/Terrorism-+Obstacle+to+Peace/Terrorism+from+Lebanon-
+Hizbullah/Preserving+Humanitarian+Principles+While+Combating+Terrorism+-
+April+2007.htm?DisplayMode=print.

115 Ibid.

116 *Canadian Law of Armed Conflict Manual* (1999), p. 4-2.

117 MFA (2007, April 1). Preserving humanitarian principles while combating
terrorism: Israel's struggle with Hezbollah in the Lebanon war. Diplomatic Notes No.
1. Israel Ministry of Foreign Affairs (MFA). Retrieved on August 19, 2008, from http://
www.mfa.gov.il/MFA/Terrorism-+Obstacle+to+Peace/Terrorism+from+Lebanon-
+Hizbullah/Preserving+Humanitarian+Principles+While+Combating+Terrorism+-
+April+2007.htm?DisplayMode=print.

118 ICRC (1987). Commentary on the additional protocols of 8 June 1977 to
the Geneva Conventions of 12 August 1949. International Committee of the Red
Cross (ICRC), pp. 632-633.

119 MFA (2007, April 1). Preserving humanitarian principles while combating
terrorism: Israel's struggle with Hezbollah in the Lebanon war. Diplomatic Notes No.
1. Israel Ministry of Foreign Affairs (MFA). Retrieved on August 19, 2008, from http://
www.mfa.gov.il/MFA/Terrorism-+Obstacle+to+Peace/Terrorism+from+Lebanon-
+Hizbullah/Preserving+Humanitarian+Principles+While+Combating+Terrorism+-
+April+2007.htm?DisplayMode=print.

Al Manar TV Station. Operating as the Hezbollah television station, Al Manar was used to relay messages to terrorists and to incite acts of terrorism. The ICRC list of accepted military objectives includes "the installations of broadcasting and television stations." Similarly, the Committee established to review the North Atlantic Treaty Organization (NATO) bombings in Yugoslavia noted in relation to NATO attacks on radio and television stations in Belgrade: "If the media is used to incite crimes, then it is a legitimate target .... Insofar as the attack actually was aimed at disrupting the communications network, it was legally acceptable."[120],[121] In this author's opinion, this makes the al-Jazeera television station also a legally acceptable target of the US should the terrorists attack our homeland with WMDs.

US Law Enforcement Officials Experience Good Security in Israel. A group of 12 highly placed law enforcement agents from around the US visited the Israel Border Police's counterterrorism training base in Beit Horon, which is located outside of Jerusalem. They went there to observe a seamless reaction to a simulated terrorist attack using a jeep and cardboard cutouts of civilians and terrorists.[122]

Special Agent Jim Cavanagh, from the Department of Alcohol, Tobacco, and Firearms (ATF) in Washington, DC, referring to the group's visit to Jerusalem's Old City, said he was particularly impressed by the Mabat 2000 project. That project is a complex network of surveillance cameras that provide security for the well-visited historical site. The group toured the "war room" where technicians constantly monitor around 60 surveillance screens. The project's primary aim is combating terrorism. However, as an added benefit, the Mabat 2000 surveillance system also proves to be a powerful tool for crime prevention. Responsible for keeping large cities safe, several of the visiting Americans felt such a system would be highly effective in their city centers and were set to embark on similar ventures.[123]

When asked about the wisdom of traveling to Israel, Cavanagh could not have been more reassuring. "It is safe to visit Israel," he proclaimed. "It's the

120 Anonymous (n.d.). *Final Report to the Prosecutor by the Committee Established to Review NATO Bombings in Yugoslavia*, para. 75-6.

121 MFA (2007, April 1). Preserving humanitarian principles while combating terrorism: Israel's struggle with Hezbollah in the Lebanon war. Diplomatic Notes No. 1. Israel Ministry of Foreign Affairs (MFA). Retrieved on August 19, 2008, from http://www.mfa.gov.il/MFA/Terrorism-+Obstacle+to+Peace/Terrorism+from+Lebanon-+Hizbullah/Preserving+Humanitarian+Principles+While+Combating+Terrorism+-+April+2007.htm?DisplayMode=print.

122 Goldstein, J. (2006, June 25). Democracy: US law enforcement officials find security in Israel. *Israel21c.com*. Retrieved August 21, 2008, from http://www.israel21c.org/bin/en.jsp?enScript=PrintVersion.jsp&enDispWho=Articles^l1340.

123 Ibid.

security that makes it safe." He added that following the group's tour of the security set-up at Ben-Gurion Airport, he believed it was "probably the safest [airport] in the world." Arieh O'Sullivan, Director of Communications at the Anti-Defamation League's (ADL's) Israel office, revealed that the group was briefed on the methods Israel adopts to prevent terrorism at Ben-Gurion. "They include profiling, using sensors, and monitoring while mobilizing elite units operating within the airport at all times," said O'Sullivan. Participants noted that the US constantly learns from Israel new ways to better protect its airports.[124] In a country like Israel, surrounded by enemies that desire to eradicate them, profiling is a necessity that cannot be ignored. The US should do likewise.

Profiling Aviation Threats. John Barham wrote that Israeli experts say screening has served the country well and should not be fundamentally changed. "It is not foolproof, but it is effective, and our record for safety shows that," says Ariel Merari, a specialist on political violence and terrorism at Tel Aviv University. "The method is justified. I do not see a moral or legal problem. Because the evidence [indicates] that danger comes from a specific group of people, so I think that there is a good reason to select this group of people for more meticulous searches," he says. "I think it is immoral to ignore these facts." Merari says Israel should not give up screening Israeli Arabs more stringently just "because people complain about political correctness." He does not deny that it is discriminatory, stating simply: "But yes, you do have to discriminate."[125] Sometimes you must do what is necessary to keep your country safe and secure from destruction. America should do likewise.

What Israeli Security and Risk Management Measures Would We Use in the US

This section covers some of Israel's good security and risk management measures that have either already been adopted by the US or other measures that are being considered for adoption.

Following the Israeli Plan. Ralph Jensen said, "When in Rome, do as the Romans [do]." To tighten up security at US airports, it might be wise to adopt novel Israeli methods using behavior-detection technology. Why Israel? Well, they do have a lot of experience in successfully protecting airports. Apparently, Homeland Security Secretary Michael Chertoff agrees because,

124 Ibid.
125 Barham, J. (2008, August). Profiling aviation threats. *Security Management.* Retrieved August 19, 2008, from http://www.securitymanagement.com/print/4454.

in an interview with Reuters, he said, "I think that it is of interest to us to see if there is any adaptation there."[126]

Jensen further went on to say, "Dare I call it profiling, but Ben-Gurion International Airport in Tel Aviv is known for its strict security measures and relies heavily on techniques that detect suspicious behavior among travelers. Wouldn't the civil libertarians have a tough time with this?" You can't deny that it works in that country because Israeli technologies detect explosives, which is exactly what Chertoff wants to accomplish in protecting US airports and other public places. Chertoff has signed an agreement with Israel to share technology and information methods to improve homeland security. One of the new systems he saw during a conference in Israel uses behavioral science and biometric sensors to detect sinister intentions among travelers.[127]

US Observing Israeli Tactics for Iraq Insurgents. Mass assaults by covert squads of soldiers to confound guerrillas and swoops by troops posing as Arabs are among Israeli tactics US forces are studying for use in Iraq, Israeli security sources said. Israeli measures have been honed against a three-year-old Palestinian revolt in the West Bank and Gaza Strip. Washington is watching and recently sent military brass to consult with its chief Middle East ally. "The Americans now realize their forces are in Iraq for the long haul, and are reorganizing accordingly," a senior Israeli security source said. "Israel has been providing advice on how to shift from a reliance on heavy, armored occupation troops to mobile forces that are more effective in quelling urban resistance and cause less friction with the general populace."[128]

IDF Teaches US Soldiers Guerrilla Response. In order to improve their skills and learn firsthand tactics adopted by the IDF in urban and guerrilla warfare in the West Bank and Gaza, US Army units underwent training in 2004 in the special anti-terror school located in the Adam base near Modi'in. After completing their training, the units returned to Iraq. The IDF spokesman said, "The Army does not comment on cooperation with foreign armies," but did not deny US forces were currently training in Israel. In November 2003, US generals visited Israel to study tactics adopted by the IDF in its ongoing war against terror. A report in the *New York Times* claimed US military officials were studying the tactics and strategy used by the IDF operating in the West Bank and Gaza within densely populated Palestinian areas. US Army officials

---

126 Jensen, R. C. (2008, July 23). Following the Israeli plan. *Security Products*. Retrieved August 19, 2008, from http://www.secprodonline.com/print.aspx?aid=65682.

127 Ibid.

128 Kirkhope (2007, December 9). Article (terrorism): US eyeing Israeli tactics for Iraq insurgents. Retrieved August 20, 2008, from http://www.terrorism.com/modules.php?op=modload&name=News&file=article&sid=18239.

later adopted the IDF's policy of demolishing houses belonging to terrorists suspected of attacking US troops in Iraq, set up checkpoints similar to those in the West Bank, deployed sniffer dogs to seek out explosives, and in a number of cases, arrested relatives of terror suspects to glean information.[129]

We Can Learn from the Israelis. Americans would be wise also to study this final lesson: Perhaps the greatest danger in fighting terrorism is the polarizing effect such a campaign can have – not just internationally, but domestically. To avoid this pitfall, a strong political consensus for military action is necessary. That means the president must actively reach out to domestic opposition. Additionally, American leaders must also heed Ariel Sharon's other lessons. That means an ability to endure criticism from abroad and even to risk international isolation, a willingness to define the war on terrorism as a total war, and a commitment to focus one's political agenda on winning, not on divisive or extraneous concerns. Fulfilling those conditions does not guarantee success. However, it does make success possible – as Israel is, at great cost, showing the world.[130]

Conclusion

President George W. Bush has made clear that terrorists seeking to acquire and use WMD are our most serious national security threat. To counter an elusive and adaptive adversary, we must transform ourselves and our partnerships to deter, detect, and defeat this growing threat to our country and to the peace and security of the international community.[131]

Al-Qaeda is driven by an undiminished strategic intent to attack our homeland. We cannot permit the world's most dangerous terrorists and their regime sponsors to threaten us with the world's most destructive weapons. Hostile states and terrorists that possess WMDs represent one of the greatest security challenges facing the US. No country has been subjected to more relentless terrorism than Israel. However, Israel considers itself at war with

129 Dudkevitch, M. (2004, August 17). IDF teaches US soldiers guerrilla response. *Jerusalem Post.* Retrieved August 21, 2008, from http://www.freerepublic.com/focus/f-news/1193685/posts.

130 Halevi, Y. K., & Oren, M. B. (2004, September 20). Israel's unexpected victory over terrorism: How Sharon beat the intifada – and what the United States can learn. *Jewish World Review.* Retrieved August 21, 2008, from http://www.jewish-worldreview.com/0904/halevi_israeli_victory.php3.

131 Lehrman, T. (2006, November 7). Building transformational partnerships to combat WMD terrorism. Remarks at the US Military Academy. Washington, DC: US Department of State. Retrieved August 20, 2008, from http://www.state.gov/t/isn/rls/rm/77155.htm.

only the perpetrators of terrorism, not with the Palestinian people. Yet the Palestinian terrorists' goal is to kill the maximum number of Israeli civilians. We are dealing with an evil enemy that must be defeated.

CHAPTER 6
EXAMPLE SECURITY PLAN

Robert T. Uda, MS, MBA

*H*YPOTHETICAL SCENARIO: *In a small community near a metropolitan city, you are the Administrator of Airport Security of a commuter airport. Develop a security plan and explain the measures to implement based on the potential threats facing small airports in the United States. Include a discussion of the agencies you would contact concerning counterterrorism intelligence and support in the event of a terrorist attack. Explain the type of measures used to identify threats, recommend preemptive measures that would or should be used, and evaluate the effectiveness of the response measures chosen.*

Security Plan for the McClellan-Palomar Airport

1.0 Introduction

Because I live only seven miles away from the McClellan-Palomar Airport, I selected to prepare an example security plan for this airport. The McClellan-Palomar Airport is located in a small community (Carlsbad, CA) 30 miles north of a metropolitan city (San Diego, CA). As required by the hypothetical scenario, I serve as the administrator of airport security of this commuter airport. In developing this security plan, I explain the measures to implement based on the potential threats facing small airports in the United States.

The McClellan-Palomar Airport is located at 2192 Palomar Airport Road, Carlsbad, CA 92011. The airport is named for aviator Gerald McClellan, a North San Diego County community leader. The McClellan-Palomar Airport is a gateway to and from San Diego's North County. It serves the general aviation (GA) community with corporate aircraft and commercial services. Ground was broken in 2007 for a new terminal building to combine airline terminal/security screening with restaurant, Customs and Border Protection (CBP) facility, and other amenities. Over 344 aircraft are based at the airport. Two regularly-scheduled airlines, America West Express and United Express, provide non-stop service to Phoenix and Los Angeles with connections to the world. The airport is an important part of the community with its $108 million per year contribution to the local economy.[132]

1.1 Background

Airport security planning is the joint responsibility of the federal Transportation Security Administration (TSA), the airlines, and the individual airports. Ten airports in the Southern California Association of Governments (SCAG) region offer commercial service, and two airports offer commuter service. Additionally, over 50 GA airports in the region are available for public use including some of the most active GA airports in the country. Since the 9/11 attack on the World Trade Center, airports in the SCAG region upgraded their security systems using a variety of strategies in conjunction with local, state, and federal law enforcement. Furthermore, airports serve a vital role in recovery efforts. Airports can serve as evacuation centers and, if in working order after an incident, can serve as staging centers for relief efforts. Large, flat areas at airports provide excellent staging areas for supplies, equipment, and helicopter landing/takeoff.[133]

Security is an important component of the McClellan-Palomar Airport planning process. The McClellan-Palomar Airport planning organizations are charged with considering ways to increase the security of the airport system including aircraft based at the airport. Security has been designated as a new, stand-alone planning factor by the Safe, Accountable, Flexible, and Efficient Transportation Equity Act: A Legacy for Users (SAFETEA-LU), the current federal transportation legislation.[134]

Since 1950, the State of California has experienced nearly 300 state or federally declared disasters. Of those, roughly half were caused by wildfires, floods, or earthquakes. Together, these three hazards account for the largest losses of life among all disasters and over $55 billion in disaster costs. As a consequence of its experience with disasters, California has initiated a variety

---

132 Anonymous (n.d.). County of San Diego: McClellan-Palomar Airport. County of San Diego Website. Retrieved August 22, 2008, from http://www. sdcounty.ca.gov/dpw/airports/palomar.html.

133 SCAG (2008). *2008 Regional Transportation Plan (RTP): Making the Connections: Transportation Security Report.* Los Angeles, CA: Southern California Association of Governments (SCAG), 22 pp.

134 APO (2007, May). *Security Plan.* St. Cloud, MN: St. Cloud Area Planning Organization (APO), 23 pp.

of ongoing hazard mitigation efforts.[135],[136] Because of additional looming threats, we must be better prepared to mitigate, respond to, and recover from emergency situations.[137]

For the purposes of this security plan, we use the following definitions:[138],[139]

- "Safety" is defined as the protection of persons and property from unintentional damage or destruction caused by accidental or natural events.
- "Security" is defined as the protection of persons or property from intentional damage or destruction caused by vandalism, criminal activity, or terrorist attacks.

1.2 Purpose

The purpose of this security plan is to provide a variety of tools to help mitigate hazards, prepare for emergencies, and enhance the response and recovery phases of any emergency situation. Additionally, the purpose of this security plan is also to assist with emergency situations and major disasters by providing guidance that ensures that proper protocol is followed for different situations. Furthermore, this security plan assists communities and agencies to collaborate in planning, communicating, information-sharing, and coordinating activities before, during, and after emergency situations.

---

135 OES (2007). *State of California Multi-Hazard Mitigation Plan.* Sacramento, CA: California Office of Emergency Services (OES).

136 SCAG (2008). *2008 Regional Transportation Plan (RTP): Making the Connections: Transportation Security Report.* Los Angeles, CA: Southern California Association of Governments (SCAG), 22 pp.

137 APO (2007, May). *Security Plan.* St. Cloud, MN: St. Cloud Area Planning Organization (APO), 23 pp.

138 Dornan, D., & Maier, M. P. (2005). Incorporating security into the transportation planning process. National Cooperative Highway Research Program Report 525, Volume 3.

139 SCAG (2008). *2008 Regional Transportation Plan (RTP): Making the Connections: Transportation Security Report.* Los Angeles, CA: Southern California Association of Governments (SCAG), 22 pp.

1.3 Agencies Involved in McClellan-Palomar Airport Security Planning

1.3.1 Agencies to Contact Concerning Counterterrorism Intelligence

At the federal level, the following agencies shall be contacted concerning counterterrorism intelligence:

- Office of the Director of National Intelligence (ODNI) and National Counterterrorism Center (NCTC)
- Department of Justice (DoJ) and Federal Bureau of Intelligence (FBI), in particular, the San Diego FBI Office on Aero Drive
- Department of Homeland Security (DHS) and Transportation Security Administration (TSA)
- Central Intelligence Agency (CIA)
- Department of Defense (DoD), Defense Intelligence Agency (DIA), National Security Agency (NSA), and National Geospatial-Intelligence Agency (NGA)
- Department of State (DoS)
- Department of Energy (DoE)

At the state level, the following agencies shall be contacted concerning counterterrorism intelligence:

- The Governor's Office of Emergency Services
- The California Attorney General's Office
- The California Highway Patrol (CHP)

1.3.2 Agencies to Contact for Support in the Event of a Terrorist Attack

At the federal level, the following agencies shall be contacted for support in the event of a terrorist attack:

- Federal Bureau of Intelligence (FBI), in particular, the San Diego FBI Office on Aero Drive
- Department of Homeland Security (DHS), Transportation Security Administration (TSA), and Federal Emergency Management Agency (FEMA)

- US Department of Transportation (USDOT) and Federal Aviation Administration (FAA)
- National Nuclear Security Administration (NNSA) – if radiological and/or nuclear attack
- US Department of Health and Human Services (DHHS) and Centers for Disease Control and Prevention (CDC) – if chemical and/or biological attack

At the state, county, and local levels, the following agencies shall be contacted for support in the event of a terrorist attack:

- The Governor's Office of Emergency Services, the County Office of Emergency Services (OES), and the San Diego County Community Emergency Response Team (CERT)
- California Department of Forestry and Fire Protection (CDF) and Office of the State Fire Marshal
- California Emergency Medical Services Authority (EMSA) and Disaster Medical Services (DMS) Division
- The California Attorney General's Office
- California National Guard
- California Highway Patrol (CHP)
- American Red Cross
- San Diego County Health and Human Services
- San Diego County Sheriff's Department
- Carlsbad Police Department

2.0 Security Plan Implementation

2.1 Potential Threats Facing Small Airports in the US

The McClellan-Palomar Airport resides within the Southern California Association of Governments (SCAG) region. The SCAG region is vulnerable to many types of catastrophic events including earthquakes, floods, fires, hazardous material (HAZMAT) incidents, dam failures, civil unrest, transportation accidents, tsunamis, and terrorism. As a consequence of its experience with disasters, California has initiated a variety of ongoing hazard mitigation efforts.[140],[141]

The potential terrorism-related threats against the McClellan-Palomar Airport include (1) bomb threats and other threats of violence, (2) fire/arson, (3) riot/civil disorder, (4) sabotage, (5) security breaches, (6) vandalism, (7) cyber attacks, (8) terrorist assaults using chemical, biological, radiological, or nuclear agents, and/or (9) terrorist assaults using explosives, firearms, or conventional weapons (SCAG, 2008). Additionally, the following four subparagraphs show the specific terrorist threats that could be lodged against the McClellan-Palomar Airport:

- Theft of airplanes
- Shoulder-launched missiles (AKA MANPADS)
- Exploding aircraft in flight
- San Onofré Nuclear Generating Station (SONGS) at risk from Palomar Airport aircraft used as a bomb

2.1.1 Theft of Airplanes

In June 2005, two small planes were stolen and taken for joy rides. In neither case was the crime a national security threat. However, some analysts note that in this post-9/11 era, the thieves could have easily been al-Qaeda operatives and not teenagers out for a thrill. That has again raised the question of whether enough is being done to secure the more than 19,000 small airports scattered across the nation. At the same time, the incidents also put into stark relief two challenges the nation faces as it tries to secure itself against another terrorist attack. The first is how to prioritize potential threats, determine which ones would cost too much to guard against, and then educate the public that they must simply learn to live with them. The second is how to balance the need for security against individual freedoms and commerce. Both challenges are evident in the $20 billion GA industry, which includes everything from small private planes to corporate jets.[142]

---

140 OES (2007). *State of California Multi-Hazard Mitigation Plan.* Sacramento, CA: California Office of Emergency Services (OES).

141 SCAG (2008). *2008 Regional Transportation Plan (RTP): Making the Connections: Transportation Security Report.* Los Angeles, CA: Southern California Association of Governments (SCAG), 22 pp.

142 Marks, A. (2005, June 29). Two thefts of small planes renew security concerns: Some 19,000 small airports across the US have varied safeguards. *The Christian Science Monitor.* Retrieved August 22, 2008, from http://www.csmonitor.com/2005/0629/p03s02-usju.htm.

But security experts counter that al-Qaeda has a history of planning to use small aircraft in attacks. Soon after 9/11, investigators uncovered a plan to use a small plane packed with explosives to attack the US Embassy in Pakistan. Mohammad Atta, one of the 9/11 suicide hijackers, had applied for a loan to buy a crop duster. And Zacarias Massouwi [also spelled Moussaoui], the alleged 20th hijacker, had a crop-dusting manual with him when he was arrested.[143] These acts were evidently done for future potential biological and/or chemical attacks.

2.1.2 Shoulder-Launched Missiles (AKA MANPADS)

The US faces a multitude of security challenges in today's post-September 11, 2001, era. One glaring threat to the nation's economic well-being and public safety is the commercial aviation industry's vulnerability to shoulder-launched missiles, also known as MANPADS (Man-Portable Air Defense Systems). This industry sustains the flow of goods and services in today's globally connected economy and is critical to the American way of life.[144]

Currently, 27 terrorist groups, including al-Qaeda, possess MANPADS. Since 1994, there have been 10 high-profile attempts to target commercial aircraft, with four being shot down. Furthermore, MANPADS fit al-Qaeda's mode of operation perfectly and are relatively easy to use, convenient to transport, widely available, inexpensive, and lethal. This capability coupled with al-Qaeda's direction from its leader, Osama bin Laden, "to kill Americans and their allies – civilians and military," is a potentially catastrophic combination. With the means and motive to inflict harm in place and its propensity to favor economic, symbolic, and mass casualty targets, all that remains is opportunity. It is only a matter of time before al-Qaeda penetrates a seam and strikes a US carrier at home or abroad.[145] Commercial aircraft taking off from and landing at McClellan-Palomar Airport is no exception.

2.1.3 Exploding Aircraft in Flight

British police say they have arrested 21 people in connection with a terrorist plot to blow up aircraft flying from the United Kingdom (UK) to the US. The plot was "intended to be mass murder on an unimaginable scale," Metropolitan Police Deputy Commissioner Paul Stephenson said. The UK's threat warning level was raised to "critical" – meaning "an attack is expected imminently." London Heathrow Airport – one of the world's busiest airports

143 Ibid.
144 Whitmire, J. C. (2006, December). Shoulder launched missiles (A.K.A. MANPADS): The ominous threat to commercial aviation. Retrieved August 22, 2008, from http://www.stormingmedia.us/43/4351/A435164.html.
145 Ibid.

– was closed to most European flights, thereby, causing chaos for thousands of travelers. British Airways canceled all flights between the airport and points in Britain, Europe, and Libya. The plot involved hiding liquid explosives in carry-on luggage, and 6 to 10 flights would have been targeted, US officials said. A senior US congressional source said it is believed the plotters were to carry a "British version of Gatorade" onto the planes and then mix it with a gel-like substance. The explosives were to be triggered by an iPod or a cell phone, the source said.[146]

2.1.4 SONGS at Risk from Palomar Airport Aircraft Used as a Bomb

The nuclear industry beefed up security on the ground at nuclear power plants throughout the US after the September 11 terrorist attacks. However, the plants today remain as vulnerable to a hit from a plane using a nearby small airport as they were then. A *USA TODAY* analysis shows that thousands of airports are within 60 miles of plants; 52 are within five miles. Yet, aircraft based at many of these airports are largely unguarded and could reach a nuclear site within minutes. Nuclear power companies say that their plants are designed to withstand earthquakes and natural disasters and are well-protected. Furthermore, if struck by an aircraft, they would not release radiation. Even a jet crash would not cause major damage, although it could affect the ability to generate electricity, they say. However, some scientists, safety experts, and lawmakers say the real threat is the ever-increasing stockpile of used fuel stored in less-protected pools at the power plants.[147]

It is interesting to note that the San Onofré Nuclear Generating Station (SONGS) is located only 28 miles from the McClellan-Palomar Airport and only 58 miles from the San Diego International Airport. Because of lack of adequate security at the McClellan-Palomar Airport, either a US Air Express or United Express flight loaded with explosives could reach and crash into SONGS within 5-10 minutes after takeoff. These aircraft normally carry in excess of 30 passengers, so they are large enough to carry a good load of explosives. In August 2008, it is interesting to note that the author of this security plan participated as a CERT member in a San Diego County OES and FEMA-sponsored mock evacuation, reception, and contamination exercise for just such an incident at SONGS.

---

146 Anonymous (2006, August 10). Police: Plot to blow up aircraft foiled. *CNN.com*. Retrieved August 22, 2008, from http://www.cnn.com/2006/WORLD/europe/08/10/uk.terror/index.html.

147 Stoller, G. (2003, June 10). Nuclear plants near airports may be at risk. *USA Today*. Retrieved August 22, 2008, from http://www.usatoday.com/money/biztravel/2003-06-10-nuclear_x.htm.

2.2 Types of Measures Used to Identify Threats

Numerous threats/hazards were considered for inclusion in this security plan. However, not all were included for further analysis because the threats/hazards were limited to those that may most likely be related to a terrorist attack. These threats/hazards were outlined in other local and county plans that are directly relevant to the McClellan-Palomar Airport.[148]

2.3 Preemptive Measures That Would or Should Be Used

Preemptive measures that would/should be used at the McClellan-Palomar Airport include (1) preparing/implementing hazard mitigation plans, (2) using the integrated National Incident Management System (NIMS) and California Standard Emergency Management System (SEMS), (3) being knowledgeable of and familiar with working with an Incident Command System (ICS), and (4) understanding and using the national Intelligent Transportation Systems (ITS) Program and the SCAG regional ITS architecture.[149]

2.4 Measures to Implement

All four of the above measures shall be implemented because they are all required by federal and/or state law.

2.5 Evaluation of the Effectiveness of the Response Measures Chosen

Preparing and implementing hazard mitigation plans need to be accomplished as soon as possible since nothing has yet been done in this area. The NIMS and SEMS are being integrated on the state level and shall be available for use soon. The ICS has worked well in the recent wildfires in San Diego; hence, it should continue to work well for any future terrorist incident.

Regarding the ITS Program, the SCAG regional architecture did not fully examine the use of the ITS for Emergency Management. Hence, the region needs to develop an incident prevention and response system that would alert travelers (including air travelers) to dangerous conditions, improve

---

148 SCAG (2008). *2008 Regional Transportation Plan (RTP): Making the Connections: Transportation Security Report.* Los Angeles, CA: Southern California Association of Governments (SCAG), 22 pp.

149 Ibid.

early detection of incidents, activate timely and coordinated response, and significantly reduce clearance time.[150]

3.0 Conclusion

The implementation of security methods and processes in general has had a decisive impact on the aviation industry. However, efforts to coordinate effectively varied aspects of security protocols between agencies and GA components have not been adequately addressed. Overall security issues, especially with regard to planning for catastrophic terrorist events, have been neglected at the nation's smaller airports. For perspective, the term "general aviation" is generally accepted to include all flying except for military and scheduled airline operations. General aviation makes up more than $150 billion or 1 percent of the US Gross Domestic Product (GDP) and supports almost 1.3 million high-skilled jobs in professional services and manufacturing and, hence, is an important component of the aviation industry.[151],[152] Note the huge discrepancy of Sweet's $150B (above) vs. Mark's $20B (at top of page 8) for GA industry annual revenues.

In both conceptual and practical terms, we must perform proactive management of security planning and repeated security awareness training from both an individual and an organizational perspective within the GA venue. The results of a research project considered incorporating survey data from GA and small commercial airport managers as well as Transportation Security Administration (TSA) employees. Survey findings suggest that miscommunication takes place on different organizational levels and that between TSA employees and airport management, interaction can be contentious with diminished cooperation. The importance of organizational training for decreasing conflict and increasing security and preparedness is a primary implication.[153]

The data collected support the notion that catastrophe planning within the aviation community needs improvement. More specifically, focused attention needs to be given to the current threat to the GA community. It is simply too easy for perpetrators to access the facilities and to engage in nefarious

---

150 Ibid.

151 AOPA (n.d.). General aviation flying plays a critical role in the US economy. Aircraft Owners and Pilots Association (AOPA). Retrieved August 22, 2008, from http://www.gaservingamerica.com/our_economy/economy.htm.

152 Sweet, K. M. (2006). Emergency preparedness for catastrophic events at small and medium sized airports: Lacking or not? *Journal of Air Transportation, 11(3)*, pp. 110-143.

153 Ibid.

conduct without raising too much suspicion. Common sense dictates that the criminal or terrorist is more comfortable accessing the least secure facility and the one presenting the least risk. Admittedly, terrorists, unlike criminals, are rarely concerned with escape, but they still need to gain entrance to the airport system to disrupt it. To ignore the desire of terrorists possibly to use the GA community (or the McClellan-Palomar Airport) to attack a larger, more significant target (such as SONGS) suggests the old head-in-the-sand cliché may be a reality.[154]

---

154 Ibid.

CHAPTER 7
INTELLIGENCE, COUNTERMEASURES, AND POLICY

Robert T. Uda, MS, MBA

T his chapter is a catch-all that covers solutions for creating cooperation between government agencies and public officials in gathering and sharing intelligence. It also addresses the key agencies responsible for counterterrorism in the United States and their interactive role in combating terrorism. Furthermore, I present counterterrorism measures designed to prevent and respond to acts of terrorism along with a recommended countermeasure not yet suggested. Finally, I present an example of a general security policy statement. In particular, the policy statement is for the City of San Marcos, California, Community Emergency Response Team (CERT).

Cooperation and Intelligence Gathering

Two Major Solutions. Two of the major solutions for creating cooperation between government agencies and public officials that resulted from the 9/11 Commission report included establishing the position of Director of National Intelligence (DNI) and establishing the National Counterterrorism Center (NCTC). The 9/11 Commission also saw a need for a domestic intelligence agency (which we currently do not have) only if the DNI, NCTC, and other recommendations were not adopted.[155] The DNI, NCTC, and other recommendations were adopted. However, they do not appear to be working well. The DNI was purposefully made separate from the Director of Central Intelligence (DCI). These agencies are not cooperating as they should. The establishment of the NCTC has not been the panacea that people had hoped for. It suffers from both horizontal and vertical sharing problems.[156]

---

155 Burch, J. (2007, June). A domestic intelligence agency for the United States? A comparative analysis of domestic intelligence agencies and their implications for homeland security. *Homeland Security Affairs, 3(2).*

156 Kaplan, E. (2006, November 6). Examining counterterrorism culture. Council on Foreign Relations. Retrieved December 11, 2008, from http://www.cfr.

Problems that Need to Be Solved. "Stove-piping" is still a major problem among all intelligence agencies including the FBI, CIA, DoD, DOS, DIA, DHS, ODNI, NCTC, National Geospatial-Intelligence Agency (NGA), NRO, NSA, DOE, National Nuclear Security Administration (NNSA), and others. This is not to mention the information sharing problems that exist among the federal, state, local, territorial, tribal, and private sector partners. Incompatible security clearances among agencies and incompatible databases exacerbate the information sharing problem. The effectiveness of state and local fusion centers is also being questioned by public officials. The NCTC and federal/state/local law enforcement agencies are experiencing problems finding qualified candidates with the required intelligence gathering and analysis expertise; hence, positions are remaining vacant for long periods of time.

ODNI Doomed to Failure or Mediocrity. The Office of the DNI (ODNI) will not be effective unless:

- All intelligence agencies (indeed all of the Intelligence Community, IC) report directly to it with dotted line reporting to their current organizations
- The ODNI controls all intelligence budgets
- The DNI has the power and authority to hire and fire anyone working in the IC

Now, you would have an ODNI with the power and authority to get things done in an integrated fashion. However, I do not foresee this happening in the foreseeable future because public officials would not want to see so much power centered on one man and his office. As currently organized, the ODNI is doomed to failure or mediocrity.

DHS Ineffective. This is no different from the Department of Homeland Security (DHS). The DHS will never be totally effective if it does not have:

- All of the component agencies reporting directly to the Secretary of Homeland Security
- The DHS controls all of the component agency budgets
- The Secretary of HS has the power and authority to hire and fire anyone under the DHS umbrella

By not organizing the Department this way, it is no wonder that former Director Tom Ridge and the current Secretary Michael Chertoff have been rather ineffective in their positions.

org/publication/11922/examining_counterterrorism_culture.html.

FBI Ineffective at Domestic Intelligence Gathering. The Federal Bureau of Investigation (FBI) is the lead agency on domestic counterterrorism. The FBI now finds itself thrust into a domestic intelligence-gathering role for which it does not have a native skill set. Many experts have suggested the United States should create its own domestic intelligence agency, much like Britain's MI5.[157]

Intelligence Sharing

Are the agencies responsible for implementing counterterrorism measures effectively sharing intelligence information?

Slow Improvement. Prior to the 9/11 attacks, the Federal Bureau of Investigation (FBI), Central Intelligence Agency (CIA), National Security Agency (NSA), military intelligence agencies, state/local law enforcement agencies, and the aerospace/defense public sector very rarely if ever shared intelligence information much less cooperated in working together to characterize the enemy. In fact, they purposefully were territorial in nature and kept information from each other. However, after the 9/11 attacks, the administration and federal government realized that these agencies needed to share information and to work together to combat terrorists. With the establishment of the Department of Homeland Security (DHS) on November 25, 2002, and beginning of its operations on January 24, 2003, things slowly began to improve.

A Good Start. For example, in August 2004, President George W. Bush established the National Counterterrorism Center (NCTC) to serve as the primary organization in the United States Government (USG) for integrating and analyzing all intelligence pertaining to terrorism and counterterrorism and to conduct strategic operational planning by integrating all instruments of national power. In December 2004, Congress codified the NCTC in the Intelligence Reform and Terrorism Prevention Act (IRTPA) and placed the NCTC in the Office of the Director of National Intelligence (DNI). Located at the Liberty Crossing Building in Northern Virginia, the NCTC is a multi-agency organization dedicated to eliminating the terrorist threat to US interests at home and abroad.[158] At the NCTC, CIA analysts, FBI agents, and other experts from across the government sit side by side and

---

157 Ibid.
158 NCTC (2008, June 8). National Counterterrorism Center (NCTC) website. Retrieved June 8, 2008, from http://www.nctc.gov/about_us/about_nctc.html.

73

share intelligence continuously.[159] This was a good start towards solving the problem.

Closer Working Relationships and Sharing Information. The FBI is a relatively small organization with but 12,000 agents, compared to 800,000 law enforcement officers across the United States. That is why partnerships like our Joint Terrorism Task Forces (JTTFs) are so vital. Police officers and others from the federal government – including the CIA, the Secret Service (SS), and the DHS, just to name a few – work side-by-side with FBI agents and analysts, cooperating on investigations, and sharing information with their own departments and agencies.[160] Federal, state, and local agencies and the high-tech private sector companies now work closer together and share information than ever before.

Good Intelligence is the Key. By its very nature, intelligence is imperfect. Human sources may not be 100 percent reliable. Technology may not always be in the right place at the right time and may not capture everything we need to hear or read. Even with the best technology, the most reliable sources, and the most talented personnel, intelligence is an art, not a science. It is a continual process of trying to determine what we know and what we do not know and, then, finding ways to fill those gaps.[161] Good military and civilian intelligence is the key to winning 21st Century wars. The most important kind of intelligence is human intelligence (HUMINT). We need to pay good money for valuable information provided to us by the Arabs-Muslims-Islamic (AMI) people willing to sell us the gathered G-2. Money talks. Follow the money trail. There will always be someone ready to take a fist full of money for good information. Feed greed.[162]

Counterterrorism Measures

The practicality of counterterrorism measures designed to prevent and respond to acts of terrorism and a recommended countermeasure not yet suggested.

---

159 Anonymous (2007, September 9). Are we safer today? *The Washington Post*, Washington, DC, p. B.1. Retrieved February 13, 2008, from http://proquest.umi.com.proxy1.ncu.edu/pqdweb?did=1332819931&sid=1&Fmt=3&clientld=52110@RQT=309&VName=PQD.

160 Mueller, R. S., III (2006, August). Homegrown terrorism and the radicalization process. Vital Speeches of the Day, 72(20/21), pp 562-565.

161 Mueller, R. S. III (2008, April 7). Federal Bureau of Investigation – Major Executive Speeches. Chatham House, London, England. Retrieved June 8, 2008, from http://www.fbi.gov/pressrel/speeches/mueller040708.htm.

162 Uda, R. T. (2007). *Principles of Asymmetrical Warfare: How to Beat Islamofascists at Their Own Game.* Lincoln, Nebraska: iUniverse, Inc.

Available Counterterrorism Measures. Some of the available counterterrorism measures that many consider impractical, extreme, or unacceptable to the United States include:

- Abu-Ghraib-type humiliation
- Assassinations of leaders
- Blow up Muslim mosques that harbor terrorists
- Discard all rules of engagement
- Discard the Geneva Convention
- Disinformation campaign
- First strike strategy
- Genocide of all terrorists and sympathizers
- Gitmo-type prisons
- Interception of cell phone messages of citizen al-Qaeda sympathizers
- Kill family members of terrorist leaders
- Military tribunals
- Public beheadings
- Public execution of convicted American traitors
- Racial profiling
- Scorched-earth carpet bombing while ignoring collateral damage and fratricide
- Super-secret hit squads
- Take no prisoners and kill all of them
- Torture
- Use of detention, relocation, internment, or concentration camps for civilian "fellow travelers"
- Use of tactical nukes
- Use of weapons of mass destruction (WMDs) including chemical, biological, radiological, and nuclear (CBRN) weapons on terrorists and terror-supporting nations
- Wiretaps

All of these countermeasures are usually opposed by the American Civil Liberties Union (ACLU), Amnesty International, Council on American-Islamic Relations (CAIR), the Hollywood elite, extremist-radical liberals, and extremist-radical conservatives.

Offensive Counterterrorism Measures. These counterterrorism measures are offensive to many. However, we must know about these measures, understand them well, keep them at our disposal, and be able and willing to use all of them. This will be particularly so when the enemy is about to annihilate us, conquer us, and/or place us in bondage. When there is nothing left but the survival of our nation, all self-imposed limitations should be discarded and anything goes.

Available Limited Counterterrorism Measures. All other counterterrorism measures prove to be limited in effectiveness. Such countermeasures include:

- Airport screening
- Antiterrorism laws
- Armed air marshals
- Armed pilots in the cockpit
- Body armor
- Bomb-detection equipment
- Border guards
- Border inspection stations
- Closing the borders
- Conventional weapons
- Counter-cyber-terrorism tactics
- Criminal trials
- Diplomacy
- Hardening of critical infrastructure
- Intrusion-detection equipment
- Law enforcement
- Negotiations
- Non-lethal weapons
- Search warrants
- Shutting off funding sources
- Special forces
- United Nations resolutions
- Unmanned aerial vehicles (UAVs)

All of these counterterrorism measures (and many more) somewhat prevent and respond to acts of terrorism. However, there is no silver bullet. There is no panacea. None of these countermeasures by themselves can eradicate terrorism. However, a combination of them can.

Recommended Countermeasure Not Yet Suggested. A countermeasure that has not yet been suggested is the use of laser guns (death rays) from space.

Other Counterterrorism Measures. Other counterterrorism measures that can prevent and respond to acts of terrorism include:

- Bomb and destroy al-Jazeera, which is al-Qaeda's media mouth piece
- Attack and destroy those countries that harbor and support terrorists
- Liquidate terrorists one at a time without any fanfare or publicity until there are none

Example General Security Policy Statement

A general security policy statement designed to protect your local community from a terrorist attack.

Policy Statement #10

Community Emergency Response Team (CERT)

Introduction. The City of San Marcos, California, provides this general security policy statement regarding how the San Marcos Community Emergency Response Team (CERT) shall work with and support the City's first responders, i.e., police, firefighters, and emergency medical personnel, during and after a terrorist attack.

Purpose. The purpose of this policy is to ensure that the San Marcos CERT works in conjunction with and as an additional resource to first responders during and after a major terrorist incident.

General Security Policy Statement. During any terrorist incident occurring within the city limits of San Marcos, the mayor of San Marcos shall serve as the focal point for making all major decisions needed to deal with the incident. The San Marcos city manager shall serve as the mayor's deputy during any terrorist incident. The San Marcos chief of police, fire chief, head of the emergency medical team, and the CERT emergency preparedness coordinator (EPC) all shall serve on the City Response Leadership Team under the mayor and city manager and report directly to them. The City Response Leadership Team shall be responsive to the head of the San Diego County Board of Supervisors, the head of the Unified San Diego County Emergency Services Organization, the governor of the State of California, and the local head of the Federal Emergency Management Agency (FEMA) should they be on the scene.

The San Marcos CERT is managed jointly by the San Marcos Fire Department battalion chief and the CERT EPC with the battalion chief as the lead and the EPC as his deputy. The members of the San Marcos CERT shall not self-activate; however, they may self-activate as concerned citizens in their neighborhoods but may not use their official CERT vests, hardhats, and backpacks/duffel-bags of emergency equipment/supplies. The San Marcos CERT shall be activated by the CERT EPC through their amateur radio system. When activated, the members of the CERT shall don their CERT vests, hardhats, and carry needed equipment in their backpacks. The rest of their equipment and supplies shall be available to them in their duffel-bags in their car trunks if required to travel or at their homes if they work in their neighborhoods.

The members of the San Marcos CERT shall support the Fire Department, Police Department, emergency medical services team, and the American Red Cross as directed by the battalion chief and CERT EPC, who shall take their directions from the Incident Command System (ICS). Duties and responsibilities may include the following:

- Provide first-aid to victims
- Perform cardio-pulmonary resuscitation (CPR)
- Provide American Red Cross cross-shelter operations support activities
- Perform triage
- Erect shelters
- Provide San Onofré Nuclear Generating Station (SONGS) reception and decontamination traffic support
- Perform emergency radio communications
- Perform search & rescue
- Perform heavy lifting
- Perform anything else asked of the police, firemen, emergency medical service workers, and Red Cross workers

For CERT members to remain current and active members, all CERT members are required to complete four training events per year. All CERT members are also sworn in as disaster service workers (DSWs) with the Unified San Diego County Emergency Services Organization. CERT members shall wear their official ID badge from the Office of Emergency Services (OES) at all times when participating in CERT activities and when activated on emergency events.

CHAPTER 8
STRATEGIES TO COUNTER MARITIME PIRACY

Robert T. Uda, MS, MBA

Introduction

In the November 2005 *International Outreach and Coordination Strategy*, Secretary of State Condoleezza Rice wrote, "For most of our history, warfare and perils such as piracy were first on our minds when we thought of threats to maritime security. Today, however, we also face a determined and resourceful terrorist enemy who would turn the vehicles of peaceful transportation – including ships, as well as planes, trains, and trucks – into deadly instruments of destruction. This enemy will attack not only naval vessels like the USS Cole, but also commercial vessels such as the Merchant Vessel (M/V) Limburg, a French tanker."

While the variety of actors threatening the maritime domain continues to grow in number and capability, they can be broadly grouped as (1) nation-states, (2) terrorists, and (3) transnational criminals and pirates. Our foremost objective is to defeat the threat of the widely dispersed terrorist networks that present an immediate danger to US national security interests at home and abroad.[163] Additionally, modern-day pirates and other criminals are well-organized and well-equipped. They often possess advanced communications, weapons, and high-speed craft to smuggle people, drugs, weapons, and other contraband as well as to commit piracy.[164]

According to the International Maritime Bureau's (IMB's) Piracy Reporting Center, half of all pirate attacks go unreported. Many shipping companies do not report raids because they do not want bad publicity.[165]

---

163 DoS (2005, November). *International Outreach and Coordination Strategy: For the National Strategy for Maritime Security*. Washington, DC: Department of State (DoS), 47 pp.

164 MSPCC (2005, October). *National Plan to Achieve Maritime Domain Awareness: For The National Strategy for Maritime Security*. Washington, DC: Maritime Security Policy Coordinating Committee (MSPCC), 33 pp.

165 NPR (2008, August 9). Writer tracks modern-day pirates in Malaysia. *NPR.org*. Retrieved August 9, 2008, from http://www.npr.org/templates/story/story.php?storyId=15170359.

Maritime piracy attacks and their level of violence grew steadily over the past two years. Consequently, countering them is a topic of great interest to those involved in maritime security. Hence, this paper presents ideas and analysis related to developing strategies to disrupt and counter maritime piracy. Also, ideas and analysis are presented to reduce the threat and increase the security of the international maritime supply chain in accordance with the *Strategy to Enhance International Supply Chain Security*.[166]

Definition of the Problem

What is Piracy? So, piracy is back, and it is bad; but exactly what is it? According to the IMB, the definition is: "Piracy is the act of boarding any vessel with intent to commit theft or any other crime and with an intent or capacity to use force in furtherance of that act." In order to distinguish it from simple high-jacking, a piracy crime requires the involvement of two vessels in the incident. The second requirement is that the crime has been undertaken for private, not political purposes. These requirements can be important considerations when determining coverage under a policy of marine cargo insurance.[167]

An Example. In one famous British case from years ago, the marine cargo insurance policy was "warranted free of capture, seizure, and detention ... piracy excepted." All was well for payment of the claim until it was discovered that the so-called "pirates" who took the insured vessel had actually been attempting to overthrow the Bolivian government! Seizure of the vessel had been a political act and, therefore, not piracy.[168] Additionally, people seem to confuse *modern-day piracy* with *maritime terrorism*. They are quite different as shown in the next paragraph.

Difference between Pirates and Terrorists. The big differences between modern-day pirates and maritime terrorists are that pirates want to live to spend and enjoy the money and cargo/supplies that they hijack. However, pirates generally prefer the large amounts of cash on the vessel over the cargo. The maritime terrorists, on the other hand, use the money and cargo/supplies they hijack to fund their fanatical/extremist political, ideological, and/or religious causes, and they do not fear dying for their cause during the hijacking process. Terrorists will sometimes use modern-day pirates to

---

166 DHS (2007, July). *Strategy to Enhance International Supply Chain Security*. Washington, DC: Department of Homeland Security (DHS), 130 pp.

167 McDaniel, M. S. (2005, November). Modern high seas piracy. The Law Offices of Countryman & McDaniel Website. Retrieved August 9, 2008, from http://www.cargolaw.com/presentations_pirates.html.

168 Ibid.

accomplish their ends. However, modern-day pirates will almost never use maritime terrorists to accomplish their ends.

Causes of Piracy. It is important to establish the causes of piracy if we are to eliminate it. The number one reason is poverty. Many residents of coastal countries do not have a legal income. The main pirate-ridden regions – West Africa, Somalia, and Southeast Asia – do not have high living standards. In Somalia, poverty is aggravated by a seemingly endless civil war and economic collapse. This is why residents of these areas become pirates. However, the different conditions in these regions affect the kind of piracy pursued there. In Southeast Asia, for instance, pirates are usually after a precious cargo that they can sell at a profit. In war-torn Somalia, selling anything is too risky, and pirates prefer to take hostages and receive cash for their release.[169]

Threats and Illicit Activities

Transnational Criminal and Piracy Threats. The continued growth in legitimate international commerce in the maritime domain has been accompanied by growth in the use of the maritime domain for criminal purposes. The smuggling of people, drugs, weapons, and other contraband, as well as piracy and armed robbery against vessels, pose a threat to maritime security. Piracy and incidents of maritime crime tend to be concentrated in areas of heavy commercial maritime activity, especially where there is significant political and economic instability, or in regions with little or no maritime law enforcement capacity. Today's pirates and transnational criminals are usually well-organized and well-equipped with advanced communications, weapons, and high-speed craft. The capabilities to board and commandeer large underway vessels – demonstrated in numerous piracy incidents – could also be employed to facilitate terrorist acts.[170]

Illicit Maritime Activities That Fund Terrorism. The world's oceans are avenues for a nation's overseas commerce. They are also highways for the import/export of illegal commodities. Maritime drug trafficking generates vast amounts of money for international organized crime syndicates and terrorist organizations. Laundered through the international financial system, this money provides a huge source of nearly untraceable funds. These monetary assets are used to bribe government officials, bypass established financial

---

169 Kramnik, I. (2008, June 27). Outside view: Fighting pirates – Part 1. *Terradaily.com*. Retrieved August 10, 2008, from http://www.terradaily.com/reports/Outside_View_Fighting_pirates_Part_1_999.html.

170 DoD/DHS (2005, September). *The National Strategy for Maritime Security*. Washington, DC: Department of Defense (DoD) and Department of Homeland Security (DHS), 31 pp.

controls, and fund additional illegal activities, which include arms trafficking, migrant smuggling, and terrorist operations. Further, these illicit activities can ensure a steady supply of weapons and cash for terrorist operatives as well as the means for their clandestine movement.[171]

Pirate Attack Strategy. Modern-day pirates do not operate in a single-ship network. They operate in organized gangs that coordinate multiple-boat attacks on a single ship. A pirate boat sails in front of the target ship causing the bridge (where the captain sits) to get distracted and to attempt to avoid hitting the pirate boat in front of them. While they slow the ship down to maneuver, pirates on two other boats board the ship, undetected, from the aft end of the ship.[172]

Piracy on the Rise and Most Dangerous Waters. It is a common misconception that piracy is on the way out. In fact, it is the opposite. From 1993 to 2003, the incidence of pirate attacks tripled when compared to the previous decade. The most dangerous waters are those around Indonesia and Somalia. In 2004, the Indonesian government started cracking down on pirates, and the Indonesian navy has made numerous arrests. While things have improved around Indonesia, they have worsened in the waters around Somalia.[173]

Strategies for Countering Piracy

No Common Strategy and Tactics. What is the major reason for the continuing international problem of piracy on the high seas in the 21st century? The world's leading nations possess neither a common strategy nor tactics to create a scourge that would prevent piracy in key regions. As a result, pirates almost always go unpunished. To lift Somalia out of its war and consequent poverty would take many years of work, enormous spending, and almost definite loss of life while peacemaking. Even then, there would be no guaranteed success. Negotiations with the pirates – who should be equated with terrorists – should be held only to gain time to prepare a rescue operation. Deterrent measures deserve special mention.[174]

---

171 Ibid.

172 Williams Kherkher (2008). Admiralty lawyer & attorney: Modern-day pirates. Williams Kherkher website. Retrieved August 9, 2008, from http://www.admiraltylawsuitattorney.com/admiralty_lawsuit_article_modern-day_pirates.aspx.

173 Ibid.

174 Kramnik, I. (2008, June 27). Outside view: Fighting pirates – Part 2. *Terradaily.com*. Retrieved August 13, 2008, from http://www.terradaily.com/reports/Outside_View_Fighting_pirates_Part_2_999.html.

US Maritime Strategic Concept. The Sea Services must become adept at forging international partnerships in coordination with the other US services and government departments. To this end, the Global Maritime Partnerships initiative seeks a cooperative approach to maritime security, which promotes the rule of law by countering piracy, terrorism, weapons proliferation, drug trafficking, and other illicit activities. Maritime forces work with others to ensure an adequate level of security and awareness in the maritime domain. In doing so, they constrain transnational threats. These threats include terrorists and extremists; proliferators of weapons of mass destruction (WMDs); pirates; traffickers in persons, drugs, and conventional weapons; and other such criminals.[175]

Multinational Naval Force. The most realistic way to combat piracy is for militarily strong countries to cooperate and protect navigation in problem areas. A united squadron of ships organized as a broad coalition could effectively counter piracy off Somalia or in any other trouble spot. These coalitions may be comprised of the North Atlantic Treaty Organization (NATO) countries, Russia, and the Gulf States.[176] Thus, Spain and France are looking for allies to create a multinational naval force to fight piracy off the coast of Somalia. According to the IMB (a United Nations agency), pirates seized more than 25 ships in Somali coastal waters during 2007. Spain and France subsequently brought international pressure to bear and the UN Security Council passed a resolution in June 2008 authorizing member countries to send warships temporarily into Somali waters to pursue pirates.[177]

Cooperation in Asia Paying Off. Unprecedented cooperation among Asian government maritime authorities is paying off with serious acts of piracy declining in that region. However, Voice of America (VOA) correspondent Steve Herman from Nalaguraidhoo, Maldives, reports that officials agree that more needs to be done as maritime attacks increase in the Horn of Africa and elsewhere. Nicholas Teo serves as the deputy director of the Information Sharing Center of the Regional Cooperation Agreement on Combating Piracy and Armed Robbery against Ships in Asia (ReCAAP). Initiated by

---

175 DON/USMC/USCG (2007, October). *A Cooperative Strategy for 21st Century Seapower.* Washington, DC: Department of the Navy (DON), United States Marine Corps (USMC), and United States Coast Guard (USCG), 20 pp.

176 Kramnik, I. (2008, June 27). Outside view: Fighting pirates – Part 2. *Terradaily.com.* Retrieved August 13, 2008, from http://www.terradaily.com/reports/Outside_View_Fighting_pirates_Part_2_999.html.

177 Staff Writers (2008, July 30). Madrid and Paris seek allies to fight piracy off Somalia coast. *Terradaily.com.* Retrieved August 10, 2008, from http://www.terradaily.com/reports/Madrid_and_Paris_seek_allies_to_fight_piracy_off_Somalia_coast_999.html.

Japan and heavily funded by Singapore, 14 countries now endorse ReCAAP. The Agreement came into force in September 2006.[178]

Singapore, Malaysia, and Indonesia conduct unprecedented sea and air patrols in the Strait of Malacca, which is a busy global shipping choke point. These patrols have caused Southeast Asia to no longer be regarded as the world's most dangerous piracy zone. ReCAAP Deputy Director Teo says that data sharing among Asian militaries and maritime law enforcement agencies has also made a difference.[179]

Indirect Routes and Training. To avoid getting hijacked, ships have begun taking a more indirect but costly route near Yemen, which takes them 200 to 300 kilometers away from the Somali coast. This strategy forces Somalia's buccaneers, who use speedboats, to venture much further offshore to hunt their prey, which thereby puts them at greater risk. To deal with the pirates, sailors on Canadian warships now in the Indian Ocean were schooled in the Law of the Sea, small arms, and hand-to-hand combat as well as the arcane art of rappelling up the sides of suspect vessels.[180]

Other Methods of Combating Piracy. Legal measures are also important. The UN Security Council's mandate will eventually make piracy too dangerous as an occupation. The mandate provides for the invasion of Somalia's territorial waters, use of arms against the pirates, and allocation of the required forces and equipment. Required forces and equipment include reconnaissance aviation, deck helicopters, radars, and Marines and Special Forces trained in boarding and releasing hostages. The strategy would be well enough just to set up a squadron of five or six warships and one light helicopter carrier as a flagship. Warships from different navies would rotate patrol duty with shifts lasting for several months. In the most dangerous areas, merchant vessels could be escorted by ships, helicopters, and/or armed motorboats. Importantly, patrols are effective only if the struggle against piracy overrides the inviolability of territorial waters. Otherwise, pirates will almost always escape punishment.[181]

---

178 Herman, S. (2008, May 21). Cooperation in Asia paying off in fight against maritime piracy. GlobalSecurity.org. Retrieved August 10, 2008, from http://www.globalsecurity.org/military/library/news/2008/05/mil-080521-voa10.htm.

179 Ibid.

180 Fisher, M. (2008, July 13). Canadian warships hunt modern-day pirates. *Politics & Current Affairs Public Debate Forum.* Retrieved August 10, 2008, from http://www.politicsandcurrentaffairs.co.uk/Forum/world-events/50768-canadian-warships-hunt-modern.html.

181 Kramnik, I. (2008, June 27). Outside view: Fighting pirates – Part 2. *Terradaily.com.* Retrieved August 13, 2008, from http://www.terradaily.com/reports/Outside_View_Fighting_pirates_Part_2_999.html.

Implementing the Strategy

Creating and maintaining security at sea are essential to mitigating threats short of war. These threats include piracy, terrorism, weapons proliferation, drug trafficking, and other illicit activities. Countering these irregular and transnational threats protects our homeland, enhances global stability, and secures freedom of navigation for the benefit of all nations.[182]

Use of Technology in Combating Pirates

Ship Security Alert System. As piracy and terrorist attacks have increased over the years, the International Maritime Organization (IMO) has defined a set of mandatory requirements in the Safety of Life at Sea (SOLAS) Resolution XI-2/6 to improve security for ships. The new SOLAS resolution 6 states that the Ship Security Alert System (SSAS) shall provide ships with two alarm buttons, which can be activated in case of a pirate or terrorist attack. The alarm is a covert signal, which will have no sound and no flashing lights so that it is in no way obvious to any intruders on-board the ship.[183]

The SOLAS Resolution XI-2/6 requires vessels of +500 GT (Gross Tons) constructed prior to 01 July 2004 to install an SSAS no later than the first radio survey after 01 July 2004. Other Cargo ships of +500 GT and mobile offshore drilling units constructed prior to 01 July 2004 must be fitted no later than the first radio survey after 01 July 2006.[184]

Approaches Shipping Firms Take to Prevent Attacks. Preventing attacks has become a bigger challenge for shipping firms. The IMB provides a warning system about suspicious craft, and ships can be kitted with non-lethal defensive devices. In November 2005, the luxury cruise liner Seabourn Spirit was attacked off Somalia. The invaders shot at the ship with a grenade launcher and machineguns. The invaders were repelled by a sonic blaster, which delivers an extremely loud and debilitating noise. Mr. Singer of Securewest International says it is now commonplace for ships to take on security staff if

---

182 DON/USMC/USCG (2007, October). *A Cooperative Strategy for 21st Century Seapower.* Washington, DC: Department of the Navy (DON), United States Marine Corps (USMC), and United States Coast Guard (USCG), 20 pp.

183 Anonymous (n.d.). Ship security alert system: SOLAS Resolution XI-2/6. Thrane & Thrane website. Retrieved August 10, 2008, from http://www.thrane.com/ Maritime/Introduction/Ship%20Security%20Alert%20System.aspx.

184 Ibid.

their course crosses pirate territory. His own company provides teams of ex-servicemen including former Gurkhas.[185]

What are Gurkhas? "Gurkhas" are quite fierce ex-British Army troops that are the stuff of many movies. Ship owners retain the unique services of a British company known as "Gurkha International Manpower Services." That company supplies teams of ex-British Gurkhas for cruise line security and anti-piracy patrol services. Expect the trend of hiring "private navies" for combating piracy to increase.[186]

High-tech Defenses. As the frequency of piracy on the high seas grows, many ship owners and insurers are not willing to wait for the navy to help them. Instead, they are turning to an array of high-tech defenses to keep freebooters at bay. For commercial shipping vessels and yachts operating in high-risk areas of Southeast Asia, the Red Sea, and the Horn of Africa, such products can mean the difference between smooth sailing and high-seas distress. Among the offerings are those shown in the following table:[187]

High-tech Equipment	Function	Supplier
Night-vision equipment	Able to see pirates during night hours.	
High-powered water guns	Knock pirates off the boat as they board.	
Ear-splitting klaxons	Irritates the ears and even injures the eardrums and, therefore, the hearing ability of pirates.	
Lubricant foam	Makes it difficult for pirates to get their footing.	

---

185 Coughlan, S. (2006, July 6). Rise of modern-day pirates. *BBC News Magazine*. Retrieved August 9, 2008, from http://newsvote.bbc.co.uk/mpapps/pagetools/print/news.bbc.co.uk/2/hi/uk_news/magazine/5146582.stm.

186 McDaniel, M. S. (2005, November). Modern high seas piracy. The Law Offices of Countryman & McDaniel Website. Retrieved August 9, 2008, from http://www.cargolaw.com/presentations_pirates.html.

187 Siegelbaum, D. J. (2008, April 18). Piracy sparks high-tech defenses. *Time* in partnership with CNN. Retrieved August 9, 2008, from http://www.time.com/time/printout/0,8816,1732125,00.html.

Secure-Ship	A high-voltage fencing product similar to those used to enclose military bases. Wires strung from poles on deck emit 9000 volts, a non-lethal charge, but enough to deter intruders.	Secure-Marine, a Netherlands-based company
Virtual fence underwater	Adapted its military underwater sonar system, Cerberus, into the private yacht market, which creates an underwater acoustic perimeter around a vessel that triggers an alert when broken. It would identify an underwater swimmer, scuba diver, or vehicle coming in under the water.	British defense firm QinetiQ
Ships send out robot snoops like the Sentry	A jet ski–sized remote-controlled scout to ferret out fakers.	QinetiQ
Protector (robotic boat)	A 30-foot unmanned surface vessel (USV) equipped with a 7.62 mm remote-controlled machine gun used for commercial protection to investigate and intercept boats up to 10 miles away.	BAE Systems, Lockheed Martin, and an Israeli defense firm
Mobility Denial System	A non-lethal weapon with a fancy name for a slippery chemical spray that coats surfaces and greatly reduces traction, thereby, making boarding and hijacking vessels difficult.	US Marine Corps
Long-range acoustic device (LRAD)	This 33-inch dish emits a sound blast of up to 150 decibels, deafening and driving away would-be attackers. It proved remarkably effective in foiling a pirate attack on a British cruise ship off the Horn of Africa in 2005.	Originally developed by the US military & manufactured by American Technology Corporation

Negating the Element of Surprise. Michael McDaniel spoke about an effective brace of merchant weapons include the fire hose, flare gun, and ship's horn. Used together, an alert crew can startle, blind, and hose a pirate group off the deck before an attack takes hold. The key here is robbing pirates of their chief weapon, i.e., the element of surprise. Diligence and better practices are starting to make a difference. Some of these approaches include the following:[188]

- Substitutes for cash carried in the ship's safe
- 24-hour radio watches
- Pre-charged fire hose at the ready
- Anti-pirate watches have accounted for dozens of repelled attacks
- Bridge and engine room doors that do not open from the outside create safe havens for crew members against less determined pirate attackers

Increased Public Awareness Required. On the technology side, all sorts of gadgets have been proposed including a recent display in London of a bullet-proof lifejacket! A particularly effective system is the "Shiploc," which uses a hidden personal computer (PC) aboard ship to monitor position by Global Positioning System (GPS) satellite 24 hours a day. If anyone should breach a fiber-optic network stretched around the vessel's perimeter, an automatic signal is provided both to the ship's crew and authorities ashore. All 450 ships of "K" Line are equipped with a similar system known as the "Seajack" alarm. Another competitor known as "Tigers Gate" immediately sounds an alarm for alerting the crew of pirate boarders. Whatever the gun, gimmick, or Gurkha, it seems clear that increased public awareness of modern high-sea piracy is going to be required before this deadly trend is truly reversed.[189]

Summary of Findings

Modern-day pirates and transnational criminals are well-organized and well-equipped. Half of all piracy attacks go unreported. The number one cause of piracy is poverty. The most realistic way to combat piracy is for militarily strong countries to cooperate and protect navigation in problem areas.

Unprecedented cooperation among Asian government maritime authorities is paying off with serious acts of piracy declining in that region. Sea and air patrols in the Strait of Malacca have caused Southeast Asia to no longer be regarded as the world's most dangerous piracy zone. It is important to note that patrols are effective only if the struggle against piracy overrides

---

188 McDaniel, M. S. (2005, November). Modern high seas piracy. The Law Offices of Countryman & McDaniel Website. Retrieved August 9, 2008, from http://www.cargolaw.com/presentations_pirates.html.

189 Ibid.

the inviolability of territorial waters. Otherwise, pirates would almost always escape punishment.

The key to combating pirates is to rob them of their chief weapon, which is the element of surprise. Additionally, diligence and better practices are beginning to make a difference. It is clear that increased public awareness of modern high-sea piracy is required before this deadly trend can be reversed.

Conclusion

Maritime piracy grew dramatically. The number of attacks and level of violence increased steadily over the years. The world community is concerned as to what strategy it should develop to counter and disrupt maritime piracy. Also, the world community is concerned about the threat to the international maritime supply chain and how to increase its security. This chapter presents some creative ideas and analysis of such strategies for countering and disrupting the piracy threat to the international maritime supply chain.

Captain Noel Choong, a former master mariner in Singapore and current head of the Piracy Reporting Center in Kuala Lumpur, said, "We'll never see the end of piracy, just as we'll never see the end of robbery on land. But we're doing everything we can."[190] Yes, piracy may never be entirely eradicated; however, it can be severely curtailed to a manageable level. Consequently, controlling piracy and transnational crime protects our homeland, enhances global stability, and secures freedom of navigation for the benefit of all nations.

---

190 Raffaele, P. (2007, August). The pirate hunter. *Smithsonian* magazine. Retrieved August 10, 2008, from http://www.printthis.clickability.com/pt/cpt?acti on=cpt&title=The+Pirate+Hunters+|+People+&+Places+|+Smithsonian+Magazine &expire=&urlID=24211033&fb=Y&url=http://www.smithsonianmag.com/people-places/pirate_main.html&partnerID=253162.

CHAPTER 9
PROTECTING AMERICA'S
CRITICAL INFRASTRUCTURES

1st Lt. Michael W. Halter Jr., US Army, MBA

Introduction

Asymmetric warfare has emerged as the term of choice for the modern war against terrorism that the United States and its numerous allies are currently confronting. Nothing other than a re-fabricated term to loosely describe unconventional warfare, asymmetrical warfare delves beyond the traditional means of conflict. In fact, conventional warfare utilizes numerous tactics that stem away from prior established understandings and mechanisms of conflict.

The current war against terrorism highlights the most complex establishments of parties to a particular conflict by drifting away from the notorious state versus state capacity as in the past. Furthermore, advanced strategies for conducting asymmetrical warfare must notably deal with factions such as counterinsurgency. Nonetheless, perhaps the best approach to understand asymmetrical warfare is by assessing the various strengths and impairments of the United States homeland, since, after all, the global fight against terrorism seeks to destroy and eliminate terrorists away from the homeland. Thus, the recently established critical infrastructures of the United States are essential in comprehending the potential asymmetric vulnerabilities that may potentially be used against the nation.

Critical Infrastructure Protection

Once considered a consequential and reactive term to assess potential hazards such as natural disasters and minor network outages with the early advent of the Internet, the methods of critical infrastructure protection have emerged into widespread sectors throughout the United States. Understanding the strengths, weaknesses, opportunities, and threats of America's critical infrastructures creates benchmark advantages for American citizens, while promoting such advancements as international trade through globalization for various nations throughout the world. However, analyzing the requirements necessary to protect these sectors is first vital to truly comprehend any notions of geopolitical or economical successes that are so commonly discussed in the media, as well as government. Thus, the following examination considers the correlation of national and homeland security as significant predictors of safety through proactive infrastructure protection. Critical infrastructures are defined according to various sectors necessary for enhancing security efforts. Furthermore, the infrastructures of cyberspace, border security, and the transportation network are assessed as potential asymmetric warfare strategies for attacking the vulnerabilities of the United States.

Critical infrastructure is commonly vocalized by numerous governmental and non-governmental officials in American society today; however, few truly understand the significance of infrastructure protection to the national and international political economy. "Because the American economy is dependent on networks of physical infrastructure such as energy and transportation systems and virtual networks such as information systems, an attack against one or more of these may disrupt an entire system and cause significant damage to the nation."[191] Therefore, it is pertinent that all levels of government, local, federal, and state, fully comprehend and develop mechanisms for securing critical infrastructures. Moreover, for the ease of classifying critical infrastructures, component sectors may be used to differentiate the needs and precautions associated with each infrastructure.

Not until a few weeks following the September 11, 2001, terrorist attacks, did the United States government clearly define the importance of critical infrastructure protection. Upon the creation of the President's Critical Infrastructure Protection Board (PCIPB), the federal government finally stressed the emerging need for consistent proactive measures concerning such sectors as information systems and telecommunications. In December 2003, President Bush further advanced the focus on infrastructure protection with the activation of HSPD-7 (Homeland Security Presidential Directive #7), which details specific sectors and responsible departments and agencies that would assure proper accountability, plans, and resources to protect designated industries.[192] Nonetheless, regardless of assignment, homeland security obviously requires shared and often overlapping responsibilities across all governmental bounds.

---

191 Sullivant, J. (2007). *Strategies for Protecting National Critical Infrastructure Assets: A Focus on Problem-Solving*, p. 38. Hoboken, NJ: John Wiley & Sons, Inc.

192 Lewis, T. (2006). *Critical Infrastructure Protection Homeland Security: Defending a Networked Nation*, pp. 30-38. Hoboken, NJ: John Wiley & Sons, Inc.

HSPD-7

HSPD-7 tasked various governmental agencies with ensuring the minimization of critical infrastructure vulnerabilities. Fourteen industries were deemed critical including: Agriculture/Food, Public Health/Food, Drinking Water and Treatment Systems, Energy, Nuclear Power Plants, Banking and Finance, Defense Industrial Base, Cyber-Security, Chemical, Transportation Systems, Emergency Services, Postal and Shipping, National Monuments, and key assets, such as dams, government facilities, and commercial facilities. Moreover, various government agencies were assigned the ultimate authority for maintaining particular industries. For example, the Department of Agriculture would control the Agriculture/Food industry. On the other hand, some industries such as Emergency Services and Postal and Shipping were not assigned a specific responsible department, while Nuclear Power Plants were assigned the Department of Homeland Security, Nuclear Regulatory Commission, and Department of Energy.[193]

As the HSPD-7 is assessed, one may quickly become confused at the message delivered. For instance, there is no particular mention of border security as an infrastructure deemed critical. However, based on one's perception, border security may be classified under the Transportation Systems, Postal and Shipping, Key Assets, or Defense Industrial Base industries. Or, border security may not be critical at all according to our federal government. Although this statement is blatantly false, it alludes to the uncertainty that exists within the national and local levels of determining the requirements for protecting such obvious key assets. Subsequently, no solid procedures exist for agencies to interact with one another. In a RAND study conducted by Bruce Don and David Mussington, the lack of appropriate contact among various agencies was concluded as potentially adding disarray to an already confusing political environment.[194] Thus, numerous requirements beyond presidential directives exist for protecting critical infrastructures. Nonetheless, presidential directives, such as the *National Strategy to Secure Cyberspace*, are excellent foundations to guide interrelations among federal, state, and local leaders.

---

193 Homeland Security Presidential Directive/HSPD-7 (2003, 17 December). Retrieved August 12, 2008, from http://www.whitehouse.gov/pcipb/cyberspace_strategy.pdf.

194 Don, B., & Mussington, D. (2002, Summer). Protecting critical infrastructure. *RAND Publications*. Retrieved August 12, 2008, from http://www.rand.org/publications/randreview/issues/rr.08.02/infrastructure.html.

Securing Cyberspace

Cyberspace has emerged as one of the potentially most hazardous homeland security and asymmetrical threats to the United States. Unlike most other infrastructures deemed critical, an attack on cyberspace activities may quickly, efficiently, and completely destroy such quality areas as manufacturing, utilities, banking, and communications. In essence, all sectors of the United States economy are interlinked with cyberspace through single or multiple networks of technology and data. Thus, the United States now entirely depends on cyberspace to perform functions as simple as devising airline schedules and as complex as accurately depicting communications and pipeline routes underground. The threats and vulnerabilities to cyberspace consequently are immense with a single virus or worm possessing the perplexity to destroy an entire nation's operations.[195]

Securing cyberspace requires extensive training and continuity of operations. Perhaps, more importantly, cyberspace security mandates invaluable integrity and reliability among its operators and maintainers. Numerous corporations, especially organizations such as the military, utilize common cyber-security methods through enterprise systems. An enterprise system is nothing more than a consolidated system that is comprised of an organization's central data operations. The main premise of securing cyberspace is thus a complicated array of systems maintained by trusted individuals who strive to avoid any losses of service, data, or security at all costs. Nonetheless, losses of service many times occur due to scheduled or accidental power outages, while losses of data regularly happen for various reasons such as corrupted files or improper deletions of files by operators. Losses of security in cyberspace, in contrast, usually occur for various reasons.

Losses of security in cyberspace actually occur more commonly than thought. Password infringements are the most frequent contributors to losses of security in cyberspace and enterprise system failures. Attackers often easily obtain passwords and logins simply by attempting various number or word strings until a computer accepts. This is why passwords should never consist of real words, but rather combinations of letters that have no significance or meaning. With that said, technology does exist to minimize potential attacks. An example is the use of encryption to manage and authenticate passwords through specialized certificates.[196] Technology, conversely, is only as strong as its governing policies.

195 *National Strategy to Secure Cyberspace* (2003, February). Retrieved August 12, 2008, from http://www.whitehouse.gov/pcipb/cyberspace_strategy.pdf.

196 Lewis, T. (2006). *Critical Infrastructure Protection Homeland Security: Defending a Networked Nation*, pp. 434-457. Hoboken, NJ: John Wiley & Sons,

Five Cyberspace Priorities

To avoid potential cyber attacks against the United States, policies must be devised and adhered at all levels of government and management. Information assurance is prone to battle with convenience, but decision-makers must choose acceptable, quantifiable minimum standards.

The *National Strategy to Secure Cyberspace* suggests and establishes five priorities that agencies such as the Department of Homeland Security should centralize. First, a national cyberspace security response system is a necessity. The federal government has already created cyber security-related network operation centers that devote much attention to distributing analysis and risk management. However, corporations and colleges and universities must strictly participate in such programs to enable trained specialists in cyber security in order to make network operation centers successful. Next, a national cyberspace security threat and vulnerability reduction program is vital for the coordination among different agencies. The Department of Homeland Security essentially must establish and implement protocols to securely share information and promote structural processes with the Department of Commerce and other related private sector and public sector agencies. Third, a national cyberspace security awareness and training program is required. The Department of Education must actively pursue mechanisms for teaching current and potential practices needed for managing, troubleshooting, and developing concrete cyber security. Fourth, the governments' cyberspace must be secured. The federal government is unable to afford weaknesses in authentication or encryption devices. More importantly, the federal government must devise a minimum requirement for all private and public sector IT (Information Technology) security programs. Finally, international cyberspace security practices must effectively counter the capabilities of espionage and other terrorist initiatives.[197]

Border Security

Although not specifically considered a critical infrastructure by HSPD-7, but mentioned in the *National Strategy for the Protection of Physical Infrastructures and Key Assets*, border security should exist at the center of the widespread homeland security requirements. Unlike cyberspace security, border security is publically scrutinized and is obviously a vulnerability of securing

---

Inc.

197 *National Strategy to Secure Cyberspace* (2003, February, pp. 55-59). Retrieved August 12, 2008, from http://www.whitehouse.gov/pcipb/cyberspace_strategy.pdf.

the United States. In fact, statistics regarding the nation's vulnerabilities are astonishing. K. Jack Riley articulates some interesting points:

> *The United States has more than 100 international airports, through which some 88 million foreign visitors pass annually. It also has numerous major ports; for instance, Los Angeles and Long Beach together constitute one of the world's largest container port facilities, handling approximately half of the seaborne trade entering or leaving the country. Every day more than 16,000 large shipping containers arrive at American ports. Also, the United States protects thousands of miles of land border with Canada and Mexico. Daily truck and passenger traffic at key land ports of entry, such as Detroit (Michigan), Vancouver (Washington), and San Diego (California), numbers in the millions.*[198]

Border security has attentively increased since September 11, 2001. The 1990s witnessed low, if any, priorities to accommodate issues among border surveillance. Unfortunately, political bounds have placed much wrongful emphasis on border control mechanisms today. Border policy has become bureaucratically inappropriate and misguided in focus. Requirements to protect the United States borders must instead generate cooperative cross-border initiatives. The US-Mexico Border Partnership Agreement of 2002 outlines the necessity to "de-border" border controls through trafficking beyond sole ports of entry. In other words, border control officials should work deeper into the territories surrounding the border. However, advanced counterterrorism practices must be implemented in order to make any effort of "de-bordering" successful. These practices must promote realistic expectations. Therefore, the random vehicle halts and inspections at the border should end immediately, so the focus may shift to the more pertinent area of seeking the few high-risk crossers, rather than holding up the majority low-risk enterers. Yes, this would create political unrest, but too much time is wasted with tactics that naturally regulate nothing other than delay in travel and trade. Standardizing other facets such as the labor market may, in turn, prevent unsuccessful border security. "Emphasizing labor market regulation with a focus on the workplace and more tamperproof documents rather than on border control with a narrow focus on the borderline would put most migrant smuggling organizations out of business."[199]

---

198 Riley, K. (2006, pp. 587-588). Border control. In David G. Kamien (Ed.). *The McGraw-Hill Homeland Security Handbook (pp. 587-612)*. New York: The McGraw-Hill Companies, Inc.

199 Andreas, P. (2006). Politics on edge: Managing the US-Mexico border. *Current History, 105(688)*, 64-68. Retrieved August 22, 2008, from Research Library

Transportation Network

A final area of emphasis regarding homeland security requirements concerns the management of transportation networks. Three primary areas worthy of assessment deal with travel by air, railroad, and ship. Travel by air is obviously the most publicized since the terrorist attacks of September 11, 2001. From skyrocketing ticket prices to frequent delays at airports, homeland security requirements are immense proponents of compromises for safety, rather than comfort and convenience to most. In retrospect, sophisticated technology continues to appear that not only enhances security, but also reintegrates convenience. For instance, the release of a new device in 20 of the nation's busiest airports that enables an X-ray beam to emit radio frequency waves to screen passengers is set to debut in the latter months of 2008. Passengers simply will be able to walk into the machine that detects any suspect materials underneath the travelers' clothing within 12 seconds. Those passengers that feel uncomfortable with such measures will continue to be physically patted-down. Most importantly, however, at the cost of some comfort, convenience, and check-in speed, safety will be boosted.[200]

Railroad and ship transportation require almost the same methods and strategies as airline safety practices. Technology is also vital as tracking mechanisms are needed to assess the movement of parts, ships, vehicles, and personnel. Furthermore, potential choke points such as critical railroad crossings and large harbors are also vital to secure. Employees should receive quality training and conduct meticulous inspections prior to any transport of foreign containers. Truthful risk assessments are necessary to combat possible terrorist initiatives.[201]

Conclusion

United States critical infrastructures must be proactively maintained and consistently updated. Vast advances through technology combined with loosely affiliated terrorists place many pressures on the nation to remain consistent with its policies, tactics, and procedures for avoiding destructive

database. (Document ID: 986385911)

200 Wong, C. (2008, August 11). FOR THEIR EYES ONLY? Scans airport security staff sees would shock passengers, critics say. *Boston Globe*, p. B.5. Retrieved August 13, 2008, from Business Dateline database. (Document ID: 1529735241)

201 Gamst, F. (2007). RAILROAD SAFETY: AN UNFINISHED INVEST-MENT COMMENTARY. *Journal of Transportation Law, Logistics, and Policy, 74(1)*, 124-127. Retrieved August 22, 2008, from ABI/INFORM Global database. (Document ID: 1332631491)

attacks. Merely defining the ramifications of critical infrastructure weaknesses or asymmetrical threats is not sufficient enough for effectively securing the nation. Moreover, formulating this foundation is vital for leading individuals into a solid direction of safety. Therefore, future analysis should assess various recommendations to successfully integrate local citizens' ideals with federal government policies and plans.

CHAPTER 10
FIGHTING CYBER-CRIME, CYBER-TERRORISM, & CYBER-WARFARE

Darrin L. Todd, MS

It would be difficult to address the myriad of ways in which someone could commit cyber-crimes, cyber-terrorism, or cyber-warfare within the scope of one small chapter. In fact, there are numerous books that discuss a variety of technological devices and defensive techniques that may be employed to defend against cyber attacks. However, within the scope of this chapter, we can discuss a high-level or 'birds-eye' view of defending against various cyber attacks and attackers using some simple principles of information security process management.

Perspectives on Information Security

Though often erroneously thought to be synonymous with computer security, information security defines the broader scope of information asset protection. As with computer security, information security includes the core fundamental protective criteria of confidentiality, integrity, and availability as well as the expanded parameters of authenticity, accountability, and non-repudiation. Employing all of these criteria should ensure a comprehensive organizational security program.

The reality of information security is that it is a continuous process of persistently redefining and assessing risks, threats, and probable targets of cyber-attacks. The growing dependence upon information assets, the global nature of today's information security threats, the increasing numbers of attached systems and networks, and the rising complexity of system capabilities creates additional requirements for sound information security practices.

Information Security Process Management

Information security process management is a term that I've coined to get people out of the habit of believing that information security is a definable object that can be possessed or obtained. Rather, information security should be thought of as a perpetual process of steps taken to preserve or increase the security posture of an organization. It is a cyclical process; a never-ending procedure involving the constant review of attacks, attack trends, and the defensive measures and strategies deployed to counter them. Thinking of security as a continuously replenishing 'shopping list' versus a one-time purchase will provide the best climate for a strong defense against cyber-attacks.

Management of Information Security

There are a series of fundamental steps that may be taken to help 'secure' your network from a cyber-attacker; most of which do not involve yet another plug-in device to add more network latency and a false sense-of-security. Don't get me wrong. Technology certainly has its place within a good information security program, yet it is the exclusive reliance upon security devices that often creates a euphoric feeling among information security professionals and organizational managers alike. The belief that technology solutions alone will secure a network can be demonstrably shown to have led to some of the largest, most devastating security failures in modern times; leading to untold billions of dollars in losses to corporations. Information security is a management problem, not a technology problem.[202]

A sound information security program begins with the appointment of an information security manager. The information security manager serves to enumerate security threats, analyze them, and assess risks to the organization and organizational assets. However, information security entails much more than appointing a great information security manager and charging them with the security of the organization's information infrastructure. It involves a top-to-bottom organizational commitment to information security.

If the information security personnel in an organization do not possess the authority to enforce security policies, they cannot be expected to control the conduct of the security program. The actions of the organizational users cannot be controlled if the security program has no enforceability or "teeth." Enforcement is a basic principle of information security. In order to be effective, the organizational security policy must have real repercussions for those that fail to abide by its tenets.[203]

202 Panko, R.R. (2003). *Corporate Computer and Network Security*. Upper Saddle River, NJ: Prentice Hall Publishing.

203 Pfleeger, C., & Pfleeger, S. (2003). *Security in Computing* (Third Edition). Upper Saddle River, NJ: Prentice Hall.

Many security programs are based upon an unrealistic notion that security is a black and white proposition. In fact, there are many shades of grey in-between. The organizational comfort level associated with the security of information systems relies heavily upon the information security manager's declaration that organizational information systems are secure. However, such an assurance is a placebo and does nothing for the security of the information assets. In order to secure organizational information assets, we must be willing to concede that there is no such thing as one hundred percent security, though that is the goal.

Organizational managers should never be led to believe information assets are one hundred percent secure. Your candor and assurance that policies and measures are constantly being reviewed, updated, and enforced is an acknowledgement that you are aware of the complexities of security and the unknown quantity and quality of the cyber-attacker. Managers should know that information security always carries some element of risk. It is the job of the information security manager to convey those risks to higher management. Some security risks may be minimized, managed, or controlled and others must be accepted as part of 'playing the game.'[204] What appeared to be relatively secure yesterday may not be secure today.

We can now discuss the basics of security that must be applied to ensure a foundation for the tight, consistent control of an information security program that provides for comprehensive protection against a wide variety of attackers and attack types. It's nice to discuss management concepts, yet it is the omnipresent and complex daily tasks of managing an information security program that presents the challenge. There is a continuous stream of security issues that information security managers must deal with while managing the threat of cyber-attacks.

Managing IT Facilities from a Security Viewpoint

Well-written and incorporated operations and contingency plans are essential to the safeguarding of information assets and preparing for operational emergencies. Safeguarding contains three essential elements; anticipating risks and threats, developing and employing countermeasures, and employing mechanisms to negate or minimize damage should preventative measures fail.

To effectively prepare IT facilities for risks and threats, information security managers must review every process and every detail from a security perspective. Nothing should be taken for granted. Effective risk management

204 Panko, R.R. (2003). *Corporate Computer and Network Security*. Upper Saddle River, NJ: Prentice Hall Publishing.

entails measurement of risks and their potential costs to the organization, should they become a reality. Spending excessive funds to secure a low-priority asset is not cost-effective and drains funds that may otherwise be used for other security priorities. As Goodman and Ramer[205] noted "Risk management must be cost effective. All vulnerabilities are not equal. An unlocked door is not a problem in a garden shed but if it leads to a bank vault or a data center that is another story."

Preparation for unforeseen circumstances entails meticulous requirements for the documentation of all routine and emergency procedures. All organizations should develop a crisis management plan that anticipates a wide range of scenarios. This plan should be heavily integrated with the organizational security policy and developed to conform to corporate security policies and directives. The IT facility security policy combines the corporate security philosophy and guidance, the specific requirements of the IT facility and the changing operating environment. The security policy is the element from which the IT facility reviews every process, task, and asset to determine and counter risks and threats. A sound security policy is the foundation of any successful security program.

Many security programs place emphasis on protections that guard against external threats with little regard for internal threats. There are many motives that can fuel an employee's desire to commit a criminal act that could jeopardize an information asset. Separation and rotation of duties, along with thorough system auditing and routine data backups can greatly assist with sabotage risks and threats.

Government organizations can differ from civilian organizations as the complexity of organizational intermingling can often create difficulties in assigning an information asset owner, though all government agencies maintain information security programs in full compliance with a set of similar security criteria. Government organizations are often targeted for different reasons by cyber criminals and are a prime target of espionage.

Malicious Software

Malicious software (virus software) has come to typify the concept of a security threat. There are many ways to minimize the threat of virus infections on a system and network. Organizations must educate employees about the hazard, including detection, defense, and reporting. Rigorous patch management and automated virus checking routines ensure the systems and

---

205 Goodman, S., & Ramer, R. (2007). Identify and mitigate the risks of global IT outsourcing. *Journal of Global Information Technology Management, 10(4)*. Retrieved February 5, 2008, from ProQuest database.

networks are as resistant to known viruses as possible. Unauthorized software should be kept off the organizational network and Internet usage policies should be implemented; denoting what users can and cannot do using a corporate computer asset. As well, networks should be structured to contain or isolate virus outbreaks and minimize the damage to corporate systems.

Physical Security

Physical security is a component of information security and the overall security program. Physical security is the collection of protective strategies, controls, and devices that serve to disallow physical access to resources requiring protection. As with any security measure, physical protective measures are often a balancing act between allowing access to authorized personnel while disallowing access to unauthorized personnel. Physical security programs protect valuable assets, establish boundaries, conceal the nature of assets, protect information, provide for safety, prevent theft, and adapt to other situational criteria as required.

All security measures essentially begin with physical security. If you tightly control physical access to a device, you have taken a first step toward delaying or denying an attack. Physical security and physical asset control is the foundation upon which all other security measures are built. How will a high-technology solution prevent damage from an attack when an attacker gains access to the machine room and simply walks away with a server under-arm? If you deny an opportunity by locking and controlling access to the physical network components, you have taken a major step towards securing your network.

Current trends reveal that terrorists prefer physical attacks, though this could change. Cyber assets may be backed up by network defensive systems and measures, but physical attacks may create harm not only to networks and systems but to personnel and other assets within the facility being protected. Physical security measures are designed and implemented to minimize these vulnerabilities and risks, though some level of risk will always be present.

Some measures should be implemented to scrutinize personnel with authorized access to ensure their worthiness to retain access. The program should also provide for understanding of organizational policies for all personnel and provide user training in security and security response measures. Terrorists and other criminals may seek employment to gain access to information resources, to fund their activities or to provide legitimate activities to conceal their objectives. It is important to institute a strong personnel access security program.

Software Security

Fast-paced software releases virtually guarantee that software will be rushed to market before it has passed rigorous security scrutiny. In a hasty effort to meet deadlines and add enhanced, up-to-date features to their software, manufacturers often do not thoroughly security-test their products prior to their release. It is unconscionable to think that software manufacturers release products without thoroughly security-testing them, yet this is the reality of a competitive software marketplace. These manufacturers do this in hopes that security bugs can be fixed later by software patches. Therefore, a major portion of a security manager's job is to ensure that software being placed on the network has been designed with security in mind and thoroughly reviewed and tested prior to being placed on the network.

Assuming you have accomplished the aforementioned steps, your job of maintaining the software is not done. In fact, it is just beginning. Significant time may have passed since the time of the software's release from the developer; exposing previously unknown security flaws and weaknesses. It is for this reason that continued monitoring of all system software releases and updates is crucial to system security. Administrators should ensure system patches and updates are conducted as soon as possible.

Patches and fixes must be applied as soon as they become available, with one caveat; test software fixes on your test systems prior to administering them on your live network. This provides extra assurance that fixes do not cause damage to live network systems. Moreover, software fixes may have a ripple effect … causing unintended problems with other software on the workstations/servers. It is much easier to address these unintended consequences in a localized setting, such as a five-workstation test lab rather than on a live network of 7,000 workstations after the software patch has already been applied.

Identification and Authentication Methods

When a user provides identifying credentials, the authentication subsystem of the information system uses the credentials to authenticate the user to the system. In modern systems, passwords are checked against a stored, encrypted password file.

Though strong passwords are a deterrent against password guessing and cracking, they have a correlative side effect; as the requirements for the passwords elevate, users become more likely to write passwords down and store them where unauthorized users may access them. The methods most useful in preventing these insecure practices are user education and random sweeps through organizational areas. Users should be required to adhere to organizational policies regarding the safeguarding of passwords and must affirm their understanding of the policy.

User and administrator accounts that allow root access are particularly dangerous. If an attacker gains access to these accounts, they can read and delete files, and install 'backdoor' software to allow re-entry at a later time.[206] User education is a must to prevent reckless handling of passwords and access cards and to prevent other hazards such as shoulder surfing, piggybacking and social engineering attacks. Dual user authentication methods are also a must.

Passwords were once the bastion upon which all system authentication routines were based, though recently taking an increasing role in two-factor authentication schemes (passwords and key cards, for example). The decreasing reliance upon password authentication is due to their dependence upon users to maintain password control. Passwords have often been compromised via social engineering attacks, weak password usage, leaving passwords unsecured, sharing passwords with unauthorized users or by other means. Strong user authentication schemes must rely on two-factor methods to establish that identity of the user.

Systems may use identifying credentials other than passwords to authenticate a user, such as crypto cards and keys, and biometrics. When used in conjunction with strong passwords, these methods enable an extra layer of protection. Most government systems now require all user systems to use a combination of two or more identification factors … typically a password and crypto card combination.

Biometric identification methods (e.g., fingerprint scanners, facial recognition, etc.) are relatively new, are expensive to implement, and require significant maintenance by qualified personnel. The slow acceptance of biometric authentication methods as a viable form of identification is due to their acceptance rate (the rate at which they deny access to authorized users and allow access for unauthorized users). As biometric technology becomes more reliable, easier-to-implement, and less expensive, it becomes more attractive to organizations. It remains to be seen whether biometrics becomes a mainstay for authentication.

Access Control

Let's discuss the internal operations that control access within a modern information system. After identifying and authenticating a user, access rights

206 Panko, R.R. (2003). *Corporate Computer and Network Security*. Upper Saddle River, NJ: Prentice Hall Publishing.

may be defined and given by the system utilizing a complex staging process. Within a system, access control rights may be governed by any one or a combination of mechanisms including automated terminal identification, and terminal logons to govern local and remote user logons. All accesses must be maintained in a system audit trail and continuously limited according to the system policies and the user's access rights.

Equally important is the governance of application access rights within a system. Applications should be implicitly denied access to system processes not expressly required for operation. During system and application development, objects should be designed to limit access and safeguard outputs. Most modern, proprietary operating systems provide these safeguards. Due to the adoption of a global architecture, called the Global Information Grid (GIG), government systems must be able to communicate and authenticate in a universally accepted way, which infers increasing reliance upon standardized identification, authentication, and access control methods.

Security 'Snooping' and Redundancy – The Often Overlooked Essentials

Proactive defense means occasionally stepping out from behind the desk and examining first-hand the systems under your charge. I call this 'snooping.' User diagrams tell only a portion of the story. Diagrams likely won't show you the potential emissions security hazards of errant equipment placement nor will they show you an unauthorized connection or a list of passwords displayed prominently above a user's workstation.

While working for one organization, I once experienced a major failure that catastrophically disconnected a network of 3,000 workstations and servers for almost an entire day. The failure was caused by a technician who simply placed a notebook over the cooling vent of a main network switch weeks before the failure. A network diagram will not show you this kind of catastrophic failure waiting to happen.

It is best to imagine how network systems might catastrophically fail. Are there any network components that are absolutely essential? Do you have replacement systems ready to take the place of vital systems? Is the data protected by redundant/backups? These kinds of questions enable you to envision a worst-case scenario that could destroy or disable your network or crucial network components. Tornado, flood, fire, theft, terrorist attack, cyber-attack ... when developing a system security plan, try to envision every conceivable scenario in which you could lose assets/capabilities and develop a security plan to either repair/replace the damaged assets in order to restore the network as quickly as possible following the event.

Do you have redundant storage of software/hardware assets? Are those redundant assets and facilities sufficiently geographically separated from the 'live' system? Do you periodically inventory and test redundant/backup systems to ensure their readiness in the event you need them? The best way to protect a system is to use your imagination to envision various disastrous scenarios and pre-determine the solutions or fix-actions that will counter them.

Managing Backup Media

System backups are the fail-safe mechanism of information security. If all precautions fail to prevent destruction of information and data, they will allow for the full or partial restoration of the system. As such, organizations must implement a backup program containing incremental and full system backups as necessary according to system requirements and organizational security policies. Periodically during the operation of network systems, users commit errors that cause irreparable damage to database files and other files. Incremental and full backups allow for the restoration of such files by the IT staff.

It has been the case that backups are conducted on a regular basis per the information policy, only to be found to be useless when actually required for restoration of data. Therefore, as with any other emergency procedure, it is crucial that the restoration procedure be practiced, tested and verified. Nothing should be taken for granted.

Tips for Managing Network and Remote Access Security

Computer assets are put in-place to support organizational objectives and the network should always be managed to provide maximum network availability to support them. All processes must be compartmentalized and accounted for within the information security policy; leaving nothing to chance. Where possible, encryption should be used to protect the transfer and storage of data and information. Patches for operating systems and data should be meticulously maintained. As connected or extra-organizational networks entail added risks for organizational systems, network partners should receive the same scrutiny as inter-organizational assets.

Network boundary firewalls should be capable of stateful inspection of incoming and outgoing packets. If possible, networks should be designed to defend against incoming attacks, including Distributed Denial of Service

(DDoS) attacks in which a series of remotely controlled systems are used to overwhelm the network and deny access for legitimate traffic. These types of attacks can be carried out for a variety of reasons including extortion, market competition, political sabotage, or even cyber-terrorism. Whatever the case, networks should be designed and operated to prevent unnecessary internal

> A "stateful" firewall is a firewall that keeps track of the state of network connections traveling across it. The firewall is programmed to distinguish legitimate packets for different types of connections. Only packets matching a known connection state will be allowed by the firewall; others will be rejected.

and external connections where possible. This minimizes internal and external network risk and threats and improves the overall performance of the network by limiting cross-traffic.

Threat/Risk Assessment

It is the duty of a security manager to determine the source and nature of the threat/risk, the level of risk posed, the threat exposure level, the ways in which a threat/risk may come to fruition and how those threats and risks may be countered, mitigated, or prevented. It is not necessary, nor even likely that all risks/threats can be envisioned or countered. However, by determining and developing plans for the most probable disastrous events, you take a major step towards preparing the system for plausible threats.

Threat/Risk management is the fundamental beginning of an organizational information security program and establishes the context by which the program is designed and implemented. The organizational security policy is derived from and continually refined by the results of the risk management process. Risk management for government organizations is principally not much different from that of civilian counterparts. However, government organizations must often wrangle with more complex regulatory requirements, intermingled with multiple government and non-government organizations and international entities.

Government organizations must often deal with the often antiquarian concepts of operation that characterize governments worldwide. The likelihood of exploitation is derived from the relative value of the information or information asset targeted by the attacker. Usually, risk exposure is calculated to reveal the cost effectiveness of the organization's risk management measures.[207] In regards to national secrets, the relative value must necessarily

---

207 Pfleeger, C., & Pfleeger, S. (2003). *Security in Computing* (Third Edition). Upper Saddle River, NJ: Prentice Hall.

be assumed to be high; therefore, the impact of the potential risk is also surmised to be high.

Network Security Essentials

There is a pervasive and antiquated thought process propagated by some information security managers that we must defend by creating an impenetrable boundary to keep attackers out. This has often resulted in networks becoming constriction points and providing a false sense of security. What is the point in defending a network that becomes nearly unusable to the network users due to the course of our actions? Therefore, in developing a defensive strategy against cyber-attacks, we must keep in mind that defensive measures must always be balanced with system usability.

As many cyber-criminals have found it increasingly difficult to successfully attack well-defended networks, they have turned to more effective methods of gaining entry, including the use of social engineering attacks and virus software. System users are often the most overlooked "weakness" in an otherwise good security program. User training must be provided and must be mandatory to gain network access. User policies must be provided as a matter of course and enforced.

Many security managers face a constant stream of users attempting to increase the functional capacity of the network; either by official channels or by circumventing established security measures. As a new information security manager years ago in one organization, I discovered an entire wireless network consisting of ten personal computers that had never passed security scrutiny. These systems had been undiscovered and unknown to the previous organizational network security manager for over four years and had somehow been allowed to attach to the network.

Information security involves tradeoffs. In many organizations, money is often devoted to security only after dire warnings … and begging and pleading by the information security staff. Warnings of impending doom are a good way to obtain funds, but will only get you so far before the spigot is turned off and your warnings begin to be discounted or ignored. Therefore, being truthful about threats and risks is the best policy for achieving long-term security program health.

It is crucial to evaluate and assess periodically the source, motive, likelihood, and potential severity of threats and to convey that information to upper-level management continually. Managers often pay only lip-service to information security … until a breach or damage occurs.

Security comes at the expense of other network necessities and niceties and is often lumped-in with other network items in the organizational requirements process for budgeting and forecasting purposes. This is a mistake. These are not 'convenience items' and 'nice-to-haves' as often are other network requirements. Security should always be a separate line item in the organizational budget along with forecasted and planned security enhancements.

Network Defensive Techniques

Firewalls, Intrusion Detection Systems (IDS), and the like must be replaced on a continuing and regular basis, regardless of whether operating system updates and software patches are being conducted. As with most network appliances there is only so much time before the operational capacity of these devices begins to degrade network efficiency and capacity. An old appliance become a network bottleneck, a potential point of failure and possibly risky to operate as technology passes them by.

Network protective measures should operate on the basic principle of 'Defense in Depth.' Defense in Depth simply means that no network protective measure stands alone. Redundant protection assures that at any entry point into the system an attacker will encounter at least two mechanisms designed to defeat an attack. For example, a network may have a firewall set to filter potential malicious content followed by similar filter residing on the organizational mail server. Redundant protection provides extra assurance that attacks are countered and that a mis-configuration of any one protective measure will not lead to a system compromise.

Another component of Defense in Depth to consider is that redundant protective systems should be dissimilar. For example, a network may contain CISCO firewalls on the perimeter and CheckPoint firewalls on the interior of the network. This ensures that the defeat of one security component due to an inherent flaw or programming error will not allow an attacker to bypass all network security measures as a result of the same flaw or exploit. However, this does entail additional work and training for network and information security personnel.

Finally, Defense in Depth should allow for internal segmentation of the network via security devices such as firewalls. An intruder that has defeated a perimeter network security system should never be allowed to roam freely about the internal network as a result. So to, segmentation decreases the ability of internal users to access systems and programs not under their purview.

Segmentation has many other uses. Segmentation on internal network firewalls can allow certain types of traffic to pass while blocking others, or may also allow only select systems to have access to the protected assets. For example, a computer on the operations floor may be allowed to print out documents on a printer within the accounting department while all other traffic is denied.

User Security

The weakest point in any corporate network is often its users. Too many security professionals rely upon technological solutions as a means to secure a network; often overlooking that users are often the origin of significant security failures. Technology cannot prevent a social engineering attack (discussed later) in which a legitimate user is tricked by an attacker posing as a legitimate network user or authority figure. There are a myriad of ways in which users may knowingly or unknowingly compromise an otherwise great information security program.

Human nature is also a persistent threat to information security. Typically, cyber-attackers and even authorized users feel it is their right to access and use organizational and even other user's personal assets for their own benefit.[208] Cyber-terrorists likely feel even less respectful of the rights of ownership.

Information Security Awareness in the Age of Terrorism

Though terrorism has often been mistakenly assigned a random nature, in reality, terror events are planned events that often take advantage of gaps in protection. By reviewing the underlying motives of terrorism and connected causal and preventive factors, organizations can take steps to minimize risk to information assets.

The difference between terrorism and other crimes is its underlying motivation. Terrorism is committed to instill fear, which drives the party being terrorized to react in a way that is considered to be favorable or positive by the terrorist or terror organization. Fear is usually not the final objective of the terror act; it is a means to achieve objectives.

Information Assets as a Target of Terrorism

Religious beliefs and associated philosophies, deep rooted hatred for the United States and its allies and the resentment associated with being a relatively wealthy country may all be primary reasons international terrorists use to motivate themselves to commit acts of terror. Homegrown terrorists may also commit such acts for similar or more localized reasons. Whatever the

---

208 Janczewski, L., & Colarik, A. (2005). *Managerial Guide for Handling Cyber-Terrorism and Information Warfare*. Hershey, PA: Idea Group Publishing.

reason, information technology assets may be thought of as a primary target of interest to terrorists and terror organizations wishing to create significant economic and psychological damage to information oriented societies such as the United States.

Though information assets are obviously advantageous to any technology oriented nation, unprotected information infrastructures offer an inviting target for ambitious terrorists and can quickly become an Achilles heel to the societies that depend so heavily upon them. Network systems control a large share of other assets, such as telephone systems and subway trains. These have often been overlooked in the traditional view of information infrastructure protection.

Terror attacks can be directed upon IT assets, focused upon infrastructure items controlled by IT assets, or terrorists may even use these assets to further their agendas: Though information technology assets provide great economic advantages, their accessibility also provides advantages to terror organizations, who may use them to coordinate, direct or even launch attacks.

Everything from the development of critical information technology assets to the way they are employed and operated is affected by their perception as a potential and exploitable target; particularly following the attacks on September 11, 2001. For this reason, IT system and facility design must often go through a substantial review to ensure security, survivability, and maintainability in the event of an attack.

Cyber-Security

In the past, 'cyber-security' was a very nebulous term. Security programs never gathered real attention from most corporate managers until the organization had either become the victim of a malicious attack or a significant high-profile attack had sufficiently alarmed them to the organization's vulnerability. Information security budgets were often lacking and security training for organizational members was nearly non-existent. Today, most organizational managers realize the stakes and the risks, yet most information security programs are still given only tangential thought. Why is that?

To analyze this problem, it is important to remember that security awareness is a cyclical event for most organizational members. In the days and months following the September 11 attacks, cyber-security awareness peaked, with some managers becoming thoroughly convinced that professional cadres of al-Qaeda super-techies were preparing to wage cyber-warfare against U.S. financial institutions and military networks. Time and again, top government agencies issued warnings of imminent attack. Major professional organizations like the SANS Institute and InfraGard followed through to ensure that security managers received the latest news. When the predicted attacks did not occur, indifference to subsequent warnings often set in. It's a classic case of "Chicken Little" syndrome. Did these organizations overshoot their goals, thereby creating a climate of over-hyped cyber-security concern?

The clear answer is "No." These organizations were simply performing the roles that all information security managers and organizations are tasked to perform, i.e., to anticipate and predict the moves of a cyber-attacker. It is not necessary that the warnings be correct to be effective. Indeed, it is the job of cyber-security managers to anticipate the moves of their opponent ... even if the anticipated attack is never realized.

Three essential items that malicious attackers must possess prior to committing a malicious cyber-attack include method, motive, and opportunity.[209] The method of attack depends greatly upon the skill level of the attacker and the tools at their disposal. Opportunity is governed by the time and access level of the attack; as well as by the access level of the victim of the attack. Motives vary greatly and provide the intentions of the attacker. Do they want to embarrass the victimized company? Do they want to destroy a resource or capability? Are they seeking financial gain from the attack? Questions like these provide the basis for developing a security plan. When you can anticipate an attacker's methods, motives, and opportunities, you can begin to prepare an adequate defense.

Cyber-Terrorism

Terrorists differ from other attackers in that they may be driven by an ideology. They may also be domestic or international in origin. It is important to review the motives of terrorism when determining what type of threat terrorists pose to your network. For example, a terrorist may be driven to deface a government organizational website to post detrimental information, cause destruction, or disrupt web services rather than attack a web server to steal credit card information for personal gain. Though this is so, one must be aware that terrorists always seek new ways in which to finance their activities. Hence, credit card theft and other for-profit crimes cannot be ruled out as a motive for terrorist network attacks.

A wide range of Internet-born attacks can threaten information resources and provide unauthorized access, which lead to fraud, theft, web defacement attacks, or other malicious or damaging results. The advantages of cyber-attacks are numerous for a cyber terrorist. With an amazingly low probability of being caught and an even smaller chance of being prosecuted, a cyber

---

209 Pfleeger, C., & Pfleeger, S. (2003). *Security in Computing* (Third Edition). Upper Saddle River, NJ: Prentice Hall.

criminal may damage or incapacitate systems, steal or damage large volumes of data, deface websites for the humiliation of the organization, and in so doing, make a profound statement about the inability of an organization to stop the attacker. The ability to "defeat" network protective measures and deface and destroy a government web site would provide an opportunity for a terrorist to demonstrate their technical savvy and embarrass a superpower that has a decided technological advantage.

Network attacks may originate from countries that do not allow criminal extradition or are unwilling to assist an investigation into a web-borne attack. Hence, terrorist from those countries may remain anonymous and immune to prosecution. The cost of the attack may be equivalent to the cost of a personal computer, a network connection, some software, or a few hours of time. The toll of such an attack may range anywhere from defacing a government website to something more dramatic such as crashing a major financial network, thereby causing billions of dollars in losses. It is easy to see why these attacks are an attractive option for even a marginally well-financed terrorist organization.

It is important to remember that the only discernable difference between a terrorist with great computer skills and any other information warrior may be ideology. Though many of these organizations operate on shoestring budgets and are not particularly technically proficient, no one should disregard the motivation of these organizations and the threat they pose on that basis alone. It is unwise to discount these information warriors as being simple cobblers, farmers, and wristwatch repairmen who happen to own a computer. In fact, many reputedly possess sophisticated technical skills and advanced degrees in computer engineering and related fields. In order to dissuade a terror attack against your high-profile network, it is wise to accept the likelihood that the attacker possesses the method, motive, and opportunity to do so … regardless of preconceived notions.

It is worthy to note that some terror organizations, such as Hezbollah and HAMAS, are exceptionally well-funded and possess an abundance of personnel resources. To date, there have been no major network attacks known to have been attributed to these powerful regional organizations. However, that is not to say that these organizations can be discounted. It is safe to assume that it is only because network-born attacks have not been the primary focus of these organizations that they have not often engaged in them. In fact, it is almost a certainty that these powerful organizations maintain a cadre of capable information warriors willing to participate in cyber attacks for their extremist ideology at a moment's notice.

Types of Cyber-Attack and Cyber-Terror Attack

Unlike other forms of attack, which attempt to disable or destroy information assets, Denial of Service (DoS) and Distributed Denial of Service (DDoS) attacks create havoc by tying up network system resources with requests for services. The idea behind DOS and DDOS attacks is simple, i.e., to force a target system to become overloaded with activities that reduce its capacity to process legitimate tasks.[210] The attacker uses a series of zombie machines running hostile software to launch the attack that is unbeknownst to the owners of the zombie machines. Because these machines may be controlled remotely or even set to begin the attack at a predetermined time, tracing the attack back to the attacker may be extremely difficult. Even if it can be traced, the trail may ultimately lead to machines that are open to the public, such as in an Internet café.

It is difficult to predict or defend against DoS attacks. The viability of networked systems often hinges upon their ability to accept and answer the service requests that are often the basis of the attack. However, some solutions have been developed including lightweight packet-filtering mechanisms that provide enhanced traffic analysis.[211]

Some other solutions depend on using several intelligent packet-filters and redundant connections. However, these solutions are often useless when faced with an onslaught of thousands of zombie systems. Therefore, the prevailing thought behind most viable DoS solutions depends upon intelligent, stateful packet inspection capabilities. The general rule is to cut off the source of the attack.[212] Developing a rapport and a plan of defense against these attacks in cooperation with Internet service providers is also important.

Web Defacement Attacks

These types of attacks are often viewed as mere nuisances. However, they may have far-reaching implications for an organization if they damage or destroy an organization's reputation or embarrasses the web site's owner. In the case of politically oriented attackers, attacks may be predicated upon embarrassing a government, government entity, or organization the attacker opposes. This type of attack may also be used to redirect traffic to a phony

---

210 Janczewski, L., & Colarik, A. (2005). *Managerial Guide for Handling Cyber-Terrorism and Information Warfare*. Hershey, PA: Idea Group Publishing.

211 Badishi, G., Herzberg, A., & Keider, I. (2007). Keeping denial of service attackers in the dark. *IEEE Transactions on Dependable and Secure Computing, 4(3)*. Retrieved February 1, 2008, from ProQuest database.

212

website or be combined with a phishing attack to steal information from persons visiting the defaced website, thereby leading to unauthorized account access or identity theft.[213]

Defending against web defacement attacks can be extremely difficult due to the simplicity of webpage design and the plethora of available design software packages containing varying security provisions. The current, standardized key to protecting against these types of attacks is to cut off the attack and provide component redundancy.

Although expensive and difficult to maintain, normally, an offline redundant copy of the website server and software is the key to quick restoral in the case of web defacement attack. Also, using a honey-pot system (a system created on the network to purposefully attract attacks and divert attention away from valuable assets) may distract the attacker and divert the attack away from the intended target of the attack. This approach allows the administrator to disconnect the attack, analyze its components, and gather information regarding the attack source.

Domain Name Service Attacks

Domain Name Service (DNS) attacks target DNS servers that provide domain name translation. By disabling a series of DNS servers, the attacker renders useless the resolving capabilities of the service, thereby, effectively producing a DoS attack. The DNS network protocol includes no provisions for authentication and, therefore, remains relatively open to attack. The attacker essentially gains access by impersonating legitimate DNS clients or redirecting legitimate network traffic.

The answer to DNS attacks rests upon the introduction of IPsec authentication routines between DNS clients and servers. Another solution is to overlay the DNS protocol with an authenticating routine of its own, such as with DNSSEC. However, this method is greatly dependent upon all clients and servers using the DNSSEC overlay. Security administrators must ensure that one of these methods of authentication is used, that system patches are applied and security reviews are conducted on a regular basis.

Routing Vulnerabilities

Routers are the building blocks of networks. Routing capabilities allow the addressing and forwarding of traffic by specifying the locations of nodes

---

213 Janczewski, L., & Colarik, A. (2005). *Managerial Guide for Handling Cyber-Terrorism and Information Warfare*. Hershey, PA: Idea Group Publishing.

on the network. As most routing protocols were primarily designed with reliability, speed and efficiency in mind, many security loopholes have been exposed and taken advantage of by attackers, who may listen to network traffic, hijack network sessions, initiate DoS and DDoS attacks, or other forms of attack. All of these attacks can happen at the nodes or the routers controlling network information flow.[214] Attackers often masquerade or spoof legitimate traffic in order to conduct attacks.

Most routing vulnerability attacks are built upon falsified network credentials, so authentication is an important first step to be taken to prevent attacks of this nature. However, using the IPSec protocol in IP networks would not be viable due to the resulting overhead. Therefore, the use of Public Key Infrastructure (PKI) is probably the best option as it provides strong authentication with moderate overhead. However, PKI can be difficult to implement and maintain.

Identity Theft and Social Engineering Attacks

Identity theft crimes are growing at an alarming rate in comparison to other theft crimes in recent years. A March 2007 study from the Gartner Group found that, from mid-2005 to mid-2006, about 15 million Americans were victims of fraud resulting from identity theft. This was an increase of more than 50 percent from the estimated 9.9 million victims in 2003.[215] This rate of growth is only matched by the exponential increase in the level of sophistication these attacks reach as the cyber criminals learn to apply newer and more effective techniques to steal identities using increasingly creative ways. The motives for identity thefts are wide-ranging; intended to steal funds or cause damage to persons or organizations.

The most crucial yet often minimized aspect of physical security is prevention of social engineering attacks to obtain access to premises through the subversion of social standards. Personnel should be trained to look for and report suspicious activity and to protect against social engineering attacks that could inadvertently provide access to terrorists despite sophisticated and expensive physical measures. These attacks could be caused by shoulder surfing pass codes, piggybacking into the facility, or by pretending to be someone they are not, such as maintenance personnel, in order to gain access to unauthorized areas. Social engineering attacks, like other attacks, tend to follow the phased approach of target surveillance, selecting an area

---

214 Ibid.

215 Fonte, E. (2008). Who should pay the price for identity theft? *Computer and Internet Lawyer, 25(2)*. Retrieved February 1, 2008, from ProQuest database.

and method of attack, and the attack itself.[216] Once unauthorized access is provided, the terrorists may commit their acts of sabotage, damage, or other harmful deeds.

Social engineering attacks, also known as 'human hacking' or 'spoofing,' enable an attacker to elicit information from unsuspecting users to gain either personal information or information that may lead to further system or account access. In contrast to cyber-attackers using highly sophisticated computer skills, attackers using social engineering techniques gain access to the desired resources via deceptive methods perpetrated against persons possessing valid system access.[217] Some computer criminals attempt to exploit software programming errors. Attackers using social engineering techniques use methods that are comparatively uncomplicated, taking advantage of human trust and cognitive bias.[218] Attackers using social engineering techniques succeed because the victim allows them to succeed. A comprehensive user training program will assist to counter this threat.

The weak link in these types of attacks is the victim's lack of awareness concerning the problem. Though periodic user education will help to some extent, some users will always be susceptible to deception under the right circumstances. The remedy to identity theft can readily be compared to the remedies to network attacks – user education and challenge authentication – to name two. Technical security measures that may assist to prevent these attacks include providing encryption, authentication, and identification procedures.

Conclusion

Within this chapter, I have discussed some basic tenets of information security, security management, cyber-terrorism, cyber-attacks, network security, and user security. This is only a brief overview of some basic principles of information security, and I encourage you to develop a greater understanding of the principles of information security and how they relate to the security of the organization by reviewing additional, comprehensive information security resources for more thorough coverage of the subject.

---

216 Janczewski, L., & Colarik, A. (2005). *Managerial Guide for Handling Cyber-Terrorism and Information Warfare.* Hershey, PA: Idea Group Publishing.

217 Ibid.

218 Thapar, A. (2008). Social engineering: An attack vector most intricate to tackle! Retrieved September 25, 2008, from http://www.infosecwriters.com/text_resources/pdf/Social_Engineering_AThapar.pdf.

CHAPTER 11
TERRORIST PROFILING: CAN THEY BE TYPED?

David P. Hale, PhD

Introduction

Terrorists and terror groups constitute the enemy in the current Global War on Terrorism (GWOT) that the United States finds itself engaged in today. Despite the vast number of research and investigative studies that have been conducted, terrorists' personalities and behaviors still remain discombobulated data sets. In addition to the difficulty in analyzing secretive, conspiratorial groups and individuals, the variety of motivations, ideologies, and behaviors involved remain extremely diverse. Common characteristics or clearly defined traits may be apparent and simplistic; however, significant differences are more the norm.

Nevertheless, there are benefits to studying individual and group terrorist motivations and behaviors. Observations on human nature and group dynamics under conditions of stress, excitement, and social isolation can give insight into the causes of particular behaviors. Moreover, psychologist Maxwell Taylor stated that understanding the various types of motivations for particular terrorists permit assessment of their aims against their actual intent.[219]

Terrorist Behavior

The most prevalent view of terrorists is usually the unpredictable, sadistically irrational stereotype emphasized by media images and sensationalism.[220] However, as an assessment of the temperament and record of terrorism demonstrates, terrorism is a rationally selected tactic employed

---

219 Taylor, M. (1988). *The terrorist*, London, England: Brassey's.

220 Snow, N. (2006). Terrorism, public relations, and propaganda. In A. P. Kavoori and T. Fraley, *Media, terrorism, and theory: ArReader*. Lanham, MD: Rowan & Littlefield.

in pursuing political objectives.[221],[222] To lend some truth to the newsworthy stereotype, individuals or small organizations that employ terrorist tactics may not always be concerned with particular causes or affirmed dogma. Some terrorists may be motivated purely by a need to be terrorists, in whatever cause suits them, or as a *gun for hire* serving a variety of causes.[223],[224]

This contradiction is summed in the two most common approaches in analyzing terrorist group and individual behavior. They are:

- *The psychologically compelled (sociopath/psychopath) model:* This dictates that terrorists engage in terrorism as it fulfills a psychological need (not entirely a need for violence) on their part. This model of terrorism treats avowed ideology and political causes as after-the-fact rationalization for behaviors the terrorists will commit anyway.
- *The rational choice model:* Terror is a tactic selected after rational consideration of the costs and benefits in order to achieve an objective. The individual makes a conscious decision to participate in these activities (even though they may not realize in what they are involved). While it recognizes that individuals or groups may be prone to violence, this is not looked at as the influential dynamic in the choice to use or reject terror tactics.

Neither of these models is universally appropriate. All terror groups or individuals fall into one model or the other. Characteristics of both models are seen in groups and individuals. As expected, both models are found within real-world examples, and they should both be thought of when investigating the actions of terrorists.

Individual Terrorist Behaviors

Walter Laquer says that one profile does not fit terrorists in terms of their backgrounds or personal characteristics. The differences in the origins of terrorists in terms of their society, culture, and environment prevent such a universal approach that fits both international and domestic terrorists. The

---

221 Laquer, W. (1987). *The age of terrorism*. Boston: Little Brown.

222 Laquer, W. (1999). *The new terrorism: Fanaticism and the arms of mass destruction*. New York: Oxford University Press.

223 Butler, P. (2002). Terrorism and utilitarianism: Lessons from, and for, criminal law. *Journal of Criminal Law and Criminology, 93*, 20-21.

224 Schmid, A. P., & Jongman, A. J. (2005). *Political terrorism: A new guide to actors, authors, concepts, data bases, theories and literature*. Somerset, NJ: Transaction Books, pp. 39-55.

profiles developed for the typical German Red Army Faction (RAF) member 25 years ago is irrelevant to predicting the nature of an Arabian al-Qaeda recruit.[225] Attempting to profile potential terrorists, even when culturally connected, is beyond the scope of this chapter.

Utopian Worldview

Terrorists characteristically possess utopian goals, despite their intentions being political, social, territorial, nationalistic, or religious. This utopianism convincingly expresses itself as an extreme degree of intolerance with the rest of the world that validates the terrorists' extreme ideology and means of operation (MO).[226] This philosophy may be best expressed as *Tear everything up; change now and fix later.* The individual terrorist perceives a crisis too urgent to be solved other than by the most extreme MO. On the other hand, the perception is of a system too corrupt or ineffective to see or adopt the *solution* the terrorist proclaims. This sense of desperate impatience with opposition is central to the terrorist worldview. This is true of both secular and religiously motivated terrorists, although with somewhat dissimilar standpoint as to how to impress their *solutions.*

There is also a significantly impractical aspect associated with the utopian mindset. Their goals often involve either the transformation of society or a significant reordering of the status quo. Individual terrorists, even the philosophical or intellectual leaders, often are vague or uncaring as to what the future order of things will look like or how their desires will be implemented. Change, and the destructive method by which it is brought about, may be much more important than the end result.

---

225 Laquer, W. (1999). *The new terrorism: Fanaticism and the arms of mass destruction.* New York: Oxford University Press.

226 Post, J. M. (1999). Terrorist psycho-logic: Terrorist behavior as a product of psychological forces. In W. Reich (Ed.), *Origins of terrorism.* Woodrow Wilson Press: Washington, DC.

Networking with Others

Terrorists network within their groups with both other members and leadership.[227],[228],[229],[230] As with any group or association, it is common for individuals forming or joining groups to conform to the *leader principle*. As expected, this amounts to total obedience to the group's leadership. This is true of both hierarchical and networked organizations, whether large or small. This helps to explain the pervasiveness of terrorist group leaders exuding great charisma. With a penchant to view leaders and authority figures within the group as near ideal examples, such leaders can demand tremendous sacrifices from subordinates through their total conformity. This type of obedience can cause internal dissention when a leader is at odds with a group, or factions arise in the organization.

Another adaptation the individual makes is accepting an *internal-group* [i.e., us against them] mentality.[231] This results in a presupposition of habitual morality held by other group members, and the clarity of their cause and virtue of their objective. The view of the greater world may be perceived as assertively attacking or persecuting the individual and his comrades. Thus, violence is necessary for the *self-defense* of the groups and carries moral justification. In some cases, the group identifies and agrees totally with their use of violence, and it becomes to them the central characteristic of their being on both the individual and collective-group level. Groups possessing this mind-set cannot renounce violence, since it would equal renouncing their own reason for being.

De-humanizing of Non-Members

There is a de-humanization of all *external-group* non-members. This de-humanization allows violence to be aimed arbitrarily at any outer-group

---

227 Arquilla, J., & D. Ronfeldt (1996). *The advent of netwar.* Santa Monica, CA: RAND.

228 Arquilla, J., & D. Ronfeldt (2001). *Networks and netwars; The future of terror, crime, and militancy.* Santa Monica,

CA: RAND.

229 Arquilla, J., D. Ronfeldt, & M. Zanini (1999). Networks, netwar, and information-age terrorism. In Ian O. Lesser et al. (Eds.), *Countering the new terrorism.* Santa Monica, CA: RAND.

230 Sageman, M. (2004). *Understanding terror networks.* Philadelphia: University of Pennsylvania.

231 Crenshaw, M. (1998). The logic of terrorism: Terrorist behavior as a product of strategic choice. In W. Reich (Ed.), *Origins of Terrorism.* Woodrow Wilson Press: Washington, DC.

target.[232] Assuming that all those outside of the group are either enemies or neutral, terrorists feel they are justified to oppress the external populous. Since everyone outside the group is a potential enemy, circumstances can change that permit any restraints that the terrorists might have observed to be broken in the name of expediency.

De-humanizing also removes some of the onus of killing innocents. The identification of authority figures with animals makes murder a simple slaughter of inferior life. The continual picture held up to group members is that there are oppressors and oppressed; they are fighting inhuman opponents in the name of the oppressed.

This is the other aspect of de-humanization. By making *the oppressed* of *the people* an abstract concept usually to an ignorant mass, it permits the individual terrorist to claim and act on their behalf.[233] The terrorist believes these acts further the interests of some *un-awakened* social or ethnic constituency that is too oppressed or misinformed to realize its interests. They see themselves as leading the struggle on behalf of the rest of whatever constituency they represent. This terrorist vision is common to all points on the political spectrum. It is variously identified as *the revolutionary vanguard* or *true patriots*, but involves the terrorists acting for the good of the uneducated or muted masses that they believe would endorse their *struggle* if they were understood and or were free to choose.

Lifestyle Attraction

The lifestyle of a terrorist, although not appealing to those in secure societies, may offer emotional, physical, and occasionally social rewards.[234] *Emotional rewards* include a mind-set of notoriety, power, and belonging. Some societies look upon inclusion into the world of a terrorist organization as a sense of contentment through insurgence; others may view it as a boost in power or social status. For some, much like the street gang member, membership in a terror group may be emotionally gratifying. *Physical rewards* include money, authority, and adventure. This enticement can destabilize other motives as the sense of intrigue may overpower that of rational thinking. Several infamous terrorists during the 1970s and 1980s, such as Abu Nidal, became highly specialized mercenaries, disposing of their beliefs and hiring themselves out to a variety of causes and sponsors.[235] Abu Nidal is a nom de

232 Sageman, M. (2004). *Understanding terror networks*. Philadelphia: University of Pennsylvania.

233 White, J. R. (2009). Terrorist and homeland security (6th ed.). Belmont, CA: Wadsworth.

234 Ibid.

235 Ibid.

guerre for Sabri al-Banna and an international terrorist group named after its founder *Abu Nidal – Abu Nidal Organization* (ANO). Sabri al-Banna spun from notoriety in the Palestine Liberation Organization (PLO) and later broke away to develop his own terror organization. The group's ideology focused on the decimation of the state of Israel, but the group has served as a mercenary terrorist force connected to several radical regimes including Iraq, Syria, and Libya. ANO actions connect to terrorist attacks in over 20 countries with killing and injuring thousands of victims.

Behaviors within Organizations

Members of groups possess differing behaviors collectively than they do as individuals [referred to as *group-think*].[236] Terrorist organizations have changing objectives and rationale for what they believe as reality, and the way in which the organization deciphers these mores characterizes their internal group dynamics.

As a whole, terrorist organizations are usually more audacious and merciless than their individual members.[237] No member desires to appear less devoted than the others, and will not object to propositions within the group they would in no way consider personally. In an effort to lead by example, terror leaders would never risk being exposed as apprehensive, so as not to run the risk of losing control of their organization. The end result can be actions not in keeping with individual behavior patterns as far as risk and lethality but dictated by the pressure of group expectations and suppression of dissent and caution.

Group commitment stresses silence, loyalty, and submission to the organization.[238] Disputes are discouraged by the sense of the external threat represented by the outside world, and pressure to conform to the group-think. Expulsion from the organization fuels the organization's repugnance and hatred of disbelievers or deserters.[239] Even the smallest sign of betrayal by a member may result in their torture or death. Extreme ideological passion in any group makes them formidable enemies. However, it frequently turns

---

236 Myers, D. G. (2008). Social psychology (9th ed.). New York: McGraw Hill.

237 White, J. R. (2009). Terrorist and homeland security (6th ed.). Belmont, CA: Wadsworth.

238 Sageman, M. (2004). *Understanding terror networks*. Philadelphia: University of Pennsylvania.

239 Schmid, A. P., & A. J. Jongman (2005). *Political terrorism: A new guide to actors, authors, concepts, data bases, theories and literature*. Somerset, NJ: Transaction Books.

upon itself, thereby making organizations cleanse themselves so successfully that they almost ceased to exist. This, in turn, makes the existence of the group more important than its original goal. If the group continues to exist, many times it will adjust its objectives so as to have a reason for continued existence. Factions that advocate maintaining their original ideology will rouse bitter in-fighting and divisions among members. The ensuing splinter groups or dissenting members are extremely unpredictable. Hence, they run the risk of compromising the original group's mission.

Organizations experiencing troubles may increase their intensity of violence.[240] An increase in violence occurs when frustration and low morale develop within a terrorist group and when there is a perceived lack of progress or successful counter-terrorism measures that may limit freedom of action within the organization. The group may hope that changing to more *shock and awe* tactics, which result in a larger casualty list, will overcome the group's internal issues.

An example of this phenomenon is the terrorist group al-Qaeda operating in the Arabian Peninsula.[241] The regional arm of al-Qaeda in Saudi Arabia is one of many sub-groups in the larger global terrorist organization, al-Qaeda International. During a 13-month period, several members of al-Qaeda in the Arabian Peninsula were arrested and/or killed, which included the group's successive leader being killed and replaced four times. In May and June 2004, the sub-group conducted a wave of hostage taking, beheadings, and gruesome murders. An interview by *Sawt Al-Jihad*, an al-Qaeda identified journal, was conducted with the commander of the Al-Quds Brigade. The Brigade is a subordinate unit of the group that took responsibility for the May 29, 2004, Oasis Compound attack at al-Khobar, Saudi Arabia. This is where 22 people were killed. During this interview, the terrorist commander claimed they had either beheaded or cut the throats of more than 12 of their victims. Al-Qaeda in the Arabian Peninsula was also responsible for a number of other murders. These murders included the killing of Robert Jacobs, an American employee of the Vinnell Corporation, and the beheading of Paul Johnson, an American employee of Lockheed-Martin. In both of these cases, the terrorist group released gruesome videos of the murders.

---

240 White, J. R. (2009). Terrorist and homeland security (6th ed.). Belmont, CA: Wadsworth.

241 Venzke, B. (2004). Al-Qaeda in the Arabian peninsula: Shooting, hostage taking, kidnapping wave. IntelCenter. Retrieved November 24, 2008, from http://www.intelcenter.com/AQAP-SHK-PUB-v1-1.pdf.

Impact of Terrorist Goals & Motivation on Planning

Practical strategies against terrorists require consideration of the terrorist's point of view in his targeting and operations.[242] Understanding the opponents' preferences and capabilities allows for a better defense and promotes an active approach to the threat. Total interdiction of all possible targets is impossible since the defender cannot protect everything. While consistent prediction is unlikely, accurate determination of what risks are acceptable must consider the terrorists' values. The terrorists' estimate of the target's value and the costs of the terrorist operation necessary to successfully hit it are of particular importance.[243]

The propagation of terrorism expertise and the breakdown in control and adherence of international norms allow a growing number of groups to use terror as a feasible tool in achieving their goals.

There has been an increase in international radicalism as compared to recent historical conflicts.[244] As the most prominent secular democracy and largest single economic, military, and political power in the world, the US becomes an easy and appealing target for extremists. Additionally, since the US declared the GWOT, the US has become the principal opponent of extremists throughout the world.[245] Much of the current thinking and literature on terrorism developed when terrorism was closely tied to revolutionary movements and separatist movements concerned with influencing events in relation to one nation. Newer causes and ideologies such as religion, economic concerns, or environmental issues are international and global in scope.[246]

Further, the perception that the US is the single most powerful nation in the world invites targeting by terror groups regardless of ideology to demonstrate their power and status.[247] In the worldview of many terrorist groups, they perceive that the US possesses power and influence to extract concessions from third parties (e.g., prisoner release and policy changes).

242 White, J. R. (2009). Terrorist and homeland security (6th ed.). Belmont, CA: Wadsworth.

243 Sageman, M. (2004). *Understanding terror networks*. Philadelphia: University of Pennsylvania.

244 Morgan, M. (2004). The origins of the new terrorism. *Parameters Online, 34(1)*, 29-43.

245 White, J. R. (2009). Terrorist and homeland security (6th ed.). Belmont, CA: Wadsworth.

246 Morgan, M. (2004). The origins of the new terrorism. *Parameters Online, 34(1)*, 29-43.

247 Crenshaw, M. (1998). The logic of terrorism: Terrorist behavior as a product of strategic choice. In W. Reich (Ed.), *Origins of Terrorism*. Woodrow Wilson Press: Washington, DC.

Although some people may question why a comparatively small terrorist group believes it can successfully confront the US, part of the answer lies in the Afghanistan jihad fighters and their success against the Soviet Union. Many Islamic fighters were convinced that they alone had defeated the Soviet Union in Afghanistan (even though the US provided substantial support), and that they could do likewise to the United States.[248]

Terror groups may believe that the use of terrorist actions against the US is the only viable option to challenge or defeat the US. The domination of US military power leaves few alternatives for the opposition to test US interests. Adding non-state-sponsored groups of formidable capability and few restraints to the roster of potential adversaries of the US increases the likely use of terror against our forces.

Many potential adversaries view the US as particularly vulnerable to the psychological impact and uncertainties generated by terror tactics in support of other activities.[249] Terrorism and terror tactics have already been used against US forces in support of conventional and insurgent warfare. They also have been used against US forces during stability and peace support operations in attempts to influence policy.

Lessons drawn from previous uses of terror against the US have led to some commonly held perceptions about the effectiveness and impact of terrorism versus the US. Some of these perceptions may or may not be valid yet are still widely held. Consequently, terrorist groups may likely capitalize on what they perceive as vulnerabilities. They include beliefs that:

- America is casualty averse. Any loss of US military life is looked upon as unnecessary.
- The US government policies and policy makers are overly influenced by public opinion, which in turn plays into the unfavorable terroristic psychological force.
- The economic cycle of the US is opinion-motivated and, likewise, susceptible to unfavorable terroristic psychological force.
- The US military cannot sustain long-term efforts.[250]

---

248 Morgan, M. (2004). The origins of the new terrorism. *Parameters Online, 34(1)*, 29-43.

249 Crenshaw, M. (1998). The logic of terrorism: Terrorist behavior as a product of strategic choice. In W. Reich (Ed.), *Origins of Terrorism*. Woodrow Wilson Press: Washington, DC.

250 White, J. R. (2009). Terrorist and homeland security (6th Ed.). Belmont, CA: Wadsworth.

The growing polarization of some domestic political issues means that the US is also likely to see increased terror attacks on its own soil by a variety of *home-grown* terror groups. These groups may target US forces either as symbols, sources, or weapons and equipment. They may also target us at the behest of other terrorist groups in exchange for money or support elsewhere.

Terrorist Asset Cost versus Target Value

Despite certain popular perceptions, there are finite limits to the number of terrorists in the US homeland and abroad. Terrorist groups require recruitment, preparation, and integration into the operational structure of the group.[251] Recruits also require extensive vetting to assure that they are not infiltrators from enemy security forces. A group's leadership will not employ assets without seriously considering the relationship between the cost of using (and possibly losing) the asset and the potential benefits to the group. While some groups may have a greater supply of personnel assets than others, no group can expend them injudiciously. Therefore, terrorist operational planning focuses on economies of personnel and balances the likelihood of losses against the value of a target and the probability of success. For example, suicide bombings are on the increase because of effective target results for relatively low cost.

In any terrorist operation, they will commit to the operation extensive pre-operational surveillance and reconnaissance, exhaustive planning, and sufficient resources. The potential risk of exposure of these resources and demands on their time are factored into the equation when deciding to commit to an attack.

Ideology and Motivation Influences on Operations

Both ideology and motivation influence the objectives of terrorist operations, particularly regarding the casualty rate.[252] Groups with secular ideologies and non-religious goals often attempt highly selective and discriminate acts of violence to achieve a specific political aim. This often requires them to keep casualties at a minimum amount necessary to achieve the objective. This is done to avoid a backlash that might severely damage the organization. Additionally, it also maintains the appearance of a rational

---

251 Sageman, M. (2004). *Understanding terror networks*. Philadelphia: University of Pennsylvania.

252 Rapoport, D. (1984). Fear and Trembling: Terrorism in Three Religious Traditions. *American Political Science Review, 78(3)*, 658-677.

group with legitimate grievances. By limiting their attacks, they reduce the risk of undermining political and economic support.

A good illustration of a group that discriminates on target selection is the revolutionary organization called *17 November*.[253] This is a radical, leftist organization established in Greece in 1975 that is anti-Greek establishment, anti-United States, anti-Turkey, and anti-NATO. Its operations have included assassinations of senior US officials, Greek public figures, European Union facilities, and foreign firms investing in Greece. Although a violent organization, reports indicate the group did not kill a bystander until 1992. *In toto*, 17 November is alleged to have been responsible for over 100 attacks, but just 23 fatalities between 1975 and 2000. Groups that comprise a "wing" of an insurgency or are affiliated with sometimes legitimate, political organizations often operate under these constraints. The tensions caused by balancing these considerations are often a prime factor in the generation of splinter groups and internal factions within these organizations.

In contrast, religiously oriented and millenarian groups typically attempt to inflict as many casualties as possible.[254] Morgan found that an apocalyptic frame of reference may deem loss of life as irrelevant and encourage mass casualty producing incidents. Fratricidal deaths among co-religionists generate little concern because they believe that such collateral casualties reap the benefits of the afterlife. Likewise, nonbelievers, whether the intended target or collateral damage, deserve death. Therefore, killing them is considered a moral duty.

In 1998, the Kenyan bombing of the US Embassy inflicted casualties on local inhabitants in proportion to US personnel of over 20-to-1 killed. An even greater disparity prevailed in the proportion of wounded, i.e., over 5,000 Kenyans were wounded by the blast, and 95 percent of the total casualties were non-American. Fear of backlash rarely concerns these groups, as one of their goals may be to provoke overreaction by their enemies and potentially widen the conflict. In the Kenya Embassy bombing, the suicide bomber failed to penetrate the Embassy's outer perimeter – thanks to the local guards' refusal to open the gates. This tactic resulted in the large casualty rate amongst local Kenyans. With numerous dead and maimed Kenyans, the terrorists issued a statement attempting to qualify a rationale for the deaths

---

253 White, J. R. (2009). Terrorist and homeland security (6th ed.). Belmont, CA: Wadsworth.

254 Morgan, M. (2004). The origins of the new terrorism. *Parameters Online, 34(1)*, 29-43.

and to mollify critics. The type of target selected will often reflect motivations and ideologies.[255]

For groups professing secular political or social motivations, their targets are highly symbolic of authority. Examples include government offices, banks, national airlines, and multinational corporations with direct relation to the established order. Likewise, they conduct attacks on representative individuals whom they associate with economic exploitation, social injustice, or political repression.[256] While religious groups also use much of this symbolism, there is a trend to connect it to greater physical devastation. There also is a tendency to add religiously affiliated individuals, such as missionaries, and religious activities, such as worship services, to the targeting equation.

Another common form of symbolism used in terrorist targeting is striking on particular anniversaries or commemorative dates.[257] Nationalist groups may strike to commemorate battles won or lost during a conventional struggle; whereas, religious groups may strike to mark particularly appropriate observances. Many groups attempt to commemorate (1) the anniversaries of successful operations or (2) the executions or deaths of notable individuals related to their particular conflict. Likewise, striking on days of particular significance to the enemy can also provide the requisite impact. For instance, Timothy McVeigh conducted the bombing of the Murrah Federal Building on April 19th, the anniversary of the end of the Branch Davidian siege near Waco, Texas. Since there are more events than operations, assessment of the likelihood of an attack on a commemorative date is only useful when analyzed against the operational pattern of a particular group or specific members of a group's leadership cadre.

Terrorist Characteristics

Walter Laquer says no singular personality profile of a terrorist exists, and no predictive test exists that can guarantee identification of a terrorist. Numerous terrorism-related studies have analyzed the biographical and social data on known terrorists in an attempt to develop some form of terrorist profile. Laquer found that, in general, terrorists are people who often feel alienated from society, have a grievance, or regard themselves as victims of an

---

255 White, J. R. (2009). Terrorist and homeland security (6th ed.). Belmont, CA: Wadsworth.

256 Sageman, M. (2004). *Understanding terror networks*. Philadelphia: University of Pennsylvania.

257 Snow, N. (2006). Terrorism, public relations, and propaganda. In A. P. Kavoori and T. Fraley, *Media, terrorism, and theory: ArReader*. Lanham, MD: Rowan & Littlefield.

injustice.[258] They are devoted to their political or religious cause and do not regard their violent actions as criminal, thereby showing no pity or remorse for their actions.[259] Although their level-of-sophistication varies depending on the individual and the specific terrorist group, terrorists skillfully and ruthlessly conduct terrorist acts. Additional to the above traits, some general characteristics appear as fairly common among terrorists. Also, some common stereotypes and misperceptions exist regarding terrorists.

Status

Contrary to the oft-repeated claim that terrorism results from poverty and despair, terrorists most commonly come from middle class backgrounds. Some actually come from extreme wealth and privilege. Guerrilla fighters and gang members often come from poor, disadvantaged backgrounds and, thus, may adopt terrorism as a tactic. Whereas, terrorist groups that specifically organize as such generally come from middle and upper social and economic strata.

Sageman, a Senior Fellow at PFRI and a former CIA case officer in Afghanistan, conducted a study of 400 Islamic terrorists. He found that 75 percent came from the upper or middle class and 90 percent came from caring, intact families. The leadership may use less educated and socially dispossessed people to conduct acts of terrorism. Even in terrorist groups that espouse the virtues of "the people" or "the proletariat," the leadership consists primarily of middle class backgrounds. However, this characteristic must be considered in context with the society from which the terrorist originates. "Middle class" or "privilege" are relative terms and will, for example, mean completely different levels of income between Western Africa and Western Europe.[260]

Education and Intellect

In general, terrorists possess more than average education, and very few Western terrorists are uneducated or illiterate. Some leaders of larger terrorist organizations possess minimal education, but this characteristic is not the norm. Left-wing terrorists, international terrorists, and the leadership echelon of right-wing groups are usually of average or better intelligence, and

---

258 Laquer, W. (1999). *The new terrorism: Fanaticism and the arms of mass destruction*. New York: Oxford University Press.

259 Morgan, M. (2004). The origins of the new terrorism. *Parameters Online, 34(1),* 29-43.

260 Sageman, M. (2004). *Understanding terror networks*. Philadelphia: University of Pennsylvania.

were exposed to advanced education. In fact, terrorist groups increasingly recruit members with expertise in communications, computer programming, engineering, finance, and the sciences. Sageman's analysis reflects 63 percent of his group went to college and three-quarters were professionals or semi-professionals, e.g., Osama bin Laden a civil engineer; Ayman al-Zawahiri a physician; and Yasser Arafat, at one time, a civil engineer. These terrorists generally are exposed to higher learning, although they usually were not highly intellectual, and are frequently dropouts or possess poor academic records.[261] Again, this is subject to the norms of the society from which they originate. In societies where religious fundamentalism is prevalent, their higher education may have been advanced religious training.

Russell and Miller's (1983) early research found that more than two-thirds of the terrorists surveyed came from middle-class or even upper-class backgrounds. Domestic and right-wing terrorists tend to come from lower educational and social levels, although they are not uneducated. Right-wing domestic groups in the US first explored the communication and organizational potential of the Internet. Typically, they possessed a high school education and were well indoctrinated in the ideological arguments they support.[262]

Age

Terrorists tend to be young.[263] Leadership, support, and training cadres can range in the 40-50-year-old age groups, but most operational members of terrorist organizations are in the 20-35-year-old age group. Practical experience and training that contribute to an effective operative are usually not present in individuals younger than the early 20s.

Guerrilla groups employ teenage individuals as soldiers. On the other hand, terrorist organizations tend not to use very young members. However, they will use them as non-operational supporters. Robert Pape found that groups that conduct suicide operations will employ very young individuals as suicide assets. However, these youths actually are not members of the organization. Instead, they simply are exploited or coerced into such operational roles. Many countries in the developing world are subjected to ethnic, political, and

---

261 White, J. R. (2009). Terrorist and homeland security (6th ed.). Belmont, CA: Wadsworth.

262 Russell, C A., & B. H. Miller (1983). Profiles of a terrorist. In L. Z. Freedman and Y. Alexander (Eds.), *Perspectives on terrorism*. Wilmington, DE: Scholarly Resources.

263 Sageman, M. (2004). *Understanding terror networks*. Philadelphia, PA: University of Pennsylvania.

religious violence. However, younger members are being recruited by terrorist organizations. Pre-teens and adolescents are often receptive to terrorist recruiting because they witness killings and see violence as the best way to deal with grievances. An example is the Liberation Tigers of Tamil Eelam (LTTE) in Sri Lanka. They recruit children to offset a manpower shortage due to casualties. Assessments by the Sri Lankan Directorate of Military Intelligence indicate a large percentage of below 18-year-old fighters.[264]

Gender

Even in primarily Islamic groups, terrorists are not exclusively male.[265,266] In these groups, women often are limited to performing support or intelligence work. However, some fundamentalist Islamic groups use women in operational roles. In groups where religious constraints do not affect women's roles, female membership may be above 50 percent with women fully integrated into the operations. Female leadership of terrorist groups is not uncommon. Female terrorists lack nothing in terms of violence and ruthlessness. For example, one-third of the LTTE cadre is made up of women. Nearly 4,000 have been killed since they began taking part in combat in 1985. Over 100 of those killed belonged to the dreaded Black Tiger suicide squad.

In August 2004, female Chechen suicide bombers were responsible for detonating improvised explosive devices (IEDs) while on Russian commercial flights. Those attacks resulted in two aircraft crashes and the death of all people on board. Within a week, another female Chechen suicide bomber detonated an IED near metro station in northeast Moscow. The explosion caused extensive property damage and injuring many people in the area.

In some right-wing groups, we make an exception to this general observation. This exception holds particularly in those groups professing neo-Nazi and Christian-Identity-oriented ideologies. Female participation and leadership are much less common in those groups.

264 Pape, R. A. (2003). The strategic logic of suicide bombing. *American Political Science Review, 97(3)*, 1-9.

265 Morgan, M. (2004). The origins of the new terrorism. *Parameters Online, 34(1)*, 29-43.

266 Sageman, M. (2004). *Understanding terror networks*. Philadelphia, PA: University of Pennsylvania.

Appearance

In individual characteristics, terrorists are often unremarkable.[267],[268] Racial diversity in organizations such as al-Qaeda signals that attempts to racially profile likely terrorist group members are an ineffective indicator. They usually do not appear extra-ordinary, and they display normal social behavior and appearance. Over the long term, elements of fanatical behavior or ruthlessness may become evident, but they are typically not immediately obvious to casual observation. An excellent example of this is the group in Greece called *17 November*. When the police captured 14 suspected members in 2002, the most striking characteristic was their ordinary nature. The group included a schoolteacher, shopkeeper, telephone operator, and other members that appeared to be members of mainstream society. Although members of sleeper cells or other covert operators may marry as part of their cover, most terrorists do not marry. However, there have been cases of married couples within terrorist organizations.

---

267 Morgan, M. (2004). The origins of the new terrorism. *Parameters Online, 34(1)*, 29-43.

268 Sageman, M. (2004). *Understanding terror networks*. Philadelphia, PA: University of Pennsylvania.

CHAPTER 12
MIDDLE EASTERN TERRORISM
AND ITS EARLY BEGINNINGS

Kevin D. Scott, MBA, MA

The Middle East

J R. White discussed and described the various aspects and origins of Middle Eastern terrorism. First and foremost, he also gave reference to the geographical boundaries encompassing the Middle East. The Middle East is a term that reflects a portion of the world that includes North Africa, Southwest Asia, and the region just south of Turkey that includes the Arabian Peninsula, Iran, and Afghanistan. White added that "some commentators also include Pakistan in their geographical definition of Middle East because it is dominated by Islamic culture."[269] This term, according to White, was given the name Middle East by an American naval strategist by the name of Alfred Thayer Mahan toward the conclusion of the 19th century. White further stated that Albert Hourani provided one of the most accurate historical pieces of information of the area. He proclaimed that "the area is dominated by two major concerns: the religion of Islam and the history of the Arab people."[270]

Muhammad

To examine the origins of Middle Eastern terrorism, we once again need to reflect back to the man who "started it all," the father of Islamic Middle Eastern culture, and that is, of course, Muhammad. It appeared to me that White was going to hit the nail on the head this time around in regards to the real origin of Middle Eastern terrorism. However, lo and behold, his account of Muhammad's life was a completely watered-down, half-truth version. He appears to be walking on eggshells when discussing the complete historical account of Muhammad's life.

---

269 White, J. R. (2002). *Terrorism: An Introduction*, pp. 92-98. Belmont, CA: Thomson Learning Inc.
270 Ibid.

Muhammad, the founder and author of the Koran (actually there is evidence he was illiterate so he most likely dictated his "revelations" to another), received a series of revelations from who he understood to be the Angel Gabriel. According to Geisler and Saleeb, Muhammad's initial reaction when confronted with this entity was that it was a demonic spirit.[271] The spirit then convinced Muhammad that it was in fact the Arch Angel Gabriel (If this incident is factual, he should have held fourth his initial inclination). White stated that Muhammad was ecstatic about his calling and began to spread the instruction he received of universalism, love, and monotheism (fancy term for rejecting Christ's deity).[272] White further stated Muhammad's message was for the most part based on love, discipline, and submission to God's will; however, he again miserably fails to document what the Koran states about Jews and Christians and all other non-Muslims.[273]

The Koran

From my study of the Islam religion, Muhammad, and their holy book, the Koran, I have come to the conclusion that Muhammad was in fact either insane or he was actually brainwashed and deceived by a demonic spirit. From studying his life, one can clearly see where Islamic/Middle Eastern terrorism came from. The following verses are taken from the Koran and are held in high esteem and applied by Muslim terrorists. I list them verbatim per Mikhail (2006).[274]

1. The prophet Muhammad urges Muslims to fight in the cause of Allah "O prophet Muhammad, urge the believers (Muslims) to fight" (Surat Al-Anfal 8:65). "Jihad (holy fighting in Allah's cause) is ordained for you" (Surat Al-Baqarah 2:216).

2. The Koran commands Muslims not to befriend Jews or Christians "O ye who believe (Muslims) take not the Jews or Christians for your friends and protectors. They are but friends and protectors to each

---

271 Geisler, N. L., Saleeb, A. (1993). *Answering Islam*, pp. 89-102. Grand Rapids, MI: Baker Books House Company.

272 White, J. R. (2002). *Terrorism: An Introduction*, pp. 92-98. Belmont, CA: Thomson Learning Inc.

273 Ibid.

274 Mikhail, L. (2006). Understanding Islam: The attack on the World Trade Center and the Pentagon. Retrieved March 14, 2006, from http://www.islamreview. com/articles/understanding.htm.

other. And he among you that turns to them (for friendship) is of them" (Surat Al-Maidah 5:51).

3. The Koran commands Muslims to fight Jews and Christians fight against those who believe not in Allah, nor in the last day, nor forbid that which has been forbidden by Allah and His Messenger (Muhammad) and those who acknowledge not the religion of truth (Islam) among the people of the scripture (Jews and Christians) until they pay the *Jizyah* with willing submission and feel themselves subdued" (Surah At-Taubah 9:29). Mikhail stated, "Jizyah is a special high tax to be paid only by Jews or Christians who do not want to renounce their religion and convert to Islam."[275]

4. The Koran commands Muslims to fight non-Muslims until they exterminate all other religions and Islam would be the only religion in the world. "And fight them until there is no more *fitnah* (disbelief and worshiping of others along with Allah) and (all and every kind of) worship is for Allah (alone). But if they cease, let there be no transgression except against *As-Zatimum* (the polytheists and wrong doers)" (Surat Al-Baqarah 2:193). Mikhail stated, "This verse is mentioned also in Surat Al-Anfal 8:39, because of the misunderstanding and ignorance of Christianity, Muslims believe that Christians are polytheists, because they believe in a Triune God. Fundamentalists look at Jews and Christians and all non-Muslims as infidels who must be killed because they have no value as human beings and must be exterminated from the face of the earth."[276] These Fundamentalists split the world into halves or camps, *Dar Al-Harb* (camp of war) where Jews and Christians remain, and *Dar Al-Sallam* (camp of peace) where Muslims remain. The Muslims adhere to the belief that holy war against the Jews and Christians should continue until they are all dead. These fundamentalists believe that there will soon be one global empire; if they can exterminate America and the Western countries, they will have this global empire.

5. The Koran declares that Muslims who fight and die in battle are promised forgiveness and a sensual luxurious life in Paradise. "And if you are killed or die in the way of Allah, forgiveness and mercy from Allah are far better than all that they amass (of worldly wealth)" (Surat Al-Imran 3:157). "Verily, Allah has purchased of the believers their

---

275 Ibid., p. 4.
276 Ibid., p. 4.

lives and their properties for (the price) that theirs shall be Paradise. They fight in Allah's cause, so they kill (others) and are killed. It is a promise in truth which is binding on Him" (Surat Al-Taubah 9:111) (p.4). Now, what can these martyrs (actually murders) expect in Paradise? Well, the Koran describes life in Paradise in the following words: "Eat and drink with happiness because of what you used to do. They will recline (with ease) on thrones arranged in ranks. And we shall marry them to *Hur* (fair females) with wide lovely eyes and we shall provide them with fruit and meat such as they desire" (Surat At-Tur 52:17-20, 22). "Water flowing constantly and fruit in plenty whose supply is not cut off and reclining on couches raised high, verily we have created them (women) of special creation and made them virgins of equal age" (Surat Al-Waqiah 56:31-37). "Gardens and vineyards and young full-breasted virgins of equal age and a full cup of wine" (Surat An-Naba 78:32-34).

Understanding the Middle East

White did, however, provide some insight into other problems and issues that the Middle East faces. He stated that one may better understand the Middle East by examining the following assumptions:[277]

1. The contemporary geographical and political structure of Middle Eastern Culture was formulated by 19th century European influence as well as the resulted effects and aftermath of WW I.

2. A large number of countries in the Arab nations apply more focus on the family unit as opposed to modern notions of government. Israel, however, being an exception, runs itself as a paramilitary democracy.

3. Modern Israel is run by a secular society of people of European descent and it is not the nation mentioned in the Christian Bible, the Jewish Torah, or the Koran (I somewhat disagree).

4. Arabs and Palestinians do not keep a monopoly on terrorist activity.

5. There has been an ongoing evolution of different religions in the region that has been going on for centuries. Fanatical religious

---

277 White, J. R. (2002). *Terrorism: An Introduction*, pp. 92-98. Belmont, CA: Thomson Learning Inc.

individuals can invoke violence and terrorist acts at any time, and this does not necessarily only pertain to Islam.

6. Israel became a recognized nation in 1948, and since then, violence has flourished throughout the Middle East and modern terrorism intensified after 1967. After 1973, terrorism developed into the established method of military assaults and operations and continues today, over three decades later.

7. In 1993, the Palestine Liberation Organization (PLO) took a stand against terrorist activity. This, however, had created a tremendous tension among the people. Some supported terrorist tactics while other renounced it. Similar instances have occurred in Israel as well. The Middle Eastern peace process is a very delicate ordeal, and the potential for terrorist activity is always present.

8. In addition to the above hardships, there is also a shortage of water as well as a diverse and complicated social structure. These nations encompass some of the wealthiest and most poverty stricken people in the world, most of which are placed in areas far away from water sources.

Palestine Islamic Jihad

The article titled "Palestine Islamic Jihad – background information" by Meir Litvak stated that the Palestine Islamic Jihad (PIJ) is the most vicious and destructive terror group operating in Palestine. It was formed in 1981 by two Islamic extremists who were operating in the Gaza Strip by the names of Dr. Fathi Abd al-Aziz Shiqaqi, a physician from Rafah, and Shaykh Abd al-Aziz Awda, a preacher from the Jabaliyya refugee camp. These two extremists had attended the Egyptian University of Zaqaziq. This university centers their curriculum on Islamic extremism. Litvak added that these two radicals rejected the mainstream approach to Islamic worship. The mainstream Muslims maintained that they needed to clean up their religion prior to destroying Israel. However, Shiqaqi argued that Israel, by its very existence, is the core reason for spiritual and moral corruption, and Muslims will never overcome their struggle until Israel is wiped off the map.[278]

---

278 Litvak, M. (2002). Palestine Islamic jihad – background information. Retrieved March 31, 2006, from http://www.jewishvirtual library.org/jsource/Terrorism/tau56.html.

Litvak stated that Islamic Jihad's ideology combined the Palestinian nationalist ideas with themes taken from three additional sources: "the ideology of the Muslim Brethren; patterns of activity of the militant Islamist groups in Egypt; and, uniquely among Sunni movements, the teachings of Ayatollah Khomeini, the Shi'i leader of the Islamic Revolution in Iran."[279]

Litvak stated that according to the proper context of the Muslim holy book, the Koran, and understanding history would form one to conclude that Palestine is the main focus of the religio-historical conflict between the Muslims and their mortal enemies, the Jews and the Christians. Litvak added that the meaning of this conflict is the Palestinian issue, which is the basis for a Western offensive that originated with Napoleon's invasion of Egypt in 1798 through 1918 with the destruction of the Ottoman Empire that symbolized Muslim unity. According to this view, Litvak added, "Palestine was always the focus of Western imperialist designs and was meant to serve as a launch pad to take over other Muslim territories."[280]

Litvak stated that Jewish presence in Palestine implies Muslim inferiority in today's Muslim view and the loyalty to Palestine cannot be regarded in the narrow confines of Palestinian nationalism. It, however, is regarded as an exclusive Muslim issue and "it is the key to every serious strategy aimed at the liberation and unification of the Islamic nation." Litvak added that this in a nutshell lays the Islamic Jihad's ideological innovation. The Palestinian Jihad encompasses a commitment of two inter-connected objectives: the freeing of Palestine and pan-Islamic return. Muslims view jihad as the sole way to free Palestine, being that Islamic victory and the disintegration of Israel are foreordained in the scripture of the Koran.[281]

Litvak stated that Shiqaqi applauded Ayatollah Khomeini for being the initial Islamic leader to provide Palestine its rightful place in his Islamic ideology. In addition, Litvak explained, the Iranian Islamic revolution was a tremendous victory in the fight against Western attempts to remove Islam from participating in political issues. Litvak further explained that Muslims were successful in producing a state founded on Islamic law. Thus, PIJ, were the sole organization that revered Khomeini as their true leader of the Islamic world.[282]

Litvak stated that PIJ started its armed terrorist activities in 1984. Shiqaqi was, however, arrested in 1986 and, subsequently, deported to Lebanon following his sidekick Awda in 1988. Shiqaqi resumed his agenda while in exile until he was whacked (assassinated) by Israeli hit men in Malta

---

279 Ibid., p. 1.
280 Ibid., p. 2.
281 Ibid., p. 2.
282 Ibid.

in 1995. His successor was Dr. Ramadan Abdallah Shallah who established his headquarters in Damascus. Litvak stated that the movement required some time before it could restart the operations because Shiqaqi was such a well respected charismatic leader, it was difficult to adjust to new leadership within the organization.[283]

HAMAS and Hizballah (also Hezbollah)

Litvak stated that although Islamic Jihad came before the establishment of HAMAS, it remained the lesser of the two organizations. Litvak further stated that HAMAS expanded and encompassed a political sub-section grounded in a wide realm network of religious and welfare institutions. However, the Islamic Jihad remained as a revolutionary vanguard for hundreds of activists. During the intifada, Litvak explains, the PIJ attempted to gain cooperation with HAMAS, but HAMAS decided not to unite.[284]

Litvak stated that Shiqaqi's relocation to Lebanon increased the organizations ties with Hizballah and Iran. Iran, therefore, became the organization's most vital financial supporter. Litvak added that Hizballah contributed training areas as well as logistical support. In turn, because of the crucial support of Hizballah, the PIJ began to grow rapidly and established networks in the Palestinian refugee camps across Lebanon. Litvak further added that "HAMAS was always an independent Palestinian movement; Islamic Jihad became an instrument of Iranian policy in the Arab-Israeli conflict."[285]

Jews a Legitimate Target

Lastly, the article entitled "UK poll: 37% of Muslims in Britain think British Jews are a 'legitimate target'" stated that almost two fifths (or 37 percent) of Muslims in England feel that British Jews are a legitimate target for terrorist attacks because they are a part of the on-going struggle for justice throughout the Middle East (I had previously seen a similar poll that listed the approval rate at 58 percent). In addition, only 52 percent feel that the state of Israel has a right to exist, with 30 percent disagreeing, a large minority. One in six Muslims questioned feel that suicide bombings at times can be justifiable in Israel, however, many less (7 percent) state the same about England. "This

---

283 Ibid.
284 Ibid.
285 Ibid.

is broadly comparable to the number justifying suicide attacks in ICM and YouGov polls of British Muslims after the July 7 attacks."[286]

---

286 Jihad Watch (2006). Uk poll: 37% of Muslims in Britain think British Jews are a "legitimate target". Retrieved March 31, 2006, from http://www.jihadwatch. org/archives/2006/02/010071print.html.

CHAPTER 13
INTERNATIONAL TERRORISM AND THE INVOLVEMENT OF PALESTINE

Kevin D. Scott, MBA, MA

Introduction

In this chapter, I discuss and describe the various aspects of international terrorism and Palestine's involvement. I also discuss the birth and acts of terror committed by the Palestine Islamic Jihad (PIJ), the most notorious terror organization of Palestine. Finally, I touch on some the tremendous dangers and hardships that Israel faces in its everyday struggle with the Palestinian government.

International Terrorism and Palestine

Yasser Arafat finally died in 2004. He leaves behind a corrupt and confused legacy. At one time, Arafat was considered the father/founder of modern international terrorism and the head "shot caller" behind the political identity of Palestine. His death threw the focus on the delicate prospects for a peace agreement between Israel and the Palestinian people who proclaim that their homeland lies within Israeli territorial boundaries.[287] White stated that Arafat is regarded as a cold-hearted terrorist to many (myself included), especially those who sympathize with Israel; to others, he was regarded as a charismatic revolutionary hero who was the mouthpiece for the Palestinian cause. Arafat was even viewed by many in the Middle East as untrustworthy and many viewed him with hatred. Furthermore, Arafat attempted to be "everything to everyone" which (in my opinion) could not be further from the truth.

---

287 Anonymous (2004, November 14). After Arafat, world waits and hopes. *South China Morning Post*. Retrieved April 6, 2006, from http://proquest.umi.com/pqdweb?did=735749191&sid=1&Fmt=3&clientId=52110&RQT=309&Vname=PQD.

However, this self-made leader of the Palestine Liberation Organization (PLO) has done more for the Palestinian Arabs than anyone else.[288]

Arafat was a symbol among his people all the way to his death in terms of the Palestinian quest for statehood. And while he was successful in proclaiming the needs and desires of the Palestinian people in regards to international circles, he never succeeded in the crucial transition from terrorist leader to statesman.[289] In other words, he didn't fool anybody.

The Palestinian Authority (PA) has not contributed the needed programs and services related to functional and modern states. Funds that were designated for welfare purposes were used elsewhere, most likely to those blind followers who supported Arafat in order to keep him in power for four decades. During that time, education and health care were placed on the backburner, and the occupied territories are drenched in poverty. Unfortunately, Arafat avoided and denounced opportunities to compromise or to accept imperfect offers for peace that may have ultimately formed the two-state solution with which the majority of the Palestinian people would have probably been satisfied.[290]

The next step very much depends on Palestinian pragmatism.[291] Now, the potential competitive factions ranging from the extremist members from HAMAS all the way to the old veterans of the PLO have displayed restraint, thus showing a desire for shared leadership and an election of a new president. As we have recently witnessed, HAMAS has now established power, but I do question the legitimacy of the elections and politics of the Palestinian people and how they view Israel and the continuing negotiations for peace.

The Palestinian Islamic Jihad Terror Organization

Now this brings us to another terrorist organization, arguably the most radical terrorist organization operating in the confines of the Palestinian arena. This organization is known as the Palestine Islamic Jihad (PIJ). Meir Litvak stated that two Islamic extremists had formed PIJ in 1981 in the Gaza Strip. The main focus of this terror organization was to:[292]

---

288 White, J. R. (2002). *Terrorism: An introduction*. Belmont, CA: Thomson Learning Inc., pp. 136-138.

289 Anonymous (2004, November 14). After Arafat, world waits and hopes. *South China Morning Post*. Retrieved April 6, 2006, from http://proquest.umi.com/pqdweb?did=735749191&sid=1&Fmt=3&clientld=52110&RQT=309&Vname=PQD.

290 Ibid.

291 Ibid.

292 Litvak, M. (2002). Palestine Islamic Jihad-Background information. Retrieved March 31, 2006, from http://www.jewishvirtuallibrary.org/jsource/Terror-

- "Clean up" Islam
- Unite as one force
- Destroy Israel quickly (sounds familiar?)

Litvak further stated that the Islamic Jihad's ideology blended Palestinian nationalist ideas with themes drawn from three other sources:[293]

- The ideology of the Muslim Brethren
- Patterns of activity of the militant Islamic groups in Egypt uniquely among Sunni movements
- The teachings of Ayatollah Khomeini, the Shi'i leader of the Islamic revolution in Iran

Now, although Islamic Jihad preceded HAMAS (established in 1988), it remained the lesser of the two organizations. HAMAS developed into a huge movement with a political section that had a stationary, widespread realm of religious and welfare institutions. However, the Islamic Jihad "remained a revolutionary vanguard of several hundred activists. During the 1987-1993 *intifada*, the PIJ sought cooperation or unity with HAMAS, but the latter was reluctant to move in this direction."[294]

Both PIJ and HAMAS denounced the 1993 Oslo Accords as a betrayal of the rights of Islam and the Palestinian people. In turn, they conducted terrorist attacks on Israeli targets in a "race" to stop the peace process. By 2000, the PIJ was responsible for murdering dozens of Israeli civilians (for the most part). During this time, the PIJ refused to acknowledge the PA as a righteous, lawful government, and it refused to participate in the 1996 PA elections. In addition, the PIJ did not debate the PA politically the way HAMAS did. However, Litvak stated that it was easier for the PA to take strong measures against the Islamic Jihad, as the smaller organization, and it closed *al-Istiqlal*, the Jihad newspaper in Gaza, and arrested some low-level activists."[295]

The September 2000 outbreak of the Israeli-Palestinian confrontation tremendously strengthened the Islamic Jihad. With the assistance and backing of HAMAS, the opinion was formed that *jihad* (i.e., holy war) was the sole way to rid Israel and drive the Israelis out of the West Bank and Gaza. This action was viewed by the Palestinians as being the first step in the process to

---

ism/tau56.html.

293 Ibid., p. 1.
294 Ibid., p. 3.
295 Ibid., p. 3.

free Palestine. The Islamic Jihad and HAMAS received mass support from many Palestinians and some logistical backing from the PA officials. On the operational level, Islamic Jihad supporters teamed up with HAMAS as well as supporters of Fatah and began executing terrorist assaults on Israeli targets. At the same time, Islamic Jihad committed itself to carry out the more dangerous and devastating attacks in order to establish and demonstrate their superiority over the other groups.[296]

Although this terror organization has enjoyed many successes, it still remains a very small group. According to numerous opinion polls, it only entails about 4-5 percent of the Palestinian population, predominately because it does not have the institutional network that HAMAS had constructed. With this in mind, it paves the way for Islamic Jihad to zero in its ideological quests and dismiss the larger political issues. As a consequence, the Islamic Jihad was not allowed a say in the Cairo discussions that took place in between Fatah and HAMAS to possibly declare a suspension of suicide bomb attacks on Israel. However, the Islamic Jihad continues today in conducting its murderous attacks.[297]

Problems Facing Israel

It is difficult to determine which move is dumber: Israel's facilitating HAMAS' involvement in the elections (a group that we all know would love nothing more than to "take out" Israel) or the government's prompting hope that future peace deal on a Fatah triumph, which is a similar yet much larger organization that has about the same amount of love for Israel as HAMAS and PIJ.[298]

As soon as the Israeli government can determine whether or not to provide support for the elections, they seem to be as if they are assuming a step in the direction of promoting a democratic Palestinian government. In essence, Israel is taking the position that terrorist organizations have a legitimate place in government. The mere assumption or accusation of Israel interfering in the Palestinian elections shows that the international community, the US being in charge, has accepted the notion that Palestinian terrorists are accepted and legitimate bodies. Ehud Olmert fears that Israel is being labeled as "meddling" in these elections. It just goes to show that he himself feels that there is some

---

296 Ibid., p. 3.
297 Ibid.
298 Glick, C. B. (2006, January 24). We needn't lose the war. *Jerusalem Post*, p. 15.

legitimacy about those whose main quest is to destroy Israel and mass murder of its citizens.[299]

The comparison of Israel's campaign toward Palestine's terrorism to America's campaign toward al-Qaeda clearly shows Israel's superior fighting abilities to ours, including everything in the realm of intelligence gathering, targeting assaults against terrorist commanders to the limiting of collateral damage. However, at the same time, on the strategic level, the US is well on its way to defeating al-Qaeda, while Israel is losing its war against the Palestinian terrorists.[300] I still say that NO ONE can deal with the Arabic Islamic terrorists better than Israel. That's what I like about Israel, i.e., not too many bleeding heart liberals, and they don't take "sorrys" either. This, however, is the only way to deal with this type of adversary because you can't reason with them, you can't bargain with them, and you can't befriend with them. I keep seeing bumper stickers stating, "War is not the answer." Well, when you are dealing with Islamic terrorism, war is the ONLY answer. Israel knows it, and in time, America may come to realize it as well.

With Israel's decline to politically contend with the realism that both groups, Fatah and HAMAS, are determined to see its destruction relates for the most part to domestic reasons. The most remarked of these is the Israeli fear that in just a matter of years, there will be an equal number of Arabs and Jews living in Judea, Samaria, and sovereign Israel. The argument that demographic realities, in a number of years, will force Israel to choose between remaining a Jewish state or remaining a democracy has been the main rationale proffered for Israel's refusal to defeat Palestinian terrorism.[301]

Conclusion

Well, I must say that given Israel's location and being surrounded by its vicious enemies, it's a miracle that they are still there and holding strong. In addition, to my knowledge, there is no race or group of people that have suffered such persecution and attempted genocide than the Jewish people, and yet, they exist stronger than ever yet remain a peaceful, democratic nation.

---

299 Ibid., p. 1.
300 Ibid., p. 1.
301 Ibid., p. 2.

CHAPTER 14
RELIGION AND TERROR

Kevin D. Scott, MBA, MA

Jonathan White discusses and describes "some" of the various aspects of religion and terrorism and how they relate to each other. He states that religion and terrorism have come together in the early years of the 21st century.[302] Both have been intertwined long before that. I don't know where Mr. White gets some of his information. There are, of course, many different types of terrorist groups and activities, but I focus this chapter on Islamic terrorism, which is what our nation currently faces.

The Process and Effects of Demonization

White states that hating one's enemy is a natural and normal emotion. Religious leaders and militaries often use this strategy with their soldiers/ militants in order to achieve maximum effectiveness against their adversaries. This use of hatred has been extremely effective for terrorist organizations in their assaults against the people who oppose them. Additionally, this use of hatred in terrorist attacks has paralleled itself by using "inflammatory diatribes in the course of war." However, whenever we involve religion, the conflict situation changes. In these so-called holy wars, adversaries do not necessarily align with people of different beliefs as witnessed in recent events. These people are viewed by terrorist militants as Satan followers that do his will. When religion becomes intertwined with any form of conflict, the situation usually goes from bad to worse. Killing people is much easier when one feels that he is doing it in the name of his god and that his actions are helping their god to rid the world of evil.[303]

Pictorial demonization of people is also very influential and damaging. In the article entitled "Graphic anti-Semitism," Dan Pattir states that if anyone believes that pictorial demonization of Jewish people is no longer produced, they need to take a look at the Arab press. The composer, who

---

302 White, J. R. (2002). *Terrorism: An introduction*. Belmont, CA: Thomson Learning Inc., pp. 46-60.
303 Ibid., p. 54.

is a seasoned researcher of editorial cartoons, is in fact the curator of many cartoon exhibitions outside as well as inside Israel.[304]

There is absolutely no restraint when it comes to producing anti-Semitic images that go from depicting the Jews assuming a Satanic force attempting to squash Islam all the way to Jews assuming an international role in aspiring to control the world including the American government, and to placing the Jews in the same category as the Nazis.[305]

The end-result of this gross anti-Semitic onslaught is that the entire Egyptian population is experiencing a major setback in the normalization process in regards to the 1979 Egyptian-Israeli Peace Treaty. It also contradicts other peace treaties that Israel has with neighboring countries, which all call for "prevention of incitement and hostile propaganda as specified in the Interim Agreement" (The Hebron Protocol of 1997). Additionally, the 1998 Wye River Memorandum states that "the Palestinian side will issue a decree prohibiting all terms of incitement to violence of terror."[306]

The Relationship Islam has with Terrorism

Now, we evaluate the basis for Islamic terror. In the book titled *Answering Islam*, Norman Geisler and Abdul Saleeb state that the Koran is the basis of the Islamic religion. The Koran claims to be God's inspired word handed down to Muhammad, which is the exact duplicate of the one in heaven. The Koran's teachings denounce Judaism and Christianity, calling them false doctrines. Other Muslims claim that the Koran is the full and final revelation of God, given to the self-proclaimed prophet Muhammad, the "last and greatest of all the prophets who supersede Moses, Jesus, and all other prophets before him."[307] For those who reject Islam, it is vital to understand how Muslims revere the Koran and Prophet Muhammad and to examine the reasons why Muslims support its teachings and commitments.

The great Sunni authority, Abu Hanifa, claimed the orthodox belief that the Koran is the truly inspired word of God and revelation. Yosuf K. Ibish, a Muslim scholar stated, "It is not a book in the ordinary sense, nor is it comparable to the Bible, either the Old or New Testaments. If you want to compare it with anything in Christianity, you must compare it with Christ

304 Pattir, D. (2006, February 12). Graphic anti-Semitism. *Jerusalem Post*, p. 15. Retrieved March 16, 2006, from http://proquest.umi.com/pqdweb?did=986497 191&sid=1&Fmt=3&clientld=52110&RQT=309&Vname=PQD.

305 Ibid.

306 Ibid.

307 Geisler, N. L., & Saleeb, A. (1993). *Answering Islam*. Grand Rapids, MI: Baker Books House Company, p.89-106.

Himself. Christ was the expression of the Divine among men, the revelation of the Divine Will. That is what the Koran is."[308] In essence, in Christianity, the Word became flesh, and in Islam, the Word became a book.

Muslims take the Koran as the very Word of God without error, so, where is the connection between Islam and terrorist activities?[309] Throughout history, people "have literalized myths" (p.49) and taken various teachings out of Holy Books such as the Koran out of context and terrorized other people who do not share in their beliefs.[310] I disagree with Jonathan White in regards to the Koran. It is a violent, evil religion. The so-called extremists abide by its teachings. They are not, as White refers to, "taking the teachings out of context." These terrorist acts inflicted upon others are extremely deadly. In essence, they express their spirituality and holiness through violent, murderous terrorist acts, and the process is continuous.

White further states that, "When people transform a non-killing religious call for universal love into a mandate to love only those who look, act, and believe like them, they introduce a formula for religious violence. The process is completed when symbols and myths are literalized. Unfortunately, this is a part of terrorism."[311] In my opinion, this is true for many other religious-based terror groups; however, it is not the "meat and potatoes" of Islam … only the vegetables. In the article titled "Understanding Islam" by Dr. Labib Mikhail, he states that those Muslims who take to the verbatim word and teachings of the Koran are known as the fundamentalists of Islam. The following versus are taken from the Koran and are held in high esteem and applied by Muslim terrorists. I will list them verbatim per Mikhail:[312]

1. The prophet Muhammad urges Muslims to fight in the cause of Allah "O prophet Muhammad, urge the believers (Muslims) to fight" (Surat Al-Anfal 8:65). "Jihad (holy fighting in Allah's cause) is ordained for you" (Surat Al-Baqarah 2:216).

2. The Koran commands Muslims not to befriend Jews or Christians "O ye who believe (Muslims) take not the Jews or Christians for your friends and protectors. They are but friends and protectors to each

---

308   Ibid., p. 179.

309   Ibid.

310   White, J. R. (2002). *Terrorism: An introduction.* Belmont, CA: Thomson Learning Inc., p. 49.

311   Ibid., p. 49.

312   Mikhail, L. (2006). *Understanding Islam: The attack on the World Trade Center and the Pentagon.* Retrieved March 14, 2006, from http://www.islamreview.com/articles/understanding.htm.

other. And he among you that turns to them (for friendship) is of them" (Surat Al-Maidah 5:51).

3. The Koran commands Muslims to fight Jews and Christians' fight against those who believe not in Allah, nor in the last day, nor forbid that which has been forbidden by Allah and His Messenger (Muhammad) and those who acknowledge not the religion of truth (Islam) among the people of the scripture (Jews and Christians) until they pay the Jizyah with willing submission and feel themselves subdued" (Surah At-Taubah 9:29).

Mikhail stated "Jizyah is a special high tax to be paid only by Jews or Christians who do not want to renounce their religion and convert to Islam."[313]

1. The Koran commands Muslims to fight non-Muslims until they exterminate all other religions, and Islam would be the only religion in the world. "And fight them until there is no more fitnah (disbelief and worshiping of others along with Allah) and [all and every kind of] worship is for Allah [alone]. But if they cease, let there be no transgression except against *As-Zatimum* (the polytheists and wrong doers)" (Surat Al-Baqarah 2:193).

Mikhail stated, "This verse is mentioned also in Surat Al-Anfal 8:39, because of the misunderstanding and ignorance of Christianity, Muslims believe that Christians are polytheists, because they believe in a Triune God. Fundamentalists look at Jews and Christians and all non-Muslims as infidels who must be killed because they have no value as human beings and must be exterminated from the face of the earth."[314] These fundamentalists split the world into halves or camps, *Dar Al-Harb* (camp of war), where Jews and Christians remain and *Dar Al-Sallam* (camp of peace) where Muslims remain. The Muslims adhere to the belief that holy war against the Jews and Christians should continue until they are all dead. These fundamentalists believe that there will soon be one global empire and that, if they can exterminate America and the western countries, they will have this global empire.

1. The Koran declares that Muslims who fight and die in battle are promised forgiveness and a sensual, luxurious life in Paradise. "And if you are killed or die in the way of Allah, forgiveness and mercy from Allah are far better than all that they amass (of worldly wealth)" (Surat

313 Ibid., p. 4.
314 Ibid., p. 4.

Al-Imran 3:157). "Verily, Allah has purchased of the believers their lives and their properties for [the price] that theirs shall be Paradise. They fight in Allah's cause, so they kill (others) and are killed. It is a promise in truth which is binding on Him" (Surat Al-Taubah 9:111). Now, what can these martyrs (actually murderers) expect in Paradise? Well, the Koran describes life in Paradise in the following words: "Eat and drink with happiness because of what you used to do. They will recline [with ease] on thrones arranged in ranks. And we shall marry them to Hur (fair females) with wide lovely eyes, and we shall provide them with fruit and meat such as they desire" (Surat At-Tur 52:17-20, 22). "Water flowing constantly and fruit in plenty whose supply is not cut off and reclining on couches raised high, verily we have created them (women) of special creation and made them virgins of equal age" (Surat Al-Waqiah 56:31-37). "Gardens and vineyards and young full-breasted virgins of equal age and a full cup of wine" (Surat An-Naba 78:32-34).

Mikhail stated that many prominent Muslim clerics refer to the suicide bombers of the World Trade Center as martyrs because, in the Koran, a martyr is provided absolute forgiveness of his past transgressions and an eternal luxurious life in Paradise where he can drink wine and have numerous wives with big breasts if you will. These so called martyrs are nothing more than selfish murderous cowards. Nineteen Muslims, who were all well-educated, murdered about 3,000 innocent people who were at the World Trade Center, the Pentagon, and on board the four planes that they had hijacked. Again, these 19 Muslims committed this act out of their deep conviction that they would go straight to heaven and enjoy all the above-mentioned pleasures and because of their deep hatred for our country that is largely populated with Christians.[315]

1. The Koran commands Muslims to terrorize and torture and kill anyone who disobeys Allah and the Prophet Muhammad: "[Remember] when your Lord revealed to the angels, "Verily I am with you, so keep firm those who have believed. I will cast terror into the hearts of those who have disbelieved, so strike them over the necks, smite over all their fingers and toes. This is because they defied and disobeyed Allah and His Messenger (Muhammad). And whoever defies and disobeys Allah and His Messenger, Allah is severe in punishment. This is [the torment], so taste it; and for the disbelievers is the torment of the Fire" (Sur Al-Anfal 8:12-14). "The recompense of those who wage

315 Ibid.

war against Allah and His Messenger (Muhammad) and do mischief in the land is only that they shall be killed or crucified or their hands and feet be cut off from opposite sides or be exiled from the land. That is their disgrace in this world and a great torment is theirs in the Hereafter" (Maidah 5:33).

2. The Koran declares that Allah loves those who fight in His cause. "Verily, Allah loves those who fight in His Cause in rows as if they were solid structures" (Surat As-Saff 61:4).

3. The Koran commands Muslims to convert non-Muslims to Islam by force. "Kill the *Mushrikun* (polytheists, Christians, and non-Muslims) wherever you find them and capture them and besiege them, and lie in wait for them in each and every ambush. But, if they repent and perform *As-Salat* (public prayer with Muslims) and give *Zakat* (Islamic alms), then leave their way free. Allah is oft-forgiving, most merciful" (Surat At-Taubah 9:5). Mathematician Blaise Pascal, who lived in 1670, stated, "Men never do evil so completely and cheerfully as when they do it from religious conviction." Mikhail stated that the heart of man is inherently evil and that evil can be ignited with religious gasoline. The teachings in the Koran ignited the evil in the hijackers' hearts and will fuel the hatred in Muslim hearts forever in the future.[316]

Conclusion

Mikhail stated that although violence is often inflicted by Muslim terrorists and is approved of by the Koran, any such violence inflicted upon others by Christians is and never will be sanctioned by the New Testament teachings.[317] Jesus Christ commanded His apostle Peter, "Put your sword in its place. For all who take the sword will perish by the sword" (Matthew 26:52).

---

316 Ibid., p. 7.
317 Ibid.

CHAPTER 15
ISLAMIC TERRORISTS AND COMMON CRIMINALS

Kevin D. Scott, MBA, MA

Introduction

In his book, *Terrorism: An Introduction*, Jonathan White discusses and describes the various aspects of individual and group behavior in terms of terrorism and criminal activity. He also explains the differences and views between terrorists and average, everyday, street criminals as well as their profiles and goals. In addition, he further explains the reasons and motives that may entice one to become a terrorist and what traits this person may have ingrained in his character that would steer him towards joining a terrorist group.

Differences between Terrorists and the Common Criminal

White states that it is important to recognize the difference between typical criminal behavior and acts of terrorism.[318] In the article titled "The mind of a terrorist" by Ernest Evans, he says that average street criminals generally have no conscience. They feel that they have no boundaries and that they can do whatever they want. Terrorists, on the other hand, obey and abide by rules and moral obligations as related to their deeds. Evans gave the example, "In tsarist Russia, the Narodnik terrorists aborted several attempts to assassinate the Tsar because of the dangers posed to innocent bystanders (They eventually killed Tsar Alexander II in 1881.). And, in an interview with former Irgun member Eli Tavin in 1975, he insisted that in the Irguns most famous attack – namely, the destruction of the British military headquarters at the King David Hotel in Jerusalem – the Irgun called to warn the British

---

318 White, J. R., (2002). *Terrorism: An Introduction*. Belmont, CA: Thomson Learning Inc., pp. 18-29.

that they must evacuate the hotel (For reasons that are still unclear, the British did not do so and several dozen people were killed.)."[319]

Evans stated that the common criminal feels that his criminal actions do not need any justification. If the opportunity for criminal behavior presents itself, the common criminal feels totally entitled to commit the illegal act without any regard for the sake and safety of others and their property. On the other hand, the terrorist will most likely go out of his way to morally justify his actions. In many Islamic terrorist cases, they feel that they are serving the will of their Islamic god, Allah.[320]

Evans goes on to state that certain heinous criminals experience a sense of sadistic pleasure and feel an extreme power trip by watching their victims suffer in agony. Hence, victims begging them for mercy are pointless. He presented the example of convicted serial murderer, Ted Bundy. Days prior to Bundy's date with the electric chair, the Reverend James Dobson urged Bundy to disclose all the information regarding his unaccounted for victims and their burial locations. Bundy refused, and to him, it was an extreme power trip situation knowing that the families of the victims were distressed beyond comprehension. Bundy even tried to negotiate a deal that he would give full disclosure of the remaining unaccounted for victims and their burial sites if his life was spared. This was the last statement he made as he was strapped into the electric chair.[321]

In many cases, the death penalty is a great deterrent in criminal cases but not so in dealing with terrorists.[322] I personally disagree, especially when dealing with extremist Muslim terrorists. Although many of these Muslim terrorists desire to die for their cause (to become a martyr) because they believe that they will reap great rewards in their afterlife. If these terrorists knew beforehand that, should they be apprehended and prior to their executions, they would be sprinkled with pig's blood, thereby, making them unclean and unable to go to their heaven, it would send a clear message to these potential terrorists and would most likely deter their terrorist acts ... thus saving countless innocent lives. Unfortunately, we are too "civilized" and "culturally sensitive" to take this type of extreme lifesaving action, and therefore, I feel that innocent people will pay the price (just my two cents).

---

319 Evans, E. (2005). The mind of a terrorist: How terrorists see strategy and morality. *World Affairs, 167 (4)*, 175-180. Retrieved March 3, 2006, from
http://proquest.umi.com/pqdweb?did=821066351&sid=2&Fmt=3&clientld=52110&RQT=309&VNAME=PQD.

320 Ibid.

321 Ibid.

322 Ibid.

Evans further states that terrorism is a type of war and, of course, in all types of war, there are many innocent victims that pay with their lives. Timothy McVeigh, at his Oklahoma City bombing trial in 1995, justified the killing of 23 children in the federal building daycare center as a form of "collateral damage" that occurs in all types of war.[323]

Justification of Terrorist Actions

White stated that when someone uses force upon another, they need to show adequate justification for their actions. This is particularly true in law enforcement situations as well as military tactics and assaults. The more force that is applied to a given situation, the greater is accountability and justification. In cases where deadly force is applied, it must warrant a tremendous amount of justification and responsibility for the action taken. White gives the example of the executioner who cannot question himself if he desires to be effective in his job.[324]

In the religion of Islam (People say that there are many peaceful Muslim groups; however, after reading the Koran, personally, I don't trust any of them.), the Koran makes numerous references about the justification of killing Jews and Christians. In the article titled "Is Islam above criticism?" Al-Maqdesi and Solomon explain some of the various aspects of the Muslim religion in terms of their justification of terrorist acts. Not very long ago, we experienced that behavior in many Muslims after the cartoon depicting Muhammad as that of being a terrorist (which he actually was). This publication fueled many Muslims to resort to boycotts, protests, and violence. Al-Maqdesi and Solomon described how many armed and angry Palestinians charged into the offices of the European Union in Gaza, screaming for an apology from Norway and Denmark. Many other like incidents soon followed.[325]

Muslims use their holy book, the Koran, as a basis for their justification to inflict terrorist acts upon others who do not share their beliefs. Al-Maqdesi and Solomon gave examples from the scriptures of the Koran that radical Muslims use as the basis of justification for their murderous, terrorist attacks on Jews, Christians, and non-Muslims. In reference to the Jews, Koran 7:176 states, "His similitude is that of a dog, if you attack him, he lolls out his tongue or if you leave him alone he still lolls out his tongue that is the similitude of those

---

323 Ibid.

324 White, J. R., (2002). *Terrorism: An Introduction*. Belmont, CA: Thomson Learning Inc.

325 Al-Maqdesi, & Solomon (2006). Answering Islam: Is Islam above criticism? Retrieved March 5, 2006, from http://www.answering-islam.org/Silas/terrorism.htm.

who reject our signs?" In addition, 7:179 states that "many are the jinns and men we have made for Hell, they have hearts they understand not, and ears wherewith they hear not. They are like cattle nay more misguided for they are headless." Al-Maqdesi and Solomon further wrote that all Islamic expositors and their manuals claim that it is the Jews who are being referenced to here. In addition, the Koran states that non-Muslims are profane; Sura 9:28, "O ye who believe, truly the pagans (non-Muslims) are profane so let them not after this year of theirs approach the sacred Mosque." By this, Mecca remains an Islamic city exclusively for Muslims.[326]

Al-Maqdesi and Solomon further stated that the Koran proclaims that Christians are apostates because they believe Jesus is the Son of God, and they (the Muslims) pray for the Christians' ultimate destruction.[327] Thus far, in the readings in White, he fails to mention what I know is the ultimate source that justifies Islamic terrorism, which of course is the teachings of their holy book, the Koran.

White wrote that terrorists undergo a process of brainwashing in order to justify their actions. He further said that terrorists are motivated by the same things that motivate everyone else; however, they just cannot accept the world on how it is.[328] I feel that White holds some truth in his writings on this particular subject; however, he continuously fails to address the real motivation and justification of Islamic terrorism (either he is ignorant or he is trying to be politically correct. I highly recommend that he picks up a copy of the Koran and read it). In addition, I feel that these so-called "moderate peaceful Muslims" are this way because they do not embrace the teachings of the Koran in its entirety. If these moderates did in fact embrace all the teachings in the Koran, terrorism would be a much bigger problem in the world today. From my past research and reading of the Koran, I believe that Islamic terrorists base the justification of their terrorist acts upon the teachings of the Koran.

Profile of the Terrorist

White described three categories of terrorists: "criminals, crazies, and crusaders."[329] He added that these three types of terrorists may encompass some of the traits from the other categories as well. The criminal category generally terrorizes its victims for monetary purposes or possibly some form

---

326 Ibid.

327 Ibid.

328 White, J. R., (2002). *Terrorism: An Introduction.* Belmont, CA: Thomson Learning Inc.

329 Ibid., p. 25.

of revenge. He further stated that the organized criminal groups may use terrorist tactics on groups of people for economic gain; however, it is the "crusaders" that are the majority when it comes to political terrorism.[330]

In an article titled "Courage in dark places: Reflections on terrorist psychology," Andrew Silke wrote that after the September 11, 2001, terrorist attacks, many commentators stated that the Al-Qaeda terrorists showed great courage when they hijacked the planes and crashed them into the World Trade Center buildings. In an article titled "Courage in dark places: Reflections on terrorist psychology," by a slaughter, they were not cowards." Ted Turner, the founder of CNN, commented at a speech at Brown University saying, "I think they [the 19 terrorists] were brave at the very least." These statements and comments describing terrorists in such a manner raised many concerns and outrage across the nation. Silke raised the question: Although these statements are extremely inflammatory, are they really inaccurate? Can terrorists possess courageous virtues? If so, what can we as a people learn from this type of courage?[331]

Silke further stated that, in essence, it is much easier to condemn terrorist acts than it is to comprehend it. When society observes violent criminal activity, they assume for the most part, that individuals who commit these horrible acts are deviant and endure considerable psychological abnormalities. Terrorist actions are often despicable. Attempting to understand these acts of terror can be seen as an implication of sympathy toward the perpetrators.[332]

Silke added that issues concerning objective insight are particularly difficult especially after an attack that leaves large numbers of casualties (which dismisses or is ignorant of the real motivations and objectives of Islamic terrorism). These horrendous attacks that claim the lives of innocent people, including children, raises a question as to the motivation, moral judgment, and psychological make-up of these people who carry out these terrorist attacks.[333]

Our perceptions of terrorists are filled with rumors and innuendos, and as terrorist attacks become more extreme, so do our perceptions. What kind of person can murder innocent people (including children) and, at the same time, take their own life? To answer this question, many have considered that it is a strong possibility that these terrorists suffer from extreme mental illness and other various forms of psychological disorders.[334] In my 16-plus years in

330 Ibid.
331 Silke, A. (2004). Courage in dark places: Reflections on terrorist psychology. *Social Research, 71(1)*, 177-199.
332 Ibid.
333 Ibid.
334 Ibid.

law enforcement, many people dismiss those who have committed the most heinous crimes as being "sick." In some cases, of course, these statements have some validity. However, many, like these Islamic terrorists, are not sick by any means. They are just downright evil!

Recent studies have shown terrorists to be very much in control of their psychological faculties when they commit these acts of mass murder and destruction. In fact, modern research has shown that terrorists are, to a much higher degree, more mentally stable than the average violent sociopath.[335]

One becomes a terrorist by beginning a slow gradual process. Socialization is the initial issue of how one assumes the identity of a terrorist. Any society can improperly influence an individual to believe that the world is evil and wants to suppress them. In many cases, of course, there are very significant reasons and causes for such a grievance. These individuals bond and identify with other individuals or groups that share the same perceptions. These established groups of individuals are the basis for creating full-fledged terrorists.[336]

Conclusion

On a final personal note (and I will be as objective as possible), the sources I used to write this chapter were very informative on the subject matter. However, it appears to me that most of these "objective" sources fail to mention where the nucleus of Islamic terrorism resides. I disagree with many who claim that it is based on peer influence and group pressure, but I do agree that it is somewhat relative. These Islamic terrorists are not courageous warriors that many commentators (particularly the ones who lean towards the left) claim them to be. They sacrifice their own lives for their own selfish gain. This behavior is, in my opinion, relative to the profile of the common criminal (which many would disagree). They are brainwashed into thinking that if they die for the Islamic movement, they will inherit eternal life and riches in heaven along with numerous spiritual wives. This comprises the spoils of their heinous criminal activity, and they do not care who or how many innocent people they kill in the process. Again, this behavior is much like the common violent criminal who couldn't care less who he injures or kills as long as he obtains some form of monetary gain.

---

335 Ibid.
336 Ibid.

CHAPTER 16
ABORTION CLINIC BOMBINGS AND TERRORISM

Kevin D. Scott, MBA, MA

Introduction

In this chapter, I discuss and describe the various aspects of terrorist attacks on abortion clinics and the people who run them. I also examine the mental reasoning and motivation of those responsible for carrying out such attacks as well as those that support these actions. In addition, I discuss the motivations and reasoning of those who are in favor of abortion and those who are very adamant about committing criminal and terrorist action on those who merely oppose the act of abortion.

Aspects of Terrorist Attacks on Abortion Clinics

Violent protests resulting in arson attacks, firebombing, and vandalism began in the 1970s in the United States. Both then and now the attacks seem to be perpetrated by the hands of religiously motivated individuals acting on their own terms and ethical standards. In recent cases that involved the killing and attempted murder of abortion providers in the United States as well other countries, many people appear to display sympathy for the perpetrators in these acts of terror.[337] During the 1980s, our country has observed nearly 40 terrorist bombings of abortion clinics in certain states. However, the 1990s brought new trends and practices. Individual workers were attacked, arson and bombing numbers have risen, and in some instances, religious fanatics have even killed some abortion providers.[338]

The escalation of violent attacks upon abortion clinics and their providers in the United States are being inflicted by the "leaders of the Religious Right." Some advocates of the Religious Right are, without doubt, inciting these acts of terror to stop the horrible act of murdering the unborn. The religious

---

337 Robinson, B. A. (2004). Violence & harassment at U.S. abortion clinics. Retrieved April 26, 2006, from http://www.religioustolerance.org/abo_viol.htm.

338 White, J. R. (2002). *Terrorism: An introduction.* Belmont, CA: Thomson Learning Inc., p. 217-218.

Right justifies their actions as doing God's will.[339] Although I am a pro-life advocate, I condemn these actions, the Bible teaches that we SHALL obey the laws of the land and fighting this way compromises God's will and breaks the law. These fanatics need to fight these atrocities not by using violence and murder because that, of course, does nothing for the cause. They must pursue other peaceful, legal, and political means as way to combat this serious issue.

There is no simple way to resolve this issue. Both sides believe that they are morally correct. The pro-abortion side feels that the Constitution defends this right. On the other hand, the pro-lifers feel that this is an act of murder, and that they are on the side of God. It does not matter which side dominates, the abortion issue represents a political issue by which both sides are viewed by the other as being extreme. In turn, this is a "perfect example of terrorism."[340]

In recent years, the term "anti-abortion has been used to label people and groups who inflict terrorist actions including murder to meet their political agendas. These extremist groups are vastly different from the majority of the pro-life movement that condemns violence and terrorist acts upon persons and property.[341] *The Freedom Writer* quoted Franky Schaeffer, son of the late Christian philosopher, Francis Schaeffer, in his book entitled *Bad News for Modern Man* (1984) as stating "abortion clinics must be picketed nonstop. Doctors who wish to murder the innocent must be harassed and driven from our communities."[342] I have no problem with this type of action.

Robinson stated that both the pro-life and anti-abortion activist movements are, in fact, driven by one concept, which is that "human personhood begins at the instant of conception."[343] Given this rationale, a newly fertilized ovum, an embryo, or "fetus" (which is a term used pro-abortion advocates to de-humanize a living human) should be granted the same rights, privileges, and protections as a child or an adult. Many people (myself included) view abortion clinics as the ethical equivalent of a Nazi death camp. The only difference is at least the Nazis had the intestinal fortitude to look at their victims when they murdered them. On the other hand, many pro-abortion

---

339 Anonymous (March, 1995). *The Freedom Writer*, p. 1. Retrieved April 26, 2006 from http://www.publiceye.org/ifas/fw/9503/10years.html.

340 White, J. R. (2002). *Terrorism: An introduction*. Belmont, CA: Thomson Learning Inc., p. 218.

341 Robinson, B. A. (2004). Violence & harassment at U.S. abortion clinics. Retrieved April 26, 2006, from http://www.religioustolerance.org/abo_viol.htm.

342 Anonymous (March, 1995). *The Freedom Writer*, p. 1. Retrieved April 26, 2006 from http://www.publiceye.org/ifas/fw/9503/10years.html.

343 Robinson, B. A. (2004). Violence & harassment at U.S. abortion clinics, p. 1. Retrieved April 26, 2006, from http://www.religioustolerance.org/abo_viol.htm.

advocates don't even acknowledge the committed atrocities. Robinson added that the pro-abortion people basically advocate that the fetus (there's that word again) becomes human further on in gestation, when it loses its neck structures (which appear like gill slits), and when it (or I should say he or she) begins to look human (Where does one draw the line?). By this viewpoint, pro-abortion advocates feel that it is within a woman's right either to seek an abortion or to keep the child. [344] Do you realize that the most dangerous place for an unborn child today is in his or her mother's womb? Scary, isn't it?

Reasoning and Motivation of Attackers and Supporters

The Freedom Writer stated that Schaeffer and attorney John Whitehead co-founded the Rutherford Institute. This organization teaches that American law should always be based on and filtered through Biblical scriptures and that "we should obey God, rather than man." The Rutherford Institute is regarded as the "legal arm of ultra-right Christian groups and organizations nationwide." However, in a televised debate with Skip Porteous, the "Reverend Jerry Falwell denied that the Moral Majority was in anyway affiliated with the Rutherford Institute. *The Freedom Writer* added that, however, in May 1983 and January 1985, the *Moral Majority Report* featured several articles about the Rutherford Institute.[345]

The Freedom Writer further stated that in Whitehead's book, *The Second American Revolution* (1982), he states, "Like it or not, the church is at war." He focused an entire chapter on the authorization of fellow Christians using physical force or terrorist tactics to combat the ungodly doings of abortionists. He further stated in his book that any law that contradicts the scriptures must be disobeyed. Additionally, the Religious Right points to certain verses in the Bible to support their anti-abortion agenda and assures themselves that abortion is against God's will.[346]

I agree with this statement above, however, again, the Bible also teaches that we must obey the laws of the land. Picketing, protesting, and most importantly, voting are ways to combat the abortionists. Bombing and murder only worsens the movement to stop abortion … abortions that we pay for with our tax dollars! Not to get too far off track, but let me set the stage and ask this question: I'm from California. Some months ago, we had a big issue here with the American Medical Association (AMA) not supporting the execution of a man named Morales who had murdered two women with

---

344 Ibid.

345 Anonymous (March, 1995). *The Freedom Writer*, p. 1. Retrieved April 26, 2006 from http://www.publiceye.org/ifas/fw/9503/10years.html.

346 Ibid.

an axe-hammer. Clearly, this guy deserved to die by execution as he was legally tried and convicted for those heinous crimes. A new law was passed and implemented because lethal injection was thought to possibly cause some "discomfort" for the condemned, and a medical doctor must be present to assure that the procedure "runs smoothly." The AMA stated that it was unethical and against their core values to participate in such an ordeal. Okay, fine. But why, then, do they allow and perform 3,000 abortions a day if they are now so high and mighty? I just don't get it. Anyway, that's something to think about.

The Freedom Writer further stated that many followers of the Religious Right are convinced that abortion is in fact murder. They are encouraged to take any steps necessary to stop acts of terror upon the unborn. This should be done even if they themselves must use terrorist tactics as well … even to the point of committing murder. In the book, *The Second American Revolution*, alternate means of terrorist action are offered. These alternatives include (1) vocal protest to unbiblical laws, (2) use of sympathetic politicians to mediate on behalf of the concerns of the Right, (3) leaving the country, which is of course out of the question, and (4) as a last resort, the use of physical force "in the defensive posture." The defensive posture, according to *The Freedom Writer*, is compared to the American Revolution, which Whitehead states was in no way a revolution, only a defense from an invading country. In addition, he states, he and other followers are enlisted in the defense of an invasion of secular humanists. Many of these people who were taken into custody and charged for terrorist bombings on abortion clinics claim that they are the defenders of the unborn. According to the writings in the book titled *The Second American Revolution*, these actions are justified and encouraged because all other avenues were met with negative results.[347]

Additionally, *The Freedom Writer* stated that although no one has come out and publicly stated "Let's go out and terrorize abortion clinics," the leadership of the Religious Right is condoning these attacks, and these same leaders, in turn, have created a problem that they are and will no longer be able to control.[348]

Statistics of Both Sides of the Issue

Robinson stated that California leads the country in violence and criminal activity. The California Senate released a report showing that abortion clinics in that state were bombed, torched, and destroyed more times than any other state in the United States: 30 incidences out of 224 crimes across the nation.

347 Ibid.
348 Ibid.

He added that the majority of the clinics responding to the survey reported terrorist activity in the form of threats, assaults, vandalism, blockades, and other crimes from 1995 to 2000. In addition, 30 percent stated that their employees were "stalked, harassed, threatened, and otherwise targeted at their homes or in other places away from clinics and medical offices." Robinson further added that other states with an excess number of attacks include: Florida with 19, Texas with 14, and New York with 9.[349]

Now I think it is important to take a different viewpoint and analyze this issue from a different perspective. A report of The Life Research Institute stated that there has been, in fact, far less violence and terrorist activity inflicted by pro-lifers toward pro-abortionists than vice versa. The study also showed more in the form of "police violence" (I call it police action) towards the pro-life side as opposed to the pro-abortion side. The report further states that in order to comprehend the aspect of the pro-abortion industry, we need to understand their definition of the word *violence*. The Life Research Institute states that "the abortion industry has defined the term for the media and for you." Now, in many instances, the abortion industry defines even legal, peaceful, constitutionally-protected praying and picketing as *violence*. They also manipulate statistics in order to fabricate and multiply the numbers of alleged incidents. The Life Research Institute gave a pro-abortionist's example of "a legal, peaceful, constitutionally-protected picket" by 100 pro-lifers will be counted as 100 acts of violence … 100 for the pro-lifers, one for the clinic, and one for the incident. The table below shows verbatim the report's findings on the violence between the two groups.[350]

Violence Between Two Groups	No. Listed	No. Guilty
Incidents by pro-life against pro-abortion	164	12
Incidents by pro-abortion against pro-life	218	15
Incidents by police against pro-abortion	0	0
Incidents by police against pro-life	29	11
Total	**411**	**38**

---

349 Robinson, B. A. (2004). Violence & harassment at U.S. abortion clinics, p. 1. Retrieved April 26, 2006, from http://www.religioustolerance.org/abo_viol.htm.

350 Anonymous (1995). Abortion-Related Violence and Alleged Violence: An Investigative Report by The Life Research Institute. The Life Research Institute. Retrieved April 26, 2006, from http://www.ewtn.com/library/PROLIFE/VIO-LENCE.TXT.

The Life Research Institute further stated that, basically, in this report, a guilty verdict comes from a court of law, not from the bias of the Life Research Institute. This obviously makes the pro-abortion movement appear to be a lot more innocent than otherwise. The Life Research Institute has examined a large number of videotapes showing obvious pro-abortion guilt, but has decided, for objectivity, not to label pro-abortion guilt outside of either court decisions or documented confessions.[351]

The Life Research Institute also lists the following findings, which I list verbatim:[352]

1. There have been more bombings of religious facilities than all types of medical facilities combined.
2. Bombings and attempted bombings of any type of medical facility have been rare.
3. There have been 230 times as many bombings against other industries, homes, and other buildings.
4. Only thirty-five one-thousandth of one percent of all US arsons can be attributed to pro-life.
5. Only one one-thousandth of one percent of all homicides can be attributed to pro-life.
6. The Bureau of Alcohol, Tobacco, and Firearms have never connected any act of violence to any pro-life organization.
7. The Federal Bureau of Investigation does not list any pro-life organization as terrorist.
8. There are many very significant reasons for the abortion industry to deceive the public.
9. The abortion industry has been unwilling and/or unable to substantiate their accusations against pro-life.
10. There are many reasons for violence against abortion facilities other than pro-life activism.
11. The media rarely portrays violence by pro-abortion, but rarely doesn't portray violence by pro-life.

Conclusion

As a final note, today's society is numb to the idea of taking violent action against practices and certain ethical values whether it be the medical procedure of killing unborn human beings or the bombing and murder of those who provide these services. History shows that notable and extreme responses to

351 Ibid.
352 Ibid.

issues disagreeable to some may cause society to take note, conceptualize, and re-evaluate previously held positions on issues such as the pro-abortion vs. pro-life movements.

CHAPTER 17
KU KLUX KLAN: THE MOST NOTORIOUS AMERICAN TERRORIST ORGANIZATION

Kevin D. Scott, MBA, MA

Introduction

In this chapter, I discuss and describe in detail the origins and components of the terror organization known as the Ku Klux Klan (KKK). I discuss its history and why and how it was formulated. I further discuss and describe how they, as a group, carried out terrorist attacks among black and other various ethnic groups and religious minorities. In addition, I discuss the modern KKK and how they operate in today's world.

Origins and Components of the Ku Klux Klan

An article titled "The Ku Klux Klan: Past and Present" by Johanna Jarvinen stated that the United States of America is seen as a melting pot of various races and cultures. At the beginning of the 16th century, the first Native Americans were introduced to the Spanish, Dutch, French, and English cultures when they colonized the New World. With this, the slave trade was also introduced at about the year 1619 when cotton production came about and intense, hard labor was essential for the survival and prosperity of Southern plantations. The slave population consisted of blacks that were a new race among European whites, and they were regarded as less human and inferior to their white counterparts. The black slaves were unable to read or write and were forbidden to learn. In the initial years of slavery, the blacks did not understand the French or English languages of the "civilized nations."[353]

Up until the civil war, blacks and whites lived together in a society of slavery. After the South lost the war, slavery was outlawed and current slaves were freed. At this turning point, society began to change rapidly. The South's economy had declined substantially and opportunities for work were slim at

---

353 Jarvinen, J. (2002). The Ku Klux Klan: Past and present, pp. 1-9. Retrieved February 15, 2006, from http://www.uta.fi/-jj73566/KKK.html.

best. As a result of this recession, both secret societies and political groups were formed ... one of those being the infamous Ku Klux Klan (KKK).[354]

The article titled "A hundred years of terror," prepared by the Southern Poverty Law Center, stated that the Ku Klux Klan's violent history evolved from the resentment and hatred that brewed up inside many white Southerners following the disastrous end of the civil war. The freed slaves, although freed from the bondage of slavery, were now faced with gross discrimination, belittlement, and a wide array of racism and terrorist attacks from white supremacy groups such as the KKK. The KKK had gained and diminished in power and numbers over time. However, it still exists and operates today in a much moderate capacity.[355]

Jarvinen stated that during the 1800s, America experienced an evolution of change that would affect American history forever. After the signing of the Declaration of Independence and the end of the Revolutionary War, all people were considered and made equal to one another. However, in reality, this declaration only pertained to white men. Women, children, and most definitely slaves were excluded from this 18th century declaration of equality. It was acceptable and even encouraged that these equal men of European descent keep and harbor slaves, particularly in the South, where free labor in the cotton fields was an essential part of Southern living.[356]

In the 19th century, the North and South began to draw apart from each other. The South embraced the concept of chivalry, proclaiming that they were the far superior half of the nation. The South boasted that they had the most beautiful women, most well mannered and distinguished gentlemen, and a lifestyle that was geared to a much slower, more enjoyable pace. On the other hand, their Northern counterparts encompassed a more fast-paced, industrial style of living. At this time, European migrants began to settle in the Midwest and the West, and favor among them accumulated towards the North.[357]

The Northern view towards slavery began to change. The North had no need for slavery on their farms. They were concerned for the treatment of slaves and began to acknowledge the absence of equality. On the contrary, the Southern states were angered at the North for their attitudes on slavery mainly because this was a means for their economical survival and livelihood.

---

354 Ibid.

355 Southern Poverty Law Center (2001). A hundred years of terror, pp.1-2 and 6-9. Retrieved February 15, 2006, from http://www.iupui.edu/-aao/kkk.html.

356 Jarvinen, J. (2002). The Ku Klux Klan: Past and present, pp. 1-9. Retrieved February 15, 2006, from http://www.uta.fi/-jj73566/KKK.html.

357 Ibid.

This, in turn, made the South ever more determined to separate from the North and maintain and promote slavery among their society.[358]

In 1860, Abraham Lincoln, a well-known opponent of slavery, was elected President of the United States. The Southern states then rebelled against the Union and formed the Confederacy. Jefferson Davis (an actual descendent of mine) was elected as the President of the Confederate States of America. The Union opposed this move and demanded that the Confederate disperse and withdraw their resignation. The South declined their resignation, which led the divided country to civil war in 1861. The South rejoiced in several initial battle victories but lost the war after suffering tremendous losses, which forced the South to surrender. As a result, slavery was outlawed and the Union was restored.[359]

After the war, the South did not like the readjustment to daily living that they were forced to undertake. Slavery was abolished, thus liberating the slaves, even the ones who were "creatures of habit" who preferred the old way of living. The plantation owners were also required by law to pay former slaves the going wage for their work and services. In addition, the South was in psychological and financial turmoil. Resentment and spiteful feelings fostered and grew within the defeated confederacy and secret clubs and societies formed … one of which was the infamous KKK.[360]

This was the environment that the KKK was formed and born into. Many veterans of the confederacy were bitter that they had lost the war and were infuriated at the new way of life with which they were faced. The freed slaves began growing in number, which fueled the anger and spite among some of their previous owners. This condition led to an extremely hostile living environment.[361] The Southern Poverty Law Center stated that the North's view of the Klan was that they were a bunch of unrepentant confederates trying to commit acts of terrorism and to accomplish what they were unable to do on the battlefield. However, this view did not explain why the Klan catered toward the South. However, there is little doubt that many veterans of the confederacy laid down their rebel gray after the war and donned the white hoods and sheets of the KKK.[362]

The origin of the Klan, as explained by The Southern Poverty Law Center, was a very well-guarded secret that continued for years.[363] Jarvinen

---

358 Ibid.
359 Ibid.
360 Ibid.
361 Ibid.
362 Southern Poverty Law Center (2001). A hundred years of terror, pp.1-2 and 6-9. Retrieved February 15, 2006, from http://www.iupui.edu/-aao/kkk.html.
363 Ibid.

stated that the Klan's history could be divided into three separate time periods beginning from the 1860s to our present day. During these time periods, the Klan responded to different types of situations, and their definition of the "enemy" evolved considerably.[364]

The name of the KKK most likely came from the Greek *Kuklos* or *Kyklos*, which translates into "a circle." Others assumed that the "Ku Klux" originated from the sound of an old fashioned firearm being cocked. The word "Klan" was added to finish the alliteration, which was derived from the Scottish term for family, "a clan."[365]

History of the KKK

With regards to the first Klan, the exact moment of its birth is sketchy at best. However, it is fairly certain that the KKK was founded in the small town of Pulaski, Tennessee. The people of Pulaski were predominately of Scottish heritage, and they were extremely proud of their ancestry. In many cases, this sense of pride was so revered and taken to heart that images of Rob Roy and Blind Harry were always a stone's throw away. The Klan was formed by six confederate veterans (all of which were in their 20s) between Christmas 1865 and June 1866. These six confederate veterans also designed and formulated the uniform of the Klansman which consisted of a white robe and a white hat/hood that covered the head and face to conceal the Klansman's identity (there were eye holes made into the hood so that the individual could see). The initial purpose of the Klan was not for political or racist/terrorist acts but only to play tricks and have fun with the citizens living among them.[366]

The initial birth of the Klan was modest at best. In order to recruit and lure citizens into their secret society, they incorporated a little mystique into their rituals. They required all new members to take an oath of secrecy to keep the intentions and agenda of the Klan a secret. Public declarations of allegiance to the Klan were also forbidden as well as exposing other members of the Klan to the general public. The Klan members were all required to attend weekly meetings in full Klan dress. This resulted in convincing many members of the black community that these Klansmen were actually ghosts of slain Confederate soldiers.[367]

As the Klan's membership began to grow, new "dens" formulated and assumed the name of the KKK. This membership then expanded first though

364 Jarvinen, J. (2002). The Ku Klux Klan: Past and present, pp. 1-9. Retrieved February 15, 2006, from http://www.uta.fi/-jj73566/KKK.html.

365 Ibid.

366 Ibid.

367 Ibid.

the states of Tennessee, Alabama, and Mississippi and then to Georgia, the Carolinas, Florida, and certain areas of Arkansas. As the KKK grew, there was a dire need for organization and management. In turn, sections and sub-sections were formed. The region in which the Klan was most heavily populated was known as "The Invisible Empire," which was divided into realms. Each realm corresponded with the states and each realm was then divided into another sub category termed "dominions." The dominions corresponded with congressional districts. Each dominion was divided into provinces that corresponded with the local counties. Finally, each province was broken down into "dens." A former Confederate general gave the title of the leader or "Grand Wizard" as Nathan Bedford Forrest. This was by no means a moral gentleman as he acquired the moniker from his Union counterparts as "a foul fiend in human shape."[368]

Terrorist Acts of the KKK

It was not long before the simple pranks of the Klan turned into vicious attacks of liberated slaves, former Union members, and allies. The Klan terrorized, threatened, exiled, whipped, shot, stabbed, mutilated, and lynched many of its victims. They were successful in driving out many of their Northern schoolteachers, shopkeepers, and politicians. They gave special attention to the prosperous former black slaves, especially the ones who spoke out against the lack of equality that they were being denied. The Klan consisted of a fairly innocent group of men that turned into a gang of angry, bloodthirsty terrorists that focused their rage primarily on the terrified black population.[369]

By 1870, the Klan was well known throughout the entire country and, for the most part, in a despicable light. Most of the atrocities committed by the Klan were done in secrecy. However, for the most part, they kept their violent actions out of the public eye. They also controlled the politicians in their areas and were able to influence the way laws were passed, which favored the Klan's agenda. However, the government forced General Nathan Forrest to disband his organization during the early to mid 1870's because of the numerous criminal acts the various sub-groups or "Klaverns" had administered. Prior to this, the Congressional Acts of 1871 and 1873 failed to dismantle the Klan even though federal troops were activated to combat the Klan. The disbandment of the original Klan occurred in 1876-1877 although Northern historians believed that it happened sometime in 1873.[370]

368 Ibid.
369 Ibid.
370 Ibid.

173

Memories of the Klan's grip on the South and the atrocities it inflicted were all but forgotten by many white Southerners who embraced their ideals.[371] The Klan was inactive for a while however sparse incidents throughout the South were still taking place. In 1915, William J. Simmons revived the Klan and established the new, revamped organization. He adopted the ideals of the Klan and took them to heart. He was also the first person to document the rituals and ceremonies in their entirety ... incorporating the majority of codes of other various fraternal orders.[372]

William J. Simmons and his two associates, Edward Young Clarke and Mrs. Elizabeth Tyler, formulated a plan to attract and recruit additional members to the new and revived Klan. They also formed a partnership with the Southern Publicity Association. The Klan was extremely successful with their recruiting of new members that, by 1921, they boasted of over 100,000 recorded members. The Klan was constantly on the move while taking action against blacks. In addition, they established a list of enemies, which included Jews, adulterers, child molesters, drug dealers, and liberals. They spread their venom throughout the country. Many Southern Protestant churches heavily supported them.[373]

During the 1920s, the Klan flourished, organized many marches, gave public speeches, and held open recruitment for aspiring members. The Klan catered to many US citizens as many of those citizens experienced growing concern with the influx of racial minorities and other undesirable people. The Klan viewed this immigration as an invasion and a threat by these other cultures and felt that it was up to them to protect their White Anglo-Saxon Protestant (WASP) birthright and survival.[374]

In 1923, Hiram W. Evans replaced Simmons, thereby stripping him of his position of authority and power. Simmons, however, did not want to give up his seat. He even dragged the Klan through several lawsuits, accusing them of conspiracy, and publicly denouncing Evans for terminating his position. Simmons and his associate, Clarke, even went so far as to establish other similar organizations up until Evans banished them altogether from the Klan in 1924. The damage inflicted, however, was sufficient enough to convince the senior Klansmen not to trust the Klan's new agenda.[375]

---

371 Southern Poverty Law Center (2001). A hundred years of terror, pp.1-2 and 6-9. Retrieved February 15, 2006, from http://www.iupui.edu/-aao/kkk.html.

372 Jarvinen, J. (2002). The Ku Klux Klan: Past and present, pp. 1-9. Retrieved February 15, 2006, from http://www.uta.fi/-jj73566/KKK.html.

373 Ibid.

374 Ibid.

375 Ibid.

The Klan began to fade out during the late 1920s. Membership drastically plunged from 100,000 members to 35,000 members by the year 1930.[376] Although this drop in the Klan's membership was severe, it was not publicly acknowledged until 1944. The reason this occurred was probably due to the political change that the Klan was undergoing along with many other internal conflicts within the organization.[377]

The Klan once again rose to power in the late 1950s with even more firepower than ever before. After the Supreme Court decision against public school segregation was implemented in 1954, Southern attitudes were fueled with rage. The Invisible Empire formed a new impetus, and a call for action was imminent. A vast majority of Southerners were outraged at this decision. Of course, the Klan saw this opportunity and exploited it. New members were recruited as the distain for black Americans flourished among many white Southerners.[378]

The Klan also heavily targeted alleged communists, as the McCarthy trials during the late 1940s and 1950s left a bad impression on the nation. The Klan was committed to gutting this cancer out of American society at all costs.[379]

This new KKK organizational realm was extremely political and acted in response to governmental decisions. It was extremely opposed to the Civil Rights Movement and abhorred Martin Luther King. However, the Klan lacked control over the organization that led to the various acts of violence and criminal activity.[380]

Once again, the Klan began to lose its power as they found it difficult to maintain political grounds for their agenda. Times were also changing as the Civil Rights Movement became accepted among Americans and terrorizing blacks became pointless. Even the majority of the Southerners were weary of the Klan's arbitrary cause. In times of crisis, the Klan may have been able to validate its agenda. However, now, the United States came together, the economic situation was positive, and, therefore, the Klan lost its luster and gradually faded in popularity and power.[381]

---

376 Southern Poverty Law Center (2001). A hundred years of terror, pp.1-2 and 6-9. Retrieved February 15, 2006, from http://www.iupui.edu/-aao/kkk.html.

377 Jarvinen, J. (2002). The Ku Klux Klan: Past and present, pp. 1-9. Retrieved February 15, 2006, from http://www.uta.fi/-jj73566/KKK.html.

378 Ibid.

379 Ibid.

380 Ibid.

381 Ibid.

The Modern Day KKK

The Klan is very much alive and operating today, always seeking new members, showing pride in its heritage and legacy, and striving to keep the white race pure. The dens are scattered pretty much throughout the Southern states. However, a few dens are sporadically located in the Northern, Midwestern, and Western states.[382]

The violent Klan of the 1960s appears to have evolved into a secret society that abides by strict rules, regulations, and honor codes. The Klansmen now are focused on protecting whites and their interpretation of Christianity. Members state that they have all the right to proclaim white power just as blacks have the right to show pride in their heritage. Most of the Klan websites attempt to be neutral. The organization is still, of course, racist. However, prior to allowing researchers to access, they warn that some of the information which appears later on in their web pages may be disturbing.[383]

Today, the Klan's main realm of action is to participate in public protests, rallies, and Internet shows.[384] The Klan also appears to be led by many who I refer to as "pseudo-religious teachers" (and we have a lot of those around I might add), such as the Rev. Jeffery L. Belly who represents the American Knights of the Ku Klux Klan, Pastor Thomas Robb who represents the Knights Party, and let's not forget the Rev. John Howard who represents the International Knights of the Ku Klux Klan. White stated that religion, as in many other terrorist organizations, plays a significant role in the processes of terrorism within the Klan. In addition, the Klan enlists itself as an instrument to purify the white race.[385] Jarvinen wrote that, in order to justify their agenda, the Klan blames the high crime rates and problems in society on the ethnic minorities ... particularly the blacks. In addition, the Klan offers many solutions on how they can put an end to these "problems."[386]

The new Klan desires to educate society on the origin and symbolism of burning crosses. They state that burning crosses is a reflection of the old Scottish tradition. They further state that they condemn burning crosses as an act of showing racism.[387]

---

382 Ibid.

383 Ibid.

384 Ibid.

385 White, J. R. (2002). *Terrorism: An Introduction*. Belmont, CA: Thompson Learning Inc. , p. 7

386 Jarvinen, J. (2002). The Ku Klux Klan: Past and present, pp. 1-9. Retrieved February 15, 2006, from http://www.uta.fi/-jj73566/KKK.html.

387 Ibid.

The KKK found its way over to Europe. The European Klan follows the same ideals of its American predecessors. Their areas of power lie in Sweden, Germany, Austria, France, and the Netherlands. These countries also encompass the majority of immigrants that keeps the European Klan (European White Knights) very busy. The European Klan is predominately partnered with neo-Nazism and Le Front National, all of which are right-wing extremist organizations.[388]

The Ku Klux Klan is very alive and active today. However, it does not carry out its violent criminal acts … the acts of its past. It has spread to parts of the world fostering its core values, however, in a much more "civilized" (if you will), peaceful manner.[389]

Conclusion

In conclusion, the Klan in the United States has evolved significantly since its birth after the Civil War. It began as a secret social club. However, it rapidly grew into a violent and racist secret society that its six founding fathers would probably not have wanted. The Ku Klux Klan is now responsible for terrorizing blacks and other racial and social minorities during its 140-year existence. The Klan still uses intimidation as its main factor when organizing marches and protests. The crosses still continue to burn, but with different connotation. However, it does not in any way promote the safety and well-being of ethnic and social minorities. Although the Klan's beliefs and ideals are resented for the most part in the United States, they are still allowed to exist and operate. American law forbids hate crimes and any sort of criminal activity; however, it defends the rights of those who lawfully organize and rally. Opinions and beliefs of those affiliated with any racist organization, no matter how disturbing they may be, will always enjoy the protections of American law.[390]

---

388 Ibid.
389 Ibid.
390 Ibid.

CHAPTER 18
AL-QAEDA AS A THREAT

Brice A. Gyurisko, Sr., MPA

The emergence of al-Qaeda came during the Soviet occupation of Afghanistan in the late 1970s. Osama bin Laden formed an alliance with the Taliban, an Islamic fundamentalist group, which brought back Sharia or Islamic law to Afghanistan after the Soviets were defeated and departed. This chapter provides historical ties to Islamic fundamentalism along with al-Qaeda organizational structure. A description is provided on how al-Qaeda received financial support including links to organized crime, which further highlight al-Qaeda as a threat to the United States and the West.

Introduction

The purpose of this chapter is to trace the emergence of al-Qaeda as a threat to Western society. The outcomes of this chapter construct the history of al-Qaeda and formulate how al-Qaeda came to rely upon the Taliban in Afghanistan. Outcomes explain how and why al-Qaeda now has contacts with international criminal organizations such as Albanian organized crime.

In introducing the topic of al-Qaeda being a threat to the US and Western society, Aldrich states that "Al-Qaeda is evidently a[n] ... organization ... dedicated to advancing certain political and religious objectives by means of terrorist acts directed against the United States and other, largely Western nations."[391] This short history of al-Qaeda includes ideology and provides reasoning of why al-Qaeda displays animosity towards and commits terrorist acts against the West.

Historical and Ideological Beginnings

Al-Qaeda's ideological beginnings started in the late 19th century when Egypt modernized and reformed its society. A movement was established

---

391 Aldrich, G. (2002). The Taliban, al-Qaeda, and the determination of illegal combatants. *The American Journal of International Law, 96(4)*, 891-898. Retrieved August 13, 2008, from Research Library database.

against modern reforms and became known as *Salafism*, which was allegedly practiced by uncorrupted Muslim predecessors. The Salafist movement idealized an uncorrupted religious community of simplified theology and rites and has been ongoing during the last century. The Salafist movement was borne from the reaction of Muslims to the Ottoman Empire and the growing dominance of the West in politics, science, and culture. A Muslim rationalist named Jamal ad-Din Al-Afghani in the late 1800s spread the ideas in Egypt that Muslim defeats at the hands of the West were due to the corruption of Islam. Consequently, this belief developed into the Salafism movement providing the seeds of discontent towards the West.

Another reformer, a student of Al-Afghani, was Muhammed 'Abduh who became Grand Mufti of Egypt in the late 1800s. Muhammed 'Abduh believed in a return to earlier Islamic fundamentalism, which was the forerunner of today's al-Qaeda. In the early 1900s, one of the first modern Islamic political movements was formed in Egypt call the Muslim Brotherhood. During that same period, *Wahabism*, which is a puritanical Sunni sect, rose and influenced the Sunni world. It was on the Arabian Peninsula and grew as oil and power came to the Saudis in the late 1960 and 1970s.

Sayyid Qutb continued the Salafist movement as a member of the Muslim Brotherhood. One of Qutb's significant contributions is that he argued to continue the movement to Islamic fundamentalism even if it meant killing Muslims. During the 1970s, Qutb's message was spread by Muhammad Abd al-Salam Faraj, a self-taught theologian, who was involved in killing Egyptian president Anwar Sadat. Faraj wrote extensively and his manifesto, *The Neglected Duty*, called for attacks against Israel, the United States, and other Western nations seen as interfering with the Muslim world.[392]

The guerrilla war against the Soviet Union in Afghanistan became a main catalyst for revolutionary *Salafist* thinking. During this period, an Egyptian physician named Ayman al-Zawahiri, who wrote extensively and became involved with Osama bin Laden in Pakistan, influenced many Arabs. Both Zawahiri and bin Laden believe in the establishment of a genuine Muslim state, which became a major goal of al-Qaeda. Zawahiri's belief is highlighted by the following quote:[393]

> *The jihad movement must...make room for the Muslim nation to participate with it in the jihad for the sake of empowerment... The one slogan that has been well understood by the nation and to which it has*

---

392 Henzel, C. (2005). The origins of al-Qaeda's ideology: Implications for US strategy. *Parameters, 35(1)*, 69-80. Retrieved August 13, 2008, from Research Library database.

393 Ibid., p. 76.

been responding for the past 50 years is the call for jihad against Israel...
[Striking at the United States would force the Americans to] personally
wage battle against the Muslims, which means that the battle will turn
into a clear-cut jihad against the infidels.

The above quote highlights that fact that al-Qaeda and the Salafist movement may not expect to defeat the United States or the West per se, but intend on uniting the different regimes of the Muslim world. "Thus al-Qaeda's immediate goal is not to destroy Israel or even drive the United States out of the Middle East; [but] rather, it is to orient the nation."[394]

The name "al-Qaeda" translates as "the base" in Arabic. As a base, al-Qaeda's evolution came mainly through the fight against the Soviets in Afghanistan and al-Qaeda's relationship with the Taliban. The term Taliban comes from the schools in Afghanistan, which were called *talibs* under the leadership of Mullah Mohammed Omar, thus becoming the Taliban. Mullah Omar was an Islamic cleric and scholar as well as a hero of the war between Afghanistan and the Soviet Union. Much unrest and lawlessness occurred after the war with the Soviets. Under Omar's leadership, the Taliban became a major power in the region. The Taliban unified the provinces and returned Afghanistan to Islamic law. The conditions in Afghanistan were prime for Osama bin Laden and his Islamic fundamentalist views.[395]

Al-Qaeda and the Taliban

The al-Qaeda link to the Taliban became firmly embedded in Afghanistan with the cooperation and ideological viewpoints of Mullah Omar and Osama bin Laden. "From the time of his arrival, bin Laden was treated as an honored guest by the Taliban. According to Islamic journalist Abu Abdul Aziz al-Afghani, the student soldiers bowed before bin Laden whenever he appeared in public."[396] Osama bin Laden's financial and material support for the Taliban and the more fundamentalist view popular with bin Laden and the Taliban leadership solidified the Taliban in Afghanistan as a main location for terrorists and a transit point for terrorist networks.[397]

---

394 Ibid., p. 77.

395 Williams, P. (2005). *The al-Qaeda connection: International terrorism, organized crime, and the coming apocalypse.* Amherst, New York: Prometheus Books, pp. 45-50.

396 Ibid., p. 50.

397 Combs, C. (2006). *Terrorism in the twenty-first century (4th ed.).* Upper Saddle River, NJ: Pearson Prentice Hall, p. 96.

Al-Qaeda Unites Muslim Sects

Al-Qaeda was created to fight the Soviets in Afghanistan. As the war ended, al-Qaeda turned into an organization that began to train individuals in their home countries to fight against those opposed to Islamic ideology. Unique in this approach is the attempt of al-Qaeda's ideology to unite all Muslims from their different sects for a jihad against occupied Islamic lands. Previous to al-Qaeda and the influence of bin Laden, various Muslim sects stayed within their respective region. For example, Hizbollah recruited only Lebanese, the Armed Islamic Group only Algerians, and the Egyptian Islamic Jihad only Egyptians. Osama bin Laden succeeded in creating a multinational organization based on the idea of uniting Muslim fundamentalists and extremists by declaring to all the Muslims of the world to declare a jihad against the Judeo-Christian alliance occupying Islamic sacred ground in Palestine and the Arabian Peninsula.[398]

Organizational Structure

In terms of organizational structure of al-Qaeda, the organization and infrastructure differs from other terrorist organizations and guerrilla groups. Al-Qaeda is neither a single group nor a coalition of groups. Al-Qaeda is "… comprised [of] a core base or bases in Afghanistan, satellite terrorist cells worldwide, a conglomerate of Islamic political parties, and other largely independent terrorist groups that it draws on for offensive actions and other responsibilities."[399]

Despite over 100 suspected al-Qaeda activists arrested in North America and Europe in the six months after the 9/11 attacks, al-Qaeda has produced new cells and managed to sustain many of the older cells. Radical Muslims previously lacked organization, which al-Qaeda has built and sustained amid secrecy. The al-Qaeda structure enables it to provide direct and indirect control over a force that is global. By issuing periodic announcements, speeches, and writings, Osama bin Laden indoctrinates, trains, and controls a core inner group and inspires and supports peripheral cadres.[400]

---

398 Trafton, J. (2007). *Countering terrorism and insurgency in the 21st century*. Westport, CT: Praeger Publishers, pp. 12-15. Retrieved August 14, 2008, from http://psi.praeger.com.proxy1.ncu.edu/doc.

399 Rohan, G. (2002). *Inside al-Qaeda: Global network of terror*. New York, NY, USA: Columbia University Press, p. 54. Retrieved August 13, 2008, from http://site.ebrary.com/lib/ncent/Doc.

400 Ibid.

In 1998, al-Qaeda was reorganized into four distinct but interconnected groups. The first group was a pyramidal structure to facilitate strategic and tactical direction. The second group was a global terrorist network. The third group was a base force for guerrilla warfare inside Afghanistan. Finally, the fourth group was a loose coalition of transnational terrorist and guerrilla groups. For example, al-Qaeda's military committee was responsible for recruiting, training, transporting, and deploying military operations in conjunction with developing tactics and acquiring and manufacturing special weapons.[401] In describing the organizational structure of al-Qaeda, Trafton wrote that "Ideology is the binding force of al-Qaeda, rather than a central command."[402]

Recruiting Efforts

In terms of recruiting supporters for the al-Qaeda cause, Osama bin Laden masterfully has used group dynamics along with religion and nationalism to achieve his goals. Bin Laden used group dynamics to "help shape terrorist thought and action"[403] into motivating and even inspiring terrorism. Bin Laden recruited and used religious zealots who already hate and fear Israel and the western civilization. The religious zealots are assured they have the moral high ground and their actions are religiously justified, coupled with the rewards they are expected to receive, such as the high number of virgins for their use in the afterlife.

Trafton further highlights that in the United States prisoners who are recent Muslim converts are natural recruits for Islamic organizations.[404] Two specific examples include (1) Richard Reid, the shoe bomber, a criminal who was converted to Islam in a British prison and (2) Jose Padilla, the dirty bomber, who also converted to Islam while in prison.[405]

---

401 Ibid., pp. 54-59.

402 Trafton, J. (2007). *Countering terrorism and insurgency in the 21st century.* Westport, CT: Praeger Publishers, pp. 14. Retrieved August 14, 2008, from http://psi.praeger.com.proxy1.ncu.edu/doc.

403 Combs, C. (2006). *Terrorism in the twenty-first century (4th ed.).* Upper Saddle River, NJ: Pearson Prentice Hall, p. 64.

404 Trafton, J. (2007). *Countering terrorism and insurgency in the 21st century.* Westport, CT: Praeger Publishers, pp. 17. Retrieved August 14, 2008, from http://psi.praeger.com.proxy1.ncu.edu/doc.

405 Acharya, A. & Rohan, G. (2007). *Denial of sanctuary.* Westport, CT: Praeger Publishers, p. 24. Retrieved August 14, 2008, from http://psi.praeger.com.proxy1.ncu.edu/doc.

Financial and Funding Support

In a speech on September 24, 2001, President Bush noted that "Money is the lifeblood of terrorist operations today."[406] The terrorists who flew the planes into the World Trade Center and the Pentagon on September 11, 2001, relied on just $500,000 in total expenditures. Nineteen terrorists entered the United States repeatedly, trained as commercial pilots, engaged in intercontinental air travel, rented cars, established personal bank accounts, obtained ATM cards, and generally live adequately funded lives in the months prior to the attack.[407]

For Islamic terrorists, funds were made available to those carrying out charitable work, including militant resistance, in Islamic outposts under siege such as Bosnia, Kosovo, Kashmir, and Chechnya. Additional funding was made available by siphoning off donations for more ordinary charitable work in many other jurisdictions within Islamic communities. These funds merely added to the seed money available on an ongoing basis from the proceeds of narcotics.[408]

Al-Qaeda financing has made use of *hawala*, which is "…an informal Islamic banking network that links bankers around the world who advance funds to depositors on a handshake and, sometimes, a password."[409] Alternatively, terrorists have had numerous opportunities to generate revenues through fraudulent conversion of social benefits, migrant smuggling, document fraud, stealing cars, gun-running, or even working for the money.[410]

Millions of dollars came from Saudi Arabia and radical mosques throughout the Muslim community, which levy taxes for bin Laden. A lucrative drug trade exists among al-Qaeda, Turkish drug lords, and the Albanian Mafia, in particular, with selling the heroin drug in Europe and the US.[411]

---

406 Trafton, J. (2007). *Countering terrorism and insurgency in the 21st century.* Westport, CT: Praeger Publishers, pp. 22. Retrieved August 14, 2008, from http://psi.praeger.com.proxy1.ncu.edu/doc.

407 Winer, J. (2003). *Financing terrorism.* Secaucus, NJ, USA: Kluwer Academic Publishers, p. 6. Retrieved August 14, 2008, from http://site.ebrary.com/lib/ncent/Doc.

408 Ibid., p. 12.

409 Combs, C. (2006). *Terrorism in the twenty-first century (4th ed.).* Upper Saddle River, NJ: Pearson Prentice Hall, p. 104.

410 Winer, J. (2003). *Financing terrorism.* Secaucus, NJ, USA: Kluwer Academic Publishers, p. 13. Retrieved August 14, 2008, from http://site.ebrary.com/lib/ncent/Doc.

411 Williams, P. (2005). *The al-Qaeda connection: International terrorism, organized crime, and the coming apocalypse.* Amherst, NY: Prometheus Books, pp. 53-55.

Al-Qaeda and Organized Crime

The drug trade is just one example of al-Qaeda interests with organized crime. An example of mutual benefit with organized crime and the drug trade is with the relationship between al-Qaeda and the Taliban, both of whom derived considerable revenues from poppy cultivation in Afghanistan.[412] Interestingly, although Islam itself does not believe in using drugs, it sees the drug trade as a weapon designed to weaken their enemy.[413] Moreover, "This violation of religious rules is necessary ... for the sake of the ultimate goal, namely, to submerge the Christian infidels in drugs."[414]

The "nexus ... between terrorist organizations and organized crime networks is based on the symbiotic relationship between the two, a dynamic that allows both entities to profit financially."[415] An example is in Albania, which is considered a terrorist transit point, where organized crime rings help smuggle terrorists from the Black Sea to Western Europe. Another example of the link with organized crime and al-Qaeda is an ex-KGB officer turned criminal named Victor Bout who supplied arms to the Taliban and al-Qaeda under the cover of a legal business organization.[416]

Summary of Main Points

Summarizing the main points of this chapter of al-Qaeda's beginning was during the Soviet war in Afghanistan. The influence of radical Islamic fundamentalists such as Jamal ad-Din Al-Afghani and the Salafist movement, Muhammed 'Abduh and the establishment of the Muslim Brotherhood, Sayyid Qutb and Muhammad Abd al-Salam Farij who espoused Islamic fundamentalism even if it meant killing Muslims, and Egyptian physician Ayman al-Zawahiri who became involved with Osama bin Laden is the historical foundation of al-Qaeda. Al-Qaeda and bin Laden's support of

412 Larsson, J. (2007). *Countering terrorism and insurgency in the 21st century*. Westport, CT: Praeger Publishers, p. 19. Retrieved August 14, 2008, from http://psi. praeger.com.proxy1.ncu.edu/doc.

413 Acharya, A. & Rohan, G. (2007). *Denial of sanctuary*. Westport, CT: Praeger Publishers, p. 22. Retrieved August 14, 2008, from http://psi.praeger.com. proxy1.ncu.edu/doc.

414 Williams, P. (2005). *The al-Qaeda connection: International terrorism, organized crime, and the coming apocalypse*. Amherst, NY: Prometheus Books, pp. 61.

415 Acharya, A. & Rohan, G. (2007). *Denial of sanctuary*. Westport, CT: Praeger Publishers, p. 17. Retrieved August 14, 2008, from http://psi.praeger.com. proxy1.ncu.edu/doc.

416 Ibid., p. 18.

the Taliban, led by Islamic fundamentalist Mullah Omar, in terms of both fighting and financial support proved to be an inextricable connection.

Al-Qaeda's unique internal organization structure is as stated by Hoffman: "Al-Qaeda has clearly shown itself to be nimble, flexible, and adaptive. Because of the group's remarkable durability, the loss of Afghanistan does not appear to have affected al-Qaeda's ability to mount terrorist attacks to the extent the US had hoped."[417]

Al-Qaeda has links with organized crime to further mutual objectives such as financing terrorist operations and profit associated with the drug trade. This relationship is based on convenience, as terrorists and criminals leverage each other's capabilities.[418]

Conclusions

Al-Qaeda represents the emergence of religious-inspired terrorist groups that possess fewer constraints about killing large numbers of people. Al-Qaeda's goals pose a significant global threat as they believe killing non-believers or infidels result in their being rewarded in the afterlife. Osama bin Laden and al-Qaeda's main purpose is to drive the US and Western influence out of the Middle East.[419]

Religious fanaticism is one of the world's greatest threats, and the "... al-Qaeda network has given the world a dramatic example of the destructive power of individuals committed to waging war on religious principles."[420] Moreover, Auerswald cites a chilling quote attributed to Osama bin Laden:[421]

> *Acquiring (WMD) weapons for the defense of Muslims is a religious duty.*
> *If I have indeed acquired these weapons, then I thank God for enabling*
> *me to do so. And if I seek to acquire these weapons, I am carrying out a*

417 Hoffman, B. (2004). *Al-Qaeda and the war on terrorism: An update. Current History, 103(677),* 423-427. Retrieved August 13, 2008, from Research Library database.

418 Acharya, A. & Rohan, G. (2007). *Denial of sanctuary.* Westport, CT: Praeger Publishers, p. 23. Retrieved August 14, 2008, from http://psi.praeger.com. proxy1.ncu.edu/doc.

419 Simon, J. (2002). The global terrorist threat. *Phi Kappa Phi Forum, 82(2),* 10-13. Retrieved April 6, 2008, from Research Library database.

420 Combs, C. (2006). *Terrorism in the twenty-first century (4th ed.).* Upper Saddle River, NJ: Pearson Prentice Hall, p. 47.

421 Auerswald, D. (2006). Deterring non-state WMD attacks. *Political Science Quarterly, 121(4),* 543-568. Retrieved May 26, 2008, from Research Library database.

duty. It would be a sin for Muslims not to try to possess the weapons that would prevent the infidels from inflicting harm on Muslims.

Chapter 19
Naval Militias and Anti-Terrorism

William R. Tubbs, Jr., MPA

Introduction

An enormous flotilla covered the waters surrounding Manhattan Island during the immediate aftermath of the terrorist attacks on the World Trade Center on September 11, 2001. In addition to all of the police and fire agencies in the area, the United States Coast Guard, Coast Guard Reserve, and Coast Guard Auxiliary all had direct roles in assisting the New York public during that period. They, along with dozens of pleasure boaters and small commercial operators, helped to evacuate citizens from Manhattan and also patrolled the waterways for days after the attacks.[422]

Another small fleet of patrol boats also plied the waters off of west Manhattan Island during that period. Several naval militia crews from New York and New Jersey provided security patrols during the evacuation of Manhattan.[423],[424] These crews were under the auspices of the New York and New Jersey National Guard, respectively, and appeared on scene to assist authorities in whatever way they were assigned. These naval militia boats and crews were an active part of their respective state defense forces.

In the past, the 3,000-member New York Naval Militia (NYNM) has responded to the 9/11 attacks, ice storms, fires, and the TWA Flight 800 crash in 1996. Currently, the NYNM participates in homeland security (HS) missions. After the attacks on the World Trade Center in 2001, the NYNM created a Military Emergency Boat Service (MEBS) to assist the Coast Guard

---

422 Mbugua, M. (2006, September 8). Study focuses on 9/11 evacuation of Manhattan by water. *UDaily*. University of Delaware Website. Retrieved from http://www.udel.edu/PR/UDaily/2007/sep/evacuation090806.html.

423 Hunter, K. (2005, February 8). Governors captain state naval militias. *Gov-Pro Media*. Retrieved from http://govpro.com/issue_20050101/gov_imp_31394/.

424 Reith, G. K. (2005, April 5). The adjutant general report to legislature on the NJ naval militia joint command (Committee Report). New Jersey National Guard Website. Retrieved from http://www.state.nj.us/military/publications/naval/tag.html.

and local law enforcement agencies in HS missions.[425],[426] It is designed and trained to conduct patrol missions with its 11 boats on New York's waterways and even assist in enforcing a security exclusion zone near nuclear power plants.[427] Enforcing security zones is normally a core function of the Coast Guard.

Until it was disbanded in 2002, the New Jersey Naval Militia (NJNM) performed similar activities albeit with a much smaller force of about 200. Like the NYNM, the NJNM patrolled key strategic assets including the major air facility at Lakehurst, nuclear power plants, and a naval weapons station ... all with the encouragement of the Coast Guard.[428] Members of the New Jersey legislature and others have made efforts to revitalize the NJNM ever since it was stood down by the State's Adjutant General in August 2002. Despite concerns that the NJNM overlapped the functions of other State agencies, Assemblyman Wilfredo Carballo insisted that the organization could serve as the "extra eyes and ears that protect our shores ...."[429]

States with Naval Militias

Today, only New York and Ohio have active naval militias.[430],[431] Texas has a "maritime unit" of the Texas State Guard although it is not technically

---

425 Yusko, D. (2008, June 3). Naval Militia shows off its agility: PB 440, one of 11 boats in emergency service, slices easily through the Hudson River. *McClatchy - Tribune Business News*. Retrieved from ProQuest database.

426 Durr, E. (Ed.). (2008, February 15). *New York State Division of Military and Naval Affairs News*. Retrieved from http://readme.readmedia.com/news/show/ New-York-Naval-Militia-Holds-Change-of-Command/63977.

427 New York Naval Militia. (2008, July 17). *New York Division of Military and Naval Affairs*. New York National Guard Website. Retrieved November 30, 2008, from http://www.dmna.state.ny.us/nynm/naval.php.

428 Anonymous (2002, January 14). Tiny naval militia aids Coast Guard; 200 N.J. volunteers gaining attention. *The Record (Bergen County, NJ)*, p. A04. Retrieved from ProQuest database.

429 Bautista, J. (2003, April 26). Volunteers refuse to give up the ships; politics, budget could scuttle Garden State's little fleet. *The Record (Bergen County, NJ)*, p. A01. Retrieved from ProQuest database.

430 Adjutant General's Department Ohio Naval Militia. (2005, April 6). Ohio's oldest and original naval homeland security unit. *Ohio Naval Militia*. Ohio National Guard Website. Retrieved November 30, 2008, from http://navalmilitia.ohio.gov/.

431 New York Naval Militia. (2008, July 17). New York Division of Military and Naval Affairs. New York National Guard Website. Retrieved November 30, 2008, from http://www.dmna.state.ny.us/nynm/naval.php.

or legally a naval militia by federal standards.[432] Several other states are in the process of activating or re-activating naval militias but are not yet past the organizational stage. New Jersey is a case in point. South Carolina reestablished its naval militia by statute in 2004.[433] Meanwhile, California's State Military Reserve has been working since at least 2003 to resurrect the naval militia that has been in state codes for decades.[434] Of the active naval militias, only New York has direct ocean access, and it is very active in assisting the Coast Guard and other government agencies in New York Harbor as well as on Lake Champlain. Ohio's naval militia assists the National Guard and other military units on Lake Erie. Based upon current levels of legal activity and publicity for both New Jersey and California, they appear to possess the inside track for re-establishing their naval militias at the earliest time. Considering the extensive port and waterway systems in both states, they will serve substantial missions once they begin.

What are Naval Militias?

Naval militias are the relatively obscure maritime units of some state defense forces (SDFs). Widely known throughout the National Guard community but little known elsewhere, SDFs, or state militias, can be succinctly characterized as the "reserves to the National Guard." State militias are part of the organized militia as provided for by federal statute. They are distinct from the self-styled unorganized militias that are privately run and have no official government sanction at any level. They are woven throughout American history and have a colorful, detailed chronology that has been documented elsewhere [see *The American home guard: The state militia in the twentieth century* by Barry M. Stentiford]. The naval militias have an equally long history in the United States but have fared less successfully over the centuries for a variety of reasons.

---

432 Texas Maritime Regiment. (2008). Texas State Guard. Texas National Guard Web site. Retrieved November 30, 2008, from http://www.gotxsg.com/index.php.

433 South Carolina Maritime Security Act, South Carolina Statute, Ch. 17, § 54-17-10 through 54-17-70 (2004).

434 Sanders, J. (2004, December 19). State may be getting new militia: Agency would draw on naval, Marine, Coast Guard reserves, adding protection at low cost. *The Sacramento Bee*, p. A3. Retrieved from ProQuest database.

No Naval Guard

Not every state has a coastline or a major waterway. Hence, some states have waterside missions while others do not. Consequently, a landside army-oriented SDF has been sufficient for most states. Those relatively few states that do have a naval militia history are located on the east, west, and gulf coasts or those that border the Great Lakes and Canada. Over the long term, the machinations among states to establish and maintain the National Guard were generally supported by most states. In contrast, since a naval presence was only important to a minority of states the lobbying pressure on Congress on behalf of naval militias was considerably less.

The Navy never saw the usefulness of the naval militias as a benefit and, in fact, tended to view naval militias as direct competition to the limited resources available to it in peacetime. In fact, at the beginning of the 20th century, legislation that established the Naval Reserve effectively killed the naval militia because the federal government finally had total control over its sailors.[435] The passage of the Naval Reserve Act in 1916 and a lack of equipment and supplies made it virtually impossible for naval militias to continue. Hence, most states simply acquiesced to the inevitable and let them slip away. The naval militias were totally eliminated by the new Naval Reserve. They never found a state niche similar to the relationship of SDFs and the Guard. After that, the only major change to the Guard came when the Air Force was established as part of the National Security Act of 1947 and the Air National Guard was concurrently established on par with their Army Guard counterparts. Even during the monumental shift in America's defense structure, there was no call for a Navy Guard. The Navy still remained a completely federal entity.

Modern Evolution

Fast-forward to the end of the 20th century. More full-scale integration of the National Guard into the plans of the Army occurred after the:

- End of World War II
- Stalemates and incongruities of Korea and Vietnam
- Multiple wars of the 1980s and 1990s (especially Desert Storm)
- Current wars in Iraq and Afghanistan

---

435 Grim, C. J. (2007, March 5). Strategic to operational: A step too far for the Navy Reserve. U.S. Army War College Website. http://oai.dtic.mil/oai/oai?&verb=g etRecord&metadataPrefix=html&identifier=ADA469670.

The competition between the National Guard and the Army Reserve continued and, to an extent, it still continues today. Over the years, the missions have been refined and duplication of effort has been minimized. Still, one overriding concern is of critical importance to the National Guard. Unless federalized, it is under the total control of the governor of each state.

National Guard programs throughout the nation redesigned their missions to accommodate the massive redesign of HS missions. They accomplished these missions on the state level while maintaining the federal government requirements. These missions included equipment acquisition, increased personnel accession, and enhancing public acceptance. There are varying numbers of Guard personnel in each state. Generally but not always, they are proportionate to population. These soldiers and airman work part time and full time for state active duty requirements. These requirements are for natural disasters such as wildfires, floods, and other natural disasters as well as for man-made problems such as civil insurrection and terrorist activity.

Since the beginning of the Global War on Terrorism (GWOT), the National Guard and Reserves have been stretched quite thin. The nation's active duty forces shrank from 2.2 million down to 1.4 million at the end of the Cold War. Additionally, Reserve/Guard forces dropped from 1.8 million to 1.2 million. All of these reductions were made with no reduction in operational commitments.[436] As a result, the proportion of forces needed to fulfill these missions requires significantly higher numbers than the total numbers available. This shows that the Guard is even less able, on a consistent basis, to staff fully for its state demands.

State Roles

The governor is the commander-in-chief of the Guardsmen and dictates their peacetime mission until individuals or units are federalized for active duty under the Army or Air Force. In the minds of the governors, there is no question as to how this works. However, with the increased operational tempo of the Guard in the GWOT, the states are finding themselves short on Guard resources needed to work on internal disaster relief efforts. Examples of such efforts include the Midwest flooding or Western wildfires, which are traditionally automatic responses by the Guard.

---

436 Anonymous (2008, January 31). Transforming the National Guard and Reserves into a 21st-century operational force. *Final Report to Congress and the Secretary of Defense*, p. E-9. Commission on the National Guard and Reserves. Retrieved from http://www.cngr.gov/Final%20Report/CNGR_final%20report%20with%20cover.pdf.

As these shortfalls become more crippling, many states reinvent their state defense forces and develop procedures for them to fill shortfalls left by mobilized Guardsmen. These forces are voluntary but must meet a variety of state standards. While not necessarily as stringent as federal standards, the tendency is towards increased professionalism in order to promote better effectiveness and public support in their missions. In some instances, the SDFs are trained to perform the same jobs as the absent Guardsmen. When they are called to duty, they are paid on similar scales ... although from state rather than federal funds.

Today, most states use their SDFs as reserve forces for their National Guard. When a Guardsman is federalized and deployed overseas to Afghanistan, Iraq, or any other national duty, there is a gap created in the state mission. When a Guardsman works either permanently or temporarily on full-time active duty in a state support role, the gap must be filled. An SDF member is one who fills that temporary vacancy. Usually, it is performed on a voluntary basis. However, for the duration, some states pay the SDF member on a scale commensurate with federal military remuneration.

The National Guard and Army Reserve became more fully integrated with the active duty Army in the early 20th century. Since then, naval militias had equal stature with and were usually integrated with land-based army militias or SDFs. The Navy never advocated for a reserve force like that of the Army. Hence, there was never a national "Navy Guard" for a naval militia to develop. The National Guard fills a dual role as a federal force and an SDF. State militias were designed to backfill for the Guard when it became federalized and, therefore, unavailable for state duty. In most states, there has never been a clear need for a naval counterpart to the National Guard. Hence, the perception is that there has never been an organization for a naval militia to backfill.

An interesting artifact of federal law is that a member of a federal reserve force cannot simultaneously be a member of a SDF. On the other hand, there is a requirement that in order to take advantage of federal resources, i.e., "vessels, material, armament, equipment, and other facilities of the Navy and the Marine Corps available to the Navy Reserve and the Marine Corps Reserve" (Title 10 USC, Sec. 7854), 95 percent of a state's naval militia members actually must be members of the Navy, Marine Corps, or Coast Guard Reserve. The former NJNM took a unique approach to this conundrum by organizing into three battalions, only one of which met the 95 percent requirement. The other two performed as pure state guard components as "operational State Naval Guard" units.[437] The end effect was

---

437 Reith, G. K. (2005, April 5). The adjutant general report to legislature on the NJ naval militia joint command (Committee Report). New Jersey National

to leverage federal resources against limited state funding and expand the potential pool of personnel.

A change to Title 10 of federal law to eliminate the 95 percent membership requirement would benefit naval militias and make their establishment and maintenance more palatable to the states. In the interim, the New Jersey approach seems like an effective and legitimate workaround.

The Forgotten Navy

The Coast Guard evolved on a totally separate track than the rest of the armed forces. It was formed by combining the Revenue Cutter Service and Lifesaving Service in 1915. This combination was further enhanced when the Lighthouse Service merged into it in 1939.[438] That same year saw the founding of the Coast Guard Auxiliary, a purely volunteer adjunct to the Coast Guard. In February 1941, the Coast Guard Reserve was established.

In response to the continuation of smuggling and excise tax evasion, the Revenue Cutter Service was originally established in 1790 as the Revenue Marine. Smuggling and excise taxing were commonplace under British rule. However, they became a severe hindrance under the new American government. The new American government was desperate to rebuild its fledgling postwar economy. Beginning under the Treasury Department, the Revenue Cutter Service moved into the Transportation Department when it was formed in 1967. It finally moved into the new Homeland Security Department in 2003. One of the five armed services, the Coast Guard has always had the possibility of being legally moved under the Navy in wartime. However, this possible move seems to be more an artifact of its service in World War II than any probability of it happening today.[439]

The Coast Guard's multi-mission tasking of pre-9/11 became much more focused on HS in post-9/11. The port security missions of the Coast Guard were generally relegated to the Reserve forces as a condition of funding from the Navy. As the potential for sabotage and other terrorist activities in the maritime sector became clear, the port security missions suddenly became the preeminent role of the entire Coast Guard. When the Coast Guard was absorbed into the Department of Homeland Security, so were all of its non-

---

Guard Website. Retrieved from http://www.state.nj.us/military/publications/naval/tag.html.

438 United States Department of Homeland Security. (2008, February 4). United States Coast Guard: About us. United States Coast Guard Website. Retrieved November 29, 2008, from http://uscg.mil/top/about/.

439 Ibid.

HS missions. These non-HS missions include such missions as search and rescue, pollution response, and others to name a few.

As the Coast Guard continues to focus on its new primary mission and still maintain minimum performance standards for its older traditional missions, it only makes sense to look to alternative and innovative means to accomplish them. Its small complement of 40,000 regular and 8,000 reservists is spread across the continental United States (CONUS) as well as Alaska, Hawaii, and several territories. Its fleet of small boats is the only military defensive force available to supplement state and local law enforcement in American waterways. The naval militia could assist the Coast Guard with its HS missions and relieve some of the pressure to maintain standards.

Even before the 9/11 attacks, it was well known throughout the maritime community that port and waterway security was inadequate within and around the more than 300 US commercial ports. The Coast Guard methodically inspects port facilities and, where needed, recommends improvements to meet basic, established standards. However, port facilities are traditionally responsible to provide their own internal security and typically do so in conjunction with local law enforcement. Waterside eyes and ears are already in place in the states that have active naval militias. Additionally, the role could be expanded as the naval militias expand to other states.

Similarly, the shipping industry must ensure security throughout a ship's movement from start to finish. With the massive growth of container shipping over the past 50 years, there are specific concerns about smuggling weapons of mass destruction or terrorists in them. Despite stated concerns about the problem prior to 9/11, only two-to-three percent of all shipping containers were inspected. Today, that percentage has risen to an estimated five-to-six percent. However, it is still an incredibly small proportion of the total traffic.[440]

There is an ongoing argument within and without the industry as to whether (as a congressional committee desires) to inspect 100 percent of all containers entering the country or to institute a program of "smart inspections" where certain groups of containers are targeted for inspection based upon their country of origin, bill of lading, and other specified factors.[441] No matter what the final decision, there will be an increased need for people to perform these inspections. Since the terrorist attacks of 9/11, there has existed

---

440 Lipton, E. (2006, April 26). Democrats want all ship containers inspected. *New York Times*. Retrieved from http://www.nytimes.com/2006/04/26/washington/26port.html?ex=1303704000&en=78927941b99cd651&ei=5088&partner=rssnyt&emc=rss.

441 Edmonson, R. G. (2008, June 23). Scan-all's great debate. *Journal of Commerce*. Retrieved from ProQuest database.

a continuous shortfall of personnel to do the necessary tasking under the HS umbrella. With proper and consistent training, naval militia personnel can supplement Customs and Coast Guard personnel in these duties.

The Reserve's Reserve

Programs exist that can and do supplement the Coast Guard and Coast Guard Reserve. The original Coast Guard Reserve, now known as the Coast Guard Auxiliary (CGA), performs thousands of boat inspections annually. Additionally, the CGA patrols local waterways to help extend the capabilities of Coast Guard small-boat stations across the country. The CGA also provides training to pleasure boaters and assists with pollution response (access the Coast Guard Auxiliary website). Emulating the World War II Coast Watch program, in 2005 the Coast Guard also established America's Waterway Watch (AWW) with the intent of having the millions of pleasure boaters keep an eye on "America's coasts, rivers, bridges, tunnels, ports, ships, military bases, and waterside industries, [which] may be the terrorists' next targets" (see the Coast Guard America's Waterway Watch website).[442]

Clearly, a perceived need exists to engage the public in helping military authorities in the GWOT in one way or another. Voluntary programs such as the CGA and AWW encourage average citizens to participate in this effort and are effective in many ways. They cannot fill every need. They do not have the capability of filling behind some of the more sensitive and military-oriented functions of the HS nor is it expected of them. For that reason, the naval militia is functionally ideal to fill the gap between the fulltime military and the purely volunteer agencies.

Increased federal funding to states and local governments has continued unabated since the 9/11 attacks and the subsequent establishment of the Department of Homeland Security.[443] Despite the increases in HS funding that have emanated from Washington, there is a limit to how much can be allocated and continuously appropriated for this purpose. Some funds are designed for one-time use in setting up otherwise non-existent programs. Other funds will be continuing appropriations to ensure ongoing maintenance of new and existing programs.

---

442 United States Coast Guard. (2005, March 7). Coast Guard launches America's Waterway Watch to encourage reporting of suspicious activity. *United States Coast Guard news [Press release]*. Department of Homeland Security Website. Retrieved November 30, 2008, from https://www.piersystem.com/go/doc/786/65244/.

443 Bullock, J. A., Haddow, G. D., Coppola, D., Ergin, E., Westerman, L., & Yeletaysi, S. (2006). *Introduction to Homeland Security, Second Edition*. Oxford, United Kingdom: Elsevier Butterworth-Heinemann, p. 65.

America's military forces have evolved significantly during the 371 years since the first militias were established in the Massachusetts Colony. Even the name "naval militia" belies the activities it currently undertakes. Most of the proposed and actual missions are more likely Coast Guard-oriented than otherwise. The discussions over naming rights have been integral during the growth of the SDF. It did not matter whether they were called state militias, SDFs, state guard, or state military reserves. Also, the original Coast Guard Reserve transitioned into the Coast Guard Auxiliary, and a new Coast Guard Reserve resulted. Continuous shifting and merging of the former organizations now constitute the modern Coast Guard.

Ever since the 1980s and 1990s when most reserve units were abolished and reserve personnel generally merged into active duty units, the Coast Guard Reserve is now more like a part-time active force. If there is future discussion over naming rights to the naval militias, it might well look towards names like the coast guard militia, coastal militia, or marine force militia. The name of an organization should be part of its definition. The term *naval militia* simply does not aptly describe its mission. However, it is part of the American lexicon, and because of that, we must understand the meanings behind the name. Those debates will continue and meanings of these terms will be resolved at another future day.

Conclusion

Naval militias present a viable alternative to cutting corners in America's waterside, HS, and anti-terrorism programs. As with any change in established organizations or programs, there will be hurdles to straddle. For example, considerable analysis and restructuring are necessary to minimize overlap and duplication of service. Additionally, complex funding streams and chains of command need to be considered.

The proactive approach of developing new and innovative programs to provide America with a protective shield should continue unabatedly. That approach needs to be combined with promoting programs that already exist and develop/maintain the capability to provide proven partnerships in the GWOT. The naval militias possess the history, energy, and potential to expand through more than just two states. It should be an integral part of our American homeland defense.

CHAPTER 20
PIRACY AND MARITIME SECURITY

Carl R. Hospedales, BS Aviation

Piracy is alive and well in the 21st century. It is an inconvenient nuisance to governments and a deadly concern to the maritime community. These are not the loveable roughs as portrayed by Hollywood. They are dyed-in-the-wool thieves and killers whose only concerns are making a profit and not getting caught. An example includes the recent rise in piracy operations conducted from Eyl in the Puntland region of Somalia in the Gulf of Aden shipping lane at the tip of the Horn of Africa. Each year, 22,000 shipping movements pass through that area. Collapse of law and order both on land and at sea in the country allows this criminal activity to flourish since Somalia has maintained no effective national government for 17 years.

The Royal Institute of International Affairs at Chatham House, London, UK, reports an estimated £17 million has been paid in ransom to these Somali based pirates. The United Nations (UN) conservatively estimates the ransom pirates earn from hijacking ships exceed $100M (£54M) a year, and even that figure is estimated at only 10 percent of the true figure. Piracy statistics vary slightly. However, according to the International Maritime Bureau (based in Malaysia), 61 attacks have occurred off the coast of Somalia this year. The pirates are holding between 12-14 ships and between 240-300 crew members. Some reports state that the pirates have seized over 30 ships already.

Maritime Insurance rates for ships passing through that area are spiraling as the pirates seize major vessels. Some of these vessels are the size of aircraft carriers. Ransoms range up to $5 million (£2.85 million) or more. Additionally, this problem affects international market prices, which only adds to an already fragile market state. Lloyd's of London, a major maritime insurer, raised its premiums this summer from 0 to 0.25 percent of the vessel's worth for each journey in this area.

Modus Operandi

From a pirate "mother ship" that travels far out to sea and launches smaller boats to attack passing vessels, pirates perpetrate opportunistic attacks

199

using machine guns and rocket-propelled grenades (RPGs). The pirates block the cargo ship or feign a ship-in-distress causing the merchant vessel to slow down or to stop. This allows the pirates to board the vessel and go directly to the ships bridge, gain control of the vessel, and force the ship's Captain to open the ships safe for a quick financial gain. Then, pirates dispose of the crew, repaint/rename the vessel, and transform it into a ghost ship. Alternatively, on occasion, they re-register the captured ship and sail it back to a pirate-friendly port. At that point, they sell what they can and ransom the rest.

Some of these pirates justify their actions by claiming that, in the absence of a functional central authority in Somalia, they are battling illegal fishing and toxic waste dumping by foreign countries. From that statement, it begs the question: When was the last time you saw a passenger ship or cargo freighter illegally fishing or toxic waste dumping?

The most recent casualty is the "Faina," a Ukrainian cargo ship flagged out of Belize and captained by Vladimir Kolobkov, a Russian. The Faina was seized by pirates sailing to the Kenyan port of Mombasa. Its 2,320 tons of cargo included 33 tanks (T-72) and other weapons and ammunition. The ship's crew-complement totaled 21 including 17 Ukrainians, 3 Russians, and a Lithuanian. Their current situation is that Capt. Kolobkov has died of a heart attack, but the remaining crew is unharmed. Currently, the vessel is moored in a Somali port, blockaded by Navy ships near the village of Hinbarwaqo, where the pirates are attempting to offload small weapons.

International Response

To say the least, international response to piracy has been poor. The inadequacy of current maritime law to address the issue has a lot to do with that situation. Fortunately, since the recent international spotlight has brought these criminal acts to the world's attention, anti-piracy operations have slightly improved. The French Navy has been conducting anti-piracy patrols for a while. The Indian Navy has had some success. Additionally, the Russia Navy has announced that it will start conducting regular anti-piracy patrols in the waters off Somalia to protect Russian citizens and ships. The Russian Navy has dispatched to the region the patrol frigate "Neustrashimy" (English translation: "Fearless") of the Baltic Fleet. In some circles, this action has raised more than a few eye brows. Some see this as another step by Russia towards increasing its global sphere of influence. This conclusion holds some credence.

Since earlier in September 2008, the Russians have conducted joint military training exercises with Venezuela in the neutral waters of the Atlantic Ocean and Caribbean Sea. Russia had dispatched two Russian Air Force

TU-160 "Blackjack" aircraft from the Saratov region of Russia to Libertador Airfield in Caracas, Venezuela. With Venezuela and Cuba, Russia conducted joint naval exercises with a task force of warships led by submarine hunter-destroyer "Admiral Chabanenko" and nuclear-powered cruiser "Peter the Great" from the Russian Northern Fleet. This action further fueled speculation of a start of a new Russian Cold War posture. If true, would this impede any potential collaboration of countries in addressing this current maritime threat?

A Western naval presence also exists in the area. That presence includes British, American, German, Danish, Canadian, and Dutch naval forces. The British Royal Navy (RN) ships have deterred up to 15 attacks during August and September 2008. The RN HMS Northumberland, a Type 23 frigate, was re-tasked as a dedicated British anti-pirate ship. Their primary mission, however, is naval escorts for protecting United Nations (UN) food agency World Food Program (WFP) famine relief vessels. They have been bringing food into Somalia and providing support for Afghanistan and Iraq Operations.

In a recent interview on October 8, 2008, with the British newspaper, *The Telegraph*, the senior RN commander in the Gulf, Commodore Keith Winstanley, headquartered in Bahrain, believes that the situation has become so serious that civilian vessels should be armed. He also said that private security companies deployed in Iraq or Afghanistan could be better used guarding ships. In pirate-infested regions, ships need a "visual deterrent" such as mounted heavy machine guns. "This coalition headquarters is advocating that as an option," said Commodore Winstanley.

In September 2008, France had circulated a draft UN resolution urging states to deploy naval vessels and aircraft to combat piracy in the Somalia area. If this resolution fails to be adopted by the UN, it will leave the flood gates open for these piracy acts to continue unabated.

On December 17, 2008, the UN Security Council voted to allow countries to conduct military raids on land and by air against pirates terrorizing the waters off Somalia. The resolution permits countries to "Use all necessary measures that are appropriate in Somalia" in pursuit of pirates, who have interfered with commerce in the Gulf of Aden. However, here is the catch: The raids will only be permitted if they have the approval of Somalia's federal government. However, with the Somalia's current state of instability, it could prove unworkable. The resolution asks UN member states to send naval vessels and military aircraft to conduct the operations. Additionally, it proposes the establishment of a regional office to coordinate the worldwide effort.

Possible solutions could be the following amendments to the International Maritime Law:

1. Allow ocean-going vessels that operate through known areas of piracy with appropriately trained security personnel to carry and use both lethal and less lethal weapons. All weapons shall be accounted for items of the ship's inventory, shall not leave the vessel when docked in foreign ports, and shall be used strictly for training and self-defense purposes only on the high seas.

2. Establish a dedicated Anti-Piracy Task Force comprised of surface, sub-surface, and aerial assets in collaboration of UN member countries' naval forces with its mission to include direct action, capture/detain pirates, and hostage rescue. The overall commander of the Anti-Piracy Task Force shall be approved by the UN Security Council. Any captured pirates shall be prosecuted by the World Court or the judicial courts of the vessel owner's home nation.

Conclusion

At the end of the day it really boils down to the drive and will-power of the international community and the maritime community to address this threat on maritime security. To date, over 60 ships have been boarded by pirates in the Somali region. The seas and oceans of the world are dangerous as is. It is inexcusable for the maritime industry to allow these acts of piracy to continue. If this crime occurred on land, society would be up in arms. However, because it takes place at sea where no witnesses are present, piracy is overlooked or, worse still, ignored.

CHAPTER 21
SUMMARY AND CONCLUSION

W e had better prepare ourselves for the coming attacks. The chapters of this book can help to educate American citizens and prepare them to combat terrorists in the United States of America. If we are prepared, we have no need to fear. We must not bury our collective heads in the sand. We must eradicate the enemy within. We must be forever vigilant.

National Strategies

Strategy provides a plan for action to combat a threat. The US must possess a strategy that effectively counters unconventional or asymmetrical warfare. The Global War on Terrorism (GWOT) is both a battle of arms and a battle of ideas. The battle of ideas helps to define the strategic intent of our National Strategy for Combating Terrorism. The National Security Strategy of the United States of America, National Strategy for Combating Terrorism, and National Strategy for Homeland Security work in unison, in coordination, and in correlation among each other. Because of that synergism and since the September 11 attacks, America is now safer but not yet safe.

Intelligence Policies and Strategies

We analyzed the US homeland security intelligence strategy and compared it to published homeland security strategy documents. We also discussed US national and homeland security intelligence policies. All of the national and homeland security intelligence documents and policies coordinate and correlate well with the national security and homeland security documents, which is an amazing accomplishment.

Doctrine of Preemption

For effective democracies, freedom is indivisible. Those democracies provide the long-term antidote to the ideology of today's terrorism. This, then, becomes a battle of ideas and winning the hearts and minds of people.

We know that laws alone will not stop terrorism. Preventive intelligence-gathering and defense measures comprise the most important weapons in the fight against extremism and terrorism. Few, if any, wars against groups using terrorist-type tactics have been won purely by defensive operations. Hence, the US anti-terrorism strategy relies heavily on the doctrine of preemption. The US has employed that doctrine in Iraq. Further, in the GWOT, the man with the money is as dangerous as the man with the gun. Thus, the successful interdiction of funds can derail terrorist operations.

Most Serious National Security Threat

President George W. Bush has made clear that terrorists seeking to acquire and use WMD are our most serious national security threat. To counter an elusive and adaptive adversary, we must transform ourselves and our partnerships to deter, detect, and defeat this growing threat to our country and to the peace and security of the international community.

An Evil Enemy That Must Be Defeated

Al-Qaeda is driven by an undiminished strategic intent to attack our homeland. We cannot permit the world's most dangerous terrorists and their regime sponsors to threaten us with the world's most destructive weapons. Hostile states and terrorists that possess WMDs represent one of the greatest security challenges facing the US. No country has been subjected to more relentless terrorism than Israel. However, Israel considers itself at war with only the perpetrators of terrorism, not with the Palestinian people. Yet the Palestinian terrorists' goal is to kill the maximum number of Israeli civilians. We are dealing with an evil enemy that must be defeated.

General Aviation

The implementation of security methods and processes in general has had a decisive impact on the aviation industry. However, efforts to coordinate effectively varied aspects of security protocols between agencies and general aviation (GA) components have not been adequately addressed. Overall security issues, especially with regard to planning for catastrophic terrorist events, have been neglected at the nation's smaller airports. For perspective, the term "general aviation" is generally accepted to include all flying except for military and scheduled airline operations. General aviation makes up more than $150 billion or 1 percent of the US Gross Domestic Product (GDP) and supports almost 1.3 million high-skilled jobs in professional services and manufacturing and, hence, is an important component of the aviation industry.

Maritime Piracy

Maritime piracy grew dramatically. The number of attacks and level of violence increased steadily over the years. The world community is concerned as to what strategy it should develop to counter and disrupt maritime piracy. Also, the world community is concerned about the threat to the international maritime supply chain and how to increase its security. We presented some creative ideas and analysis of such strategies for countering and disrupting the piracy threat to the international maritime supply chain.

Captain Noel Choong, a former master mariner in Singapore and current head of the Piracy Reporting Center in Kuala Lumpur, said, "We'll never see the end of piracy, just as we'll never see the end of robbery on land. But we're doing everything we can." Yes, piracy may never be entirely eradicated; however, it can be severely curtailed to a manageable level. Consequently, controlling piracy and transnational crime protects our homeland, enhances global stability, and secures freedom of navigation for the benefit of all nations.

Critical Infrastructure

United States critical infrastructures must be proactively maintained and consistently updated. Vast advances through technology combined with loosely affiliated terrorists place many pressures on the nation to remain consistent with its policies, tactics, and procedures for avoiding destructive attacks. Merely defining the ramifications of critical infrastructure weaknesses or asymmetrical threats is not sufficient enough for effectively securing the nation. Moreover, formulating this foundation is vital for leading individuals into a solid direction of safety. Therefore, future analysis should assess various recommendations to successfully integrate local citizens' ideals with federal government policies and plans.

Information Security

We discussed some basic tenets of information security, security management, cyber-terrorism, cyber-attacks, network security, and user security. This is only a brief overview of some basic principles of information security. Develop a greater understanding of the principles of information security and how they relate to the security of the organization by reviewing additional, comprehensive information security resources for more thorough coverage of the subject.

Terrorist Profiling

Terrorists and terror groups constitute the enemy in the current GWOT that the United States finds itself engaged in today. Despite the vast number of research and investigative studies that have been conducted, terrorists' personalities and behaviors still remain discombobulated data sets. In addition to the difficulty in analyzing secretive, conspiratorial groups and individuals, the variety of motivations, ideologies, and behaviors involved remain extremely diverse. Common characteristics or clearly defined traits may be apparent and simplistic; however, significant differences are more the norm.

Israel Stronger Than Ever

Given Israel's location and being surrounded by its vicious enemies, it's a miracle that they are still there and holding strong. In addition, to my knowledge, there is no race or group of people that have suffered such persecution and attempted genocide than the Jewish people, and yet, they exist stronger than ever yet remain a peaceful, democratic nation.

Christians Not Like Muslim Terrorists

Although violence is often inflicted by Muslim terrorists and is approved of by the Koran, any such violence inflicted upon others by Christians is and never will be sanctioned by the New Testament teachings. Jesus Christ commanded His apostle Peter, "Put your sword in its place. For all who take the sword will perish by the sword" (Matthew 26:52).

Islamic Terrorists

Islamic terrorists are not courageous warriors that many commentators (particularly the ones who lean towards the left) claim them to be. They sacrifice their own lives for their own selfish gain. This behavior is relative to the profile of the common criminal (which many would disagree). They are brainwashed into thinking that if they die for the Islamic movement, they will inherit eternal life and riches in heaven along with numerous spiritual wives. This comprises the spoils of their heinous criminal activity, and they do not care who or how many innocent people they kill in the process. Again, this behavior is much like the common violent criminal who couldn't care less who he injures or kills as long as he obtains some form of monetary gain.

Abortion Clinics

Today's society is numb to the idea of taking violent action against practices and certain ethical values whether it be the medical procedure of killing unborn human beings or the bombing and murder of those who provide these services. History shows that notable and extreme responses to issues disagreeable to some may cause society to take note, conceptualize, and re-evaluate previously held positions on issues such as the pro-abortion vs. pro-life movements.

Ku Klux Klan

The Klan in the United States has evolved significantly since its birth after the Civil War. It began as a secret social club. However, it rapidly grew into a violent and racist secret society that its six founding fathers would probably not have wanted. The Ku Klux Klan is now responsible for terrorizing blacks and other racial and social minorities during its 140-year existence. The Klan still uses intimidation as its main factor when organizing marches and protests. The crosses still continue to burn, but with different connotation. However, it does not in any way promote the safety and well-being of ethnic and social minorities. Although the Klan's beliefs and ideals are resented for the most part in the United States, they are still allowed to exist and operate. American law forbids hate crimes and any sort of criminal activity; however, it defends the rights of those who lawfully organize and rally. Opinions and beliefs of those affiliated with any racist organization, no matter how disturbing they may be, will always enjoy the protections of American law.

Al-Qaeda

Al-Qaeda represents the emergence of religious-inspired terrorist groups that possess fewer constraints about killing large numbers of people. Al-Qaeda's goals pose a significant global threat as they believe killing non-believers or infidels result in their being rewarded in the afterlife. Osama bin Laden and al-Qaeda's main purpose is to drive the US and Western influence out of the Middle East.

Naval Militias

Naval militias present a viable alternative to cutting corners in America's waterside, HS, and anti-terrorism programs. As with any change in established organizations or programs, there will be hurdles to straddle. For example, considerable analysis and restructuring are necessary to minimize overlap and duplication of service. Additionally, complex funding streams and chains of command need to be considered.

The proactive approach of developing new and innovative programs to provide America with a protective shield should continue unabatedly. That approach needs to be combined with promoting programs that already exist and develop/maintain the capability to provide proven partnerships in the GWOT. The naval militias possess the history, energy, and potential to expand through more than just two states. It should be an integral part of our American homeland defense.

Piracy and Maritime Security

At the end of the day it really boils down to the drive and will-power of the international community and the maritime community to address this threat on maritime security. The seas and oceans of the world are dangerous as is. It is inexcusable for the maritime industry to allow these acts of piracy to continue. If this crime occurred on land, society would be up in arms. However, because it takes place at sea where no witnesses are present, piracy is overlooked or, worse still, ignored.

Conclusion

In conclusion, *Combating Terrorists in the USA* provides students and researchers with thoughts and ideas for protecting the CONUS from Islamo-fascist terrorists. We must educate ourselves and know our enemies. We must develop, understand, and be prepared to use all of the counterterrorism strategies, tactics, plans, and weapons against all terrorists bent on destroying the USA. We will be fighting a good cause, which is to protect our families, religions, homes, and American way of life. As long as we are fighting for what is right and good, we will never go wrong and be defeated. To this end, will God our Heavenly Father and Jesus Christ protect us always against the formidable Islamo-fascist enemy? If we remain righteous as a people, the answer is "yes."

ABOUT THE AUTHOR

R obert T. (Bob) Uda is president and principal consultant of Bob Uda and Associates (BU&A), a counterterrorism R&D firm. He also serves as vice president of the West Coast Division of SIG Homeland Security, LLC, headquartered in Florham Park, New Jersey. Additionally, Bob serves as proposal center manager of BAE Systems Command, Control, Computing, and Intelligence (C3I) business area in San Diego, California. Bob previously served as chairman, president, and CEO of Apollo Systems Technology, Inc., a system security engineering company in Canyon Country, California. He had served in the United States Air Force (USAF) for over eight years and in the aerospace and defense industries for over a quarter century. He possesses a total of over 40 years of professional working experience in the military and aerospace/defense industries.

Bob Uda earned BS degrees in aerospace engineering from the University of Oklahoma and in general business from Regents College of the University of the State of New York (now named Excelsior College). He further earned an MS degree in astronautics from the Air Force Institute of Technology (AFIT) and an MBA degree from the University of La Verne (California). Currently, Bob works towards a PhD degree in Business Administration (BA) with specialization in Homeland Security (HS) from the Northcentral University (NCU) located in Prescott Valley, Arizona, and plans to graduate at the end of 2010. He maintains a 3.96 GPA on 27 semester credit hours.

An award-winning writer, Bob has written/published over 40 publications including 15 books. One of his books is titled *Principles of Asymmetrical Warfare: How to Beat Islamo-fascists at Their Own Game,* and the other is *Terrorism and Counterterrorism: Victory Over Islamo-fascist Jihadists.* In November 2007, he received the Honorable Mention award in the Maritime Security Expo (MSE) and NCU paper competition. His paper was titled "Detecting and Defeating Waterborne Improvised Explosive Devices (WBIEDs) Onboard Small Vessels."

Bob is certified in the Community Emergency Response Team (CERT) Program. He is a member of the City of San Marcos (California) CERT and is a disaster services worker (DSW) with the Unified San Diego County Emergency Services Organization. He earned a Certificate of Successful Completion of Examination (CSCE) Amateur Radio "Technician" License with call sign KI6SQW. Bob also holds the Certified Homeland Security Professional (CHSP) certification with specialization in Counter-Terrorism.

Furthermore, he earned the Certificate of Advanced Graduate Studies (CAGS) in Homeland Security from NCU.

Bob Uda also holds professional organizational memberships in the International Association of Law Enforcement Intelligence Analysts, Inc. (IALEIA), International Association for Counterterrorism & Security Professionals (IACSP), International Counter Terrorism Officers Association (ICTOA), San Diego InfraGard Chapter, Business Espionage Controls & Countermeasures Association (BECCA), and National Defense Industrial Association (NDIA). He has served on over 75 boards, foundations, councils, directorships, trusteeships, executive and operations committees, senate, and panels.

Internationally recognized in community service, Bob Uda appears in 46 Who's Who publications including *Who's Who in the World, Who's Who in America, Who's Who in California, Who's Who in Science and Engineering,* and *Who's Who in Finance and Industry.* Bob is also a member of Alpha Phi Sigma, the honorary fraternity for Criminal Justice and Homeland Security. Currently, he serves as vice chairman of the board of the Institute of Certified Professional Managers (ICPM) Board of Regents (BOR) headquartered at the James Madison University in Harrisonburg, Virginia.

Bob and his wife, the former Karen Elizabeth Rowland of Circleville, Ohio, sired two sons, a daughter, and are proud grandparents of five grandchildren. They live in San Marcos, California. You can contact Bob by e-mail at robert.uda@sighls.org.

CONTRIBUTING AUTHORS

Brice A. Gyurisko, Sr., served for 30 years as a US Army military police officer. He holds a Master of Public Administration degree, a BS degree in Criminal Justice, and pursues a PhD in Homeland Security from Northcentral University. He advised Army senior leaders on law enforcement, anti-terrorism matters, and strategies regarding homeland defense in the areas of physical security, law enforcement, antiterrorism, corrections, and information operations. He has served as a patrolman, patrol supervisor, chief of police, and director of public safety. He currently serves as a regional security manager for a private government security company and teaches as an adjunct professor at the University of Phoenix, College of Criminal Justice.

David P. Hale, PhD, is the founder and CEO of Talent Management Institute, a corporate psychology training and development firm. Dave is a retired Special Agent with the US Army Criminal Investigation Command (CID). During his 23-year federal law enforcement career, he held positions as the Special Agent in Charge of several CID field offices around the world, which included Saudi Arabia and Kuwait. With 11 years experience as a CID polygraph examiner, he was handpicked to develop the first war-time foreign detainee polygraph program in Iraq centering on terror suspects. Dr. Hale is a professional speaker and is on the faculty of several universities where he teaches psychology and terrorism courses. Dave can be contacted at DrDave@HiPerCoaching.com.

1LT Michael W. Halter, Jr., MBA, graduated from Northwestern State University. Upon his US Army commission, LT Halter was assigned as a platoon leader with the 69th Signal Company, Ft. Huachuca, Arizona. He led 52 soldiers in combat in support of Operation Iraqi Freedom. Halter was the communications projects liaison at Al Taji, Iraq, and planned strategic theater infrastructure upgrades. He developed the underground manhole system in Taji, a network growth from 234 to 317 end-user buildings. He also developed a plan to install 3.5 kilometers of conduit, 17 manholes for military transition teams, and the Iraqi Army Counter Insurgency School and Service Support Institute. Halter completed communications support for the Taji Theater Internment Facility Reintegration Center. The 29 buildings provide USA Corps of Engineers and Military Police with secure/unsecure phone and Internet communications. Halter completed his tour in Iraq as the 40th Expeditionary Signal Battalion HR officer. He provided personnel support in combat to 600+ soldiers and 530 civilian employees throughout the Mid-East. From medical evacuations to streamlining his unit's R&R program, Halter contributed to an often unnoticed aspect of combat.

Carl R. Hospedales holds a Bachelor's Degree in Aviation. He moved to North America from the United Kingdom after completing a successful, 22-year career in the British Armed Forces, which included Special Forces, NATO, and United Nations operations in 2001. Carl is trained and experienced in anti-terrorist operations; asset protection, intelligence, and high-risk security operations; covert operations in hostile and dangerous environments including most recently in Iraq. Currently, as a security and aviation consultant with over 29 years of training and experience, he consults, instructs, lectures, and writes for police, security professionals, and government agencies on various subjects including anti-terrorism, close protection, firearms, body armor, helicopter operations, and weapons of mass destruction (WMD).

Kevin Scott is a retired law enforcement officer and currently works with special needs children. He currently works towards a PhD in Business Administration with specialization in Homeland Security. He holds two master's degrees (one in business administration and the other in organizational management). Additionally, he holds bachelor's and associate's degrees in criminal justice. Kevin resides in the San Gabriel Valley with his wife and three children. He has been involved in the ushers' ministry at his church for the past three years. His hobbies include study in various and mixed martial arts (particularly the *Shotokan* style) and spending time with his wife, children, and their many activities.

Darrin L. Todd, MS, is an information security engineer with a quarter century of information technology (IT) experience. Taking his first programming class as a teen in 1981, he soon realized that he understood and enjoyed computers. He joined the Air Force in 1985 and spent most of his career working as an IT specialist, supervisor, and superintendent while serving a dozen assignments around the world. He eventually focused on information security. Today, Darrin Todd is a doctoral student and a contractor/consultant working for various government organizations and agencies in the Washington, DC, metro area. These organizations include the Department of Defense and the Department of Homeland Security.

William R. Tubbs, Jr., is a former Coast Guard Reserve lieutenant commander. His last assignment was as the Senior Reserve Planning Officer for the Marine Safety Office (Captain of the Port), San Francisco Bay. In this assignment, he developed and exercised port contingency plans and served as the executive secretary for the Northern California Port Readiness Committee. A graduate of several Naval War College and National Defense University reserve officer courses, he earned his BA in Government and Master of Public Administration (MPA) degrees from Sacramento State University. Recently, Bill earned a Certificate of Advanced Graduate Studies (CAGS) in Homeland Security from Northcentral University.

INDEX